D1594035

From Athens to Auschwitz

From Athens to Auschwitz

The Uses of History

CHRISTIAN MEIER

Translated by
Deborah Lucas Schneider

Harvard University Press
Cambridge, Massachusetts
London, England
2005

This work was originally published as *Von Athen bis
Auschwitz: Betrachtungen zur Lage der Geschichte,*
by Verlag C. H. Beck, copyright © Verlag C. H. Beck oHG,
Munich, 2002.

Library of Congress Cataloging-in-Publication Data

Meier, Christian, 1929–
[Von Athen bis Auschwitz. English]
From Athens to Auschwitz : the uses of history / Christian Meier ;
translated by Deborah Lucas Schneider.
p. cm.
Includes bibliographical references (p.) and index.
ISBN 0-674-01692-0 (alk. paper)
1. History—Philosophy.   I. Title.
D16.8.M4213 2005   2004060611
901—dc22

Contents

Preface

The invitation to deliver the Krupp Lectures in Essen in 2000–2001 offered an opportunity that I felt I could (and should) use to sum up the results of a great deal of research, some of it published in widely scattered places. Or, to put it more precisely, I wanted to give these studies a common context. This context existed at first only in the mind of the author. My research has been concentrated chiefly in the field of ancient history, and secondarily in the theory of historiography, but I have also worked quite intensively on the German response to the darkest chapter in our history between 1933 and 1945. Finally, I have devoted an increasing amount of time to the problems that are arising as Europe becomes a union, and the early history of Europe in ancient Greece and Rome.

Nevertheless, many of these studies had a common approach. It is expressed in the title of my inaugural lecture at the University of Basel in July 1968: "Historical Scholarship and Civic Responsibility." Since I began to study history I have found that it is not only extremely interesting, but that it can also contribute to an understanding of the present at any time, by providing people with a sense of orientation about what is important to them, and even about themselves. In other words, historians have a responsibility to their contemporaries. It ought to play a role in their work, in my opinion, although of course it would not be permissible for them to make concessions of any kind to the powers and currents of their age.

This kind of responsibility (which I'm sure I can advocate without much risk, since I'm not likely to convince anyone) is no less valid for scholars of ancient history, although the task differs slightly from that of modern and contemporary historians. All historians are influenced in some way by the era in which they live, but it is possible to deal with observations and questions of the present consciously. And this is precisely what I believe we must do, particularly for our students, in order to make a clear distinction between the past and now. It is also necessary in order to convey the unique nature of ancient phenomena, the ways in which such phenomena are distinct not only from other ages and cultures, but also from our own. And last but not least, we historians need to obtain clarity about important foundations of our own work.

In my view it would not be advisable to do so in a categorical or insistent manner. But returning repeatedly to the present, studying it and applying the questions it raises to epochs in the distant past, can be very useful, both in understanding the latter and in reflecting on current concerns, which can often look different when viewed from a distance. When I occupy myself with the present and the more recent past, in addition to the distant age in which I am a "specialist," each era can teach me a considerable amount about the others.*

If it was a mistake that I assumed, naively at the start, that this was the way to pursue the study of ancient history—looking not just at ancient historians but at historians in general, and possibly

---

* "In learning a man can only be a master in one particular field, namely, as a specialist, and in some field he should be a specialist. But if he is not to forfeit his capacity for taking a general view, or even his respect for general views, he should be an amateur at as many points as possible, privately at any rate, for the increase of his own knowledge and the enrichment of his possible standpoints. Otherwise he will remain ignorant in any field lying outside his own specialty and perhaps, as a man, a barbarian." Jacob Burckhardt, *Reflections on History,* translated by M. D. Hottinger (1943; rpt. Indianapolis: Liberty Classics, 1979), 54.

at further disciplines; that is, understanding myself first and foremost as a historian, and only secondarily as a specialist—if that was a mistake, then it at least has aroused some interest and brought me encouragement from outside the field, both of which were important to me and persuaded me to continue on this path. And I am still not entirely sure whether it was in fact to my disadvantage that I therefore never really experienced the warmth and protective boundaries of the profession and its special forms of discourse. Nevertheless, I have enjoyed good, close, and friendly relationships and scholarly contacts with many colleagues.

In any event I became persuaded early on that history must employ a comparative approach (except that unfortunately I usually failed to make explicit the contrastive background I had in mind when I formulated various statements) and that one must undertake this comparative task on one's own.* It was important to me to bring out and grasp the particular quality of the ancient world on both a large and small scale, that is, to try to see the phenomena with which ancient historians are often only too familiar in a new light. Furthermore, I found that even in its practical labors the field of history is dependent upon theory.

Nevertheless, it was not this and similar occasions, but rather my more immediate participation in the *Historikerstreit* (historians' debate) during the years 1986–1988 (which had a precursor in discussions among members of the Protestant students' association in Freiburg at the beginning of May 1965) that led to my studying such widely separated eras.

It is no simple matter to create a context for them, especially since other subjects must be added as well.

The first lecture—now "chapter"—reflects on a fact that for the greater part of my academic career either did not exist or that, if it

---

* See Ulrich Raulff, ed., *Mentalitäten-Geschichte* (Berlin: Wagenbach, 1987), 163ff.

existed, I failed to notice—namely, the absence of history (i.e., a historical orientation, a historical way of seeing things or asking questions) in the general public. This raises the question, in a new and radical sense, of the whole point of history. What does history mean, and what can it still mean in the present day? It is possible that this absence is caused by the unparalleled acceleration of change we face today, a situation with several paradoxical aspects: we are experiencing more history and historical change than almost any generation before us, and yet we take virtually no interest in it. Since the future has arrived almost before we know it—"The Future Is Today," as a recent advertisement asserts—we hardly have time to worry about the future of our society and the world.

In the ancient world there was no need to plan except in the political sphere, since people could rely on structures that remained constant. It was when these structures began to undergo great change in the modern period that "history" was discovered. Today, now that they are changing even more rapidly and more fundamentally, people are apparently unable to keep up with history. If people can count on one thing in periods of radical change, however, it is probably paradoxes. We know to expect the unexpected.

This may also be true with regard to Europe as it unites politically, a Europe that is at least not playing by the old rules, which said that when new political entities were founded, they had a particular need to define themselves in terms of their history, that is, to make sure of their own past, both good and bad, and their own commitment to it. It was agreed that this would allow them to concentrate all the more intensively on the future, on what they hoped to become and, in some sense as well, what they hoped to contribute to the world.

Such a definition, which would of necessity be based on the unique qualities of the nation, seems out of place these days, as rapid change is eroding such local and particular features more and more. And as the events of September 11, 2001, have made clearer and clearer, they really shouldn't exist at all. The particular features of the West are supposed to appear universal, such as the value attached to human rights, for example, and this is intended, although it is unmistakable that for a great many people in Asia, Africa, and elsewhere the Western identity—and with it the Western claims to superiority and dominance—is all too visible underneath the disguise of "universality." And this despite the fact that if one took a closer look, the West, and the Europe of today, would have a culture to offer of human dignity, of openness, of willingness to question itself—a culture that offers the possibility of mutual tolerance among the different cultures of a shrinking world and of respect for others and otherness.

The second and third chapters represent an attempt to show what historical scholarship might be able to accomplish, using the topic of Europe with special reference to the question of the significance of ancient cultures for—and in—European history. It is intended as an example, as an "offer" that people may feel free to accept or reject.

The fourth chapter seeks to answer the question of how history is made, or more precisely in what forms human beings participate in it, either as active forces or as passive objects, and to what extent they are responsible for it. I also discuss what it means in times of rapid, comprehensive change, when they cannot be responsible, or only in microscopic doses. And finally I deal with the question of whether new forms of history exist today.

The fifth chapter is devoted to Auschwitz, and particularly to the question of whether, to what extent, and in what terms one can understand or at least explain it. It strikes me that this enormous political and moral catastrophe marks the end of Europe's special path in history, and to this extent Athens and Auschwitz are connected by a great historical arc. What Auschwitz means for European history and world history in general, that is, to what extent earlier history must appear in a completely different light after Auschwitz, is the concluding question.

Finally, the sixth chapter asks what the possible legacy of European history might be as we enter the twenty-first century, and goes on to address the question of how historical study should be practiced in the future, and to what end.

The original lectures have been revised, and in part amplified, but in essence reproduce the text and character of the remarks I delivered in Essen.

It seemed to me unnecessary to identify citations and indicate sources in detail, as that would have entailed making the text far longer. I have identified only the direct quotations in endnotes, which also contain a number of observations on particular points for which there was no space in the text itself. I have also included a number of references to works that are often overlooked (but that provide a clearer and more comprehensive context for ideas to which I could only allude briefly in the lectures).

In conclusion I would like to express my gratitude for the invitation to deliver these lectures to Jörn Rüsen, the president of the Institute for Advanced Study in the Humanities in Essen. I would also like to thank Karl Acham and Stefan Sippell for their valuable and stimulating commentary. And finally I am grateful to Katharina Weikl, who prepared several versions of this manuscript and offered helpful suggestions and encouragement.

Munich, December 2001

From Athens to Auschwitz

1

The Absence of History

Assessing the Situation: We Are Running Out of Time

Dividing history into different periods is always problematic. Yet it cannot be totally wrong to place Athens at the start of Europe's "special path"[1] in world history and to regard Auschwitz as its definitive end. This "special path" is, according to my thesis:

—the course on which Europe embarked beginning with the Greeks, a course differing in decisive ways from that of all the other advanced civilizations—from Egypt and Mesopotamia through India and China to Central America—that developed before Europe and independently from it, and also differing from that of the great Arab civilizations of the Middle Ages;

—the course that then enabled Europe to influence the entire world from about 1500 onward, making this continent the center of world history and its driving force for several centuries;

—and the course on which Europe achieved significant breakthroughs in science, general enlightenment, political culture, and other areas, in a process of increasing rapidity, breadth, and depth, but on which it now lags behind others (chiefly the United States) and has generally fallen back into the ranks, despite its remaining distinctive features—becoming one civilization among others (if one can still apply that lofty word to it at all).

This special path will be the subject of the following chapters on the topic of history—hence they will have Europe as their main focus (with occasional references to other civilizations for purposes of comparison and contrast). This focus on Europe is the result of deliberate choice, without any intention to suggest that I take it for granted. History is no longer just the history of Europe (with the possible inclusion of North America, as we sometimes still assume, consciously or unconsciously); rather, European and North American history represents one history alongside others, even if it exerted the most profound influence on the others for a good while, and changed them all. Ignoring the history of the world outside Europe as we tend to do—particularly in Germany—is not just atavism, provincialism, or egotism; it is stupidity, a failure to make use of crucial sources of historical insight.[2]

All the same, one can't know or do everything, and so I will concentrate here on Europe and its special path.

Within this general framework, however, the following reflections have been motivated by a particular theoretical interest, which could be summed up under the heading "Historical Scholarship and Civic Responsibility." This was the title of the inaugural lecture I delivered in Basel on receiving my first professorship there in 1968.[3] It is a subject that has always concerned me.

Historical scholarship must never place itself at the service of particular forces in its own time, least of all political movements—this is the upshot of my reflections. And in no case can historians consent to serve up findings that have been requested in advance. Yet at the same time historians are members of a society and as such have a responsibility to their contemporaries and to their own age (a responsibility that, since it exists within the comprehensive processes that shape public opinion and the public will, can only be exercised as a kind of "as if": as if what they do or not do as individuals matters!).

This responsibility can and should induce historians to take an active interest in the era in which they live, and apply their professional skills to gain an understanding of it (not only to correct contemporaries' mistaken assumptions about history, but that too). This can be of great benefit to them as scholars. Often, if they pursue their research with the questions of their own time in their minds, it can shed new light on the past, while at the same time knowledge of the past will cause them to see the questions of their own era differently. How many things one can learn about antiquity, for instance, through the issues of our own times! And how much antiquity can teach us about the questions of our day!

I am aware that by calling on historians to exercise responsibility in their own era—and perhaps to recognize important features of their own time by the issues it chooses not to debate—I am in no danger of starting a stampede. Research that appears very remote from one's own century can sometimes produce results highly relevant to contemporary issues, and scholars who pursue it will not develop a bad conscience, and rightly so. Other points of view and other approaches must be granted validity as well. But it is my conviction that historians should have a public function—not only for those who happen to take a special interest in some aspect of history, but for the general public. I say this in all modesty. And it is about such a public function of history, or more precisely, about pursuing history in the public interest, that I shall speak here.

Hence I shall begin this chapter by assessing the place of history in contemporary public awareness.[4] By this I do not mean the sum of each individual's consciousness weighted equally, but rather the public awareness that coalesces around some issues and can influence—or even determine—public discourse, by which means awareness spreads still further throughout society.

History, because it by definition belongs to the past, can be present only in the memory and/or consciousness of living people. It must be visualized through inquiry and study. But the role history plays in the consciousness of the living can vary greatly from country to country and age to age. The place history occupies can thus be quite different at different times.

This is true in both a narrower and the wider sense—for local history as well as that of nations; for the history of ordinary people as well as great movements; for the history of recent generations as well as distant centuries. Which type of history stands in the foreground or center of interest will depend on circumstances, or the individual. The "larger" and "smaller" kinds of history, however, cannot be completely separated from one another, at least not as long as we are concerned with "historical consciousness" of a general kind.

It may be that history is needed, is a human need—required for an era to understand itself as part of a tradition, as an obligation to behave in a certain way, for instance, or as a stimulus to strive for a better future. History can determine how societies define their own identity: it can be a living presence in people's view of their national institutions. It can color perceptions of human affairs to a large extent and can represent a central category of public awareness in some parts of the world; this is certainly the case when a person is accustomed to viewing current events from a historical point of view. History can—but need not—play a role as transience, as a process, as a judge before whom one must give an account of oneself.

It is important for historians to recognize the situation of history in their own time, so that they know where to take up the threads of the past and from what point to set out. Its particular situation suggests approaches; it provides axioms (which in some circumstances may prove false, so that one must question them). Such questions can make it clear why there is a need for historians or, in some cases, why there is not.

For me, all this calls to mind a passage in Goethe's novel *Elective Affinities* where a character states "that one cannot get to know soon enough the character of a person one has to live with, so that one knows what to expect from them, what aspects of their personality can be improved and what must be accepted and allowed for once and for all."[5] We can apply the same principle to our contemporaries. What can we expect from them? And what, one might also ask, do they expect from historians? Do they really have direct, genuine expectations, or can historians induce them, by convincing the public that they are missing something if they lack certain historical insights? Are there real points of connection with the past nowadays, something like a sense of history, or history as a shared plane of reference?[6] Or are we historians today condemned to play the role of bikini salesmen at nudist beaches?

It is necessary to pose the question in a radical form, since hardly anything can be taken for granted today. At least that is how the gravitational forces of perception are tending.[7]

Two celebrated nineteenth-century historians, Johann Gustav Droysen, in his *Historik* ("Principles of History"),[8] and Jacob Burckhardt, in his *Reflections on History*,[9] could both start out with the history itself, without preamble—in books that aroused and still arouse interest far beyond professional circles. If they begin the same way, present-day scholars can reach only their own students and a few others with a special interest in the field, for between history and the public there is a large gap to be bridged. Why it should be so is the first question that requires an explanation.

In trying to assess the present-day situation of history, much becomes clearer if one compares these findings with those from the nineteenth and early twentieth centuries. Please don't misunderstand me. I intend to use the earlier findings solely for contrast, not as a yardstick with which to measure present-day circumstances and find them lamentable. My intention is not to lament anything, but merely to establish how things stand. We cannot go back; we can only move forward, and ahead is where we must seek our way, although by this I of course do not mean to suggest that everything from earlier times is passé and boring.

"Those who cannot draw conclusions / From three thousand

years of learning / Stay naive in dark confusions, / Day to day live undiscerning."[10] Goethe wrote these lines 180 years ago, and they have been quoted too often since then. He was right, too, that for a long time people would have felt ashamed of living from day to day in the way he meant it—that is, as a member of a community or society. (He was not referring to the shaping of private plans, or family or professional matters.) Today, I suspect, very few people would find "going with the flow" objectionable. What else can we do? In earlier times people thought that as nations became less primitive they gained more of a sense of history.[11] But a glance at Ireland or the Balkans today makes one suspect that the more important its history is to a people, the more barbarously they behave.

Jacob Burckhardt says about looking at history: "Our study . . . is not only a right and a duty; it is also a supreme need. It is our freedom in the very awareness of universal bondage and the stream of necessities."[12] Burckhardt believed that this characterization of history reflected an important condition of life in times of great change. "We should like to know on which wave in the ocean we are floating, but we ourselves are the wave."[13] People were, that is to say, simultaneously both the driving force and the driven object of history.

In the midst of this current, then, the goal had to be to create some sense of personal freedom or control. If some things were unalterable, one could at least try to recognize this, by acquiring some perspective with the help of history. For Burckhardt was living in the "historical century." People in the nineteenth century interpreted their age in terms of the historical processes they saw at work in it. Reflecting on history might make change appear desirable or, if one was not willing to embrace it, at least comprehensible. The terms "progressive" or "conservative" described not only temperaments, outlooks, or convictions, but positions with respect to historical forces.

Many people with a strong sense of history took pride in the progress achieved in the age in which they were living. Even if Burckhardt did not share it, he considered it possible to achieve a position of mastery through contemplation leading to detachment: a remarkable argument for possible human greatness! It was a way, he felt, to put some distance between oneself and history, or oneself in history, of whose might he was only too aware.

But the age when these attitudes prevailed ended a long time ago. What the loss of them meant can perhaps best be measured by the terrible disillusionment of those born in the nineteenth century who lived through the First World War. This conflict taught them the lesson that men could shift from being decent citizens to murderers and back again, without becoming essentially altered; that, in the words of Austrian writer Robert Musil, "in modern life people only do what is happening anyway."[14] This experience will serve as a reference point for my reflections.

And so we come at last to the state of history today and to the hypothesis contained in the title of this chapter—namely, that there is an absence of history in the public consciousness. I would like to begin by presenting five observations.

1

In our time we are experiencing a giant leap forward in the realm of science, namely, the discovery of human beings' genetic structure and the possibility of intervening to alter it. It raises many questions, both ethical and practical, which are being addressed. Attitudes differ: hopes are kindled, along with corresponding fears of manipulation. But in view of such an event, shouldn't one of the questions raised concern human history? What kind of history is it that began with creatures who were hunters and gatherers and who have now gained access to such stupendous possibilities? What does this history look like from our present vantage point? How do our achievements appear when placed in historical perspective? And will this history be continued in the future? After all, what is a stake here is not just a new bit of data in the history of science.

It was probably inevitable that the ancient tension between the possibilities of human power and control on the one hand and human helplessness and the threats to the environment represented in our politics and social existence on the other would become a problem and send us back to history, or to put this in other words, the tensions between the heights of our knowledge and skills and the depths of their possible uses, the tensions between the very modern and archaic components of our thought processes and behavior. We are capable of deceiving ourselves about our own motives and sometimes do; our makeup includes primitive drives, and that can make decisions about the permissible limits of research either impossible or ineffectual. We are still able, as Musil noted, to move from one extreme of the behavioral spectrum to the other without altering our essential nature.

Many terrible things exist, but as the chorus says in *Antigone,* none is more terrible than human beings. In his play Sophocles cites many magnificent achievements, of which people were then proudly conscious, and concludes that they can be used for either good or evil; indeed, the greater the achievement, the more this is the case.

In the modern era, by contrast, it was widely believed for a long time that general progress had enabled humankind to overcome this ambivalence. And for considerable stretches of time things did indeed go well—until the First World War, the Russian Revolution, the rise of Hitler, the Second World War, Auschwitz, Hiroshima and Nagasaki, the gulags, and many more things made us realize our error.

To be sure, in the second half of the twentieth century this kind of thing did not occur again, at least in the West. The veneer of civilization was repaired, and has proven relatively durable. Even the destructive potential of atomic weapons has been held in check. And even if we fail to show much character as Robert Musil defined it—namely, that others can treat us as constants[15]—still, judged on the basis of statistics, things don't look all that unfavorable. Have we succeeded then in avoiding the terrible possibilities that we have opened up for ourselves in our interactions with one another and our effect on the environment? Have we reached the goal? Or have we only reached a new, very dangerous peak in our abilities to act for both good and evil, including now the possibility of altering our own genetic makeup?

These are the questions one might put to history, and seek answers from history, if we saw ourselves in a historical context and felt a need for historical orientation. But how many people do? Would questions of this kind have any chance of striking a chord in the general public? If the answer is no, this would demonstrate an absence of history in the general consciousness (and perhaps in the consciousness of many historians as well).

2

For some time now we have to all appearances been experiencing a significant acceleration, broadening, and deepening of social change around the globe as a result of rapid progress in science and technology—especially in the field of communications (the Internet), transportation, and many forms of organization. Discoveries and knowledge double in ever shorter spans of time while their half-life of validity sinks rapidly, as more and more people, institutions, and corporations in a growing number of countries produce innovations and drive competition.[16] Most of these discoveries find practical applications within a very short time; frontiers are abolished or crossed with ease. The consequences can be felt in all areas of life, including within ourselves and our relationships with other people.

People over the age of thirty were born in a different era.[17] Those who are forty are kidding themselves if they think they have even a rough idea of the kind of world in which their ten-year-old child is growing up. If schools want to keep pace—beyond equipping their students with basic skills—they run the risk of seeing the information they teach become out of date even before students graduate.

If we stop to consider, the question is no longer *how* to keep up, but whether it is possible now at all outside a narrow field of specialization, or so at least it appears. For a long time people have been speaking of a need for orientation that is not so easily met, given all the innovations with which we are constantly confronted. It is not a question of missing a few details; I am referring to broader contexts and familiar connections, which are being altered in ways impossible to overlook.

In history one finds few parallels to this phenomenon of rapid acceleration, and those are usually quite remote, except perhaps for the rapid decline of empires. One parallel involving advance rather than decline took place in Athens in the fifth century B.C.E.[18] By our standards change proceeded quite slowly, but acceleration can be disturbing even to someone traveling at a relatively leisurely pace. Because of the numerous challenges with which the Greeks saw themselves confronted in quick succession, they created many innovations to meet them. The development of history, tragedy, the fine arts, architecture, and rhetoric are only the most notable evidence of this process that have come down to us. But music, public speaking, and many other arts and skills must have made advances at that time, too.

In some sense our entire legacy from the "classical period" of Greece, the fifth and early fourth century B.C.E., can serve as evidence of how the Greeks strove to absorb all the new data they were encountering or discovering. In other words, their accomplishment was to take all the new and difficult ideas that were so unsettling, raise them to the level of awareness, and somehow digest them. They didn't necessarily find answers to everything, mainly because the process of questioning was so intense—but for precisely that reason they achieved clarity about their own helplessness and (in extreme cases) the meaninglessness of the world. The arts and intellectual life flourished on the cutting edge as happens only very rarely—until the conditions for such flowering vanished with the collapse of Athens in 404 B.C.E.

When the fundamental interpretation of the world as a whole was called into question in fifth-century Athens, the most important Greek answer in the long run was Plato's. He found that all change on earth, as impressive as it may be, is only shadowy and trivial, not worthy of any particular attention. What was important was what remained the same: being, the ideas of the just and the good. This philosophy continued to exert an influence like no other, but it did not leave a lasting mark on political or social reality. Soon things settled down again after the extraordinary blossoming of Athens, and while changes occurred on the surface of life, society could again be viewed as static overall.

Matters stood very differently after 1789, to cite a second example of rapid change that comes to mind as particularly apt. Hannah Arendt offers a powerful description of how the leaders of the French Revolution were forced to realize that despite their free hand they had failed to become masters of events; disillusionment over what had happened "transformed itself almost immediately into a feeling of awe and wonder at the power of history itself."[19] In the preceding decades people had been coming to understand history as a slow process of improvement. Now, however, many saw it as progress. In spite of all doubts and the contradictions one might recognize, it seemed reasonable to entrust oneself to it. At that time Europeans began to reflect consciously not only about innovations, but also the process that led to them. The opponents of progress, the conservatives, also appealed to history as an important force, but most did not really want it to come to a standstill. They just wanted to slow the pace of development. Finally, as Jacob Burckhardt shows, studying history offered a third possibility—neither to embrace or resist change, but to learn to endure it by acquiring a serene philosophical detachment.[20]

The whole world became history—until it all became too much. This happened to Nietzsche before the First World War, and since then it has happened again and again. Nonetheless, the old progressive and conservative views continued to function for a long time, although confronted with more and more challenges.

Thus there were two examples, two ways to respond to accelerated change in a way that made self-determination possible—by identifying a continuity that consisted either of repetition or perpetual transformation.[21] How matters could appear in the nineteenth century is shown by Droysen, who speaks of an "infinite continuity" in which every "life work, no matter how small," forms part of the living history of mankind as a whole, but also of the history of families, nations, religious denominations, and, we could add, of classes and political parties.[22] He saw large and small histories as almost seamlessly joined.

However, is this solution, this way of understanding history as change over time, still accessible to us, so that we can find a place for history in our own view of the world, and see a place for ourselves in it? Is it possible to grasp our own era of rapid change in historical terms, as part of a larger process, except in the most superficial, habitual sense? Can we still picture ourselves as workers in or agents of history, as Droysen believed, when no matter how hard we work and strive, we still feel adrift?

One does not have the impression that historians today are engaged in developing interpretations on a similarly large scale. If they could, they might—perhaps—be able to give meaning to so many things that now seem merely painful or annoying, such as all the adaptations we have to make in our own lives, although we do so grudgingly and without really admitting it as far as possible. Our time-tested views, habits, and ideals grow old so rapidly! We are constantly overwhelmed by things we can't comprehend. Our environment and our institutions have been bulldozed or gutted, and even our German language is in danger of disappearing from use by scholars and elites. It may cease to develop or become a medium for backward ideas. Not to mention the fact that we ourselves are turning into different people, often against our own will.

It is paradoxical that following the collapse of the Socialist Eastern bloc Marx's doctrine that human beings are determined by changes in the conditions of production appears to have been confirmed on a scale that no one outside the circle of his followers could ever have believed possible.[23]

But it is just because we are being swept into the maelstrom of change—with life and limb and so much else at stake—that history has ceased to function as a provider of meaning to our lives as much as would be desirable. So why not just give it up? Faced with such rapid transformation of the world, most people have no need to identify their own place in history or acquire a long-term historical perspective; those who find this surprising may not yet have grasped the dimensions of change.

3

The faster the rush toward the future, the more urgently that future ought to command our attention. And indeed it does concern us greatly to the extent that we, as individuals or members of a corporation or network, are trying to determine how we can succeed in it. But the rapidity of the pace leaves us less time than ever to ponder the goals we wish to achieve—apart from financial security, perhaps. Before we have time to contemplate the future, we have already arrived in it.[24]

Assuredly, the future is always uncertain, especially where the course of events is concerned. But few real events (as opposed to managed ones) are taking place today, and if they do, they often result less from surprising new turns than from the unanticipated results of processes that have themselves been foreseeable for a long time. On the other hand, it is true that no age has ever had such a hard time making prognoses, because change was never so comprehensive—or the percentage of what doesn't change so small—as it is today.[25]

If we look again to the nineteenth century and large stretches of the twentieth for comparison, matters stood very differently. At that time whole classes of society, first the liberal bourgeoisie, then the proletariat, were engaged in striving for a better future, one they clearly envisioned. Others with different visions opposed them. Many young people were actively working for the fulfillment of demands that their parents and grandparents had raised and in some cases begun to achieve.[26]

Both liberals and socialists could rely in their efforts on theories—and goals—formulated by thinkers such as John Locke and Adam Smith (in an "advanced" country like Great Britain, followed by Kant in Germany), or Marx and Engels, who interpreted the process of history as an inevitable movement toward a classless society of the future. No comparable theories exist today.

There are no signs of noteworthy attempts to discern a historical process reaching from the past through the present into the future and, on that basis, to hypothesize about the path on which we now find ourselves. What appeared to be world history's main highways to the future has become a maze of branching roads. What is happening today is not easy to define, even on the surface—at least not with the aid of ideas that dominated our views of the path to the future only twenty or thirty years ago. Nor is it easy to subsume the scope of change today in one theory, or a single direction. Or is the problem just a lack of conceptual skill in joining disparate phenomena together? There is no sign at all of a concerted force pressing forward and claiming the future in its name. At least the innovations and changes brought about by many individuals, groups, and corporations around the globe are not merging into one tendency pointing toward a new or somehow better society, unless one considers as evidence the vague signs of an emerging new humanity. History, if it were still present in the general consciousness, would presumably not be able to help us on this point either.

The absence of general ideas about the future may be reflected in the widespread use of the term "postmodern" for our epoch: a society that undertakes nothing beyond its immediate concerns, that does not want (or is unable?) to define itself by what it *is*, but only by what it *comes after*. Does this mean that our era is also "posthistory"?

The notion that we find ourselves in *posthistoire* was originally an intellectual theory argued from the right, but also taken up by some on the left. As Lutz Niethammer has shown, it represents an elitist, culturally pessimistic re-evaluation of the optimistic belief in progress; it is a negative utopia.[27] But haven't the views of the general public amounted to much the same for quite some time now, to the extent that despite all the comprehensive and profound changes taking place, a future history is hardly present in our expectations, even as a possibility? Science fiction films and apocalyptic scenarios do not represent a true contradiction to this state of affairs, since they serve mainly to satisfy aesthetic needs.

On the other hand, does not every conception of a historical process extending from the past through the present into the future presuppose that a need exists to achieve something in the future that is considered necessary, and that is noticeably and painfully absent in the present? And what is noticeably lacking for us today, except perhaps for the fulfillment of dreams?[28] Those who suffer a noticeable lack of many things, even necessities, in Africa, Asia, Latin America, in Eastern Europe, and indeed even the "new poor" in the West, have few possibilities for turning their hopes—which often enough have begun to turn into doubts—into lasting expectations of future history. "It is the weaker who always seek equality and justice," observed Aristotle, "the strong give them no thought."[29] If we expand this idea and apply it to Western circumstances in the present day, it is for the sake of the weak, and in their name, that the goal of a just order is projected into the future. It is they who have need of history in the sense of a process advancing toward a better world.

For this is what the question of "post-history" really concerns. That the end of history has not arrived is self-evident.[30] But the kind of history that was conceived of in the eighteenth century as a *single* great ongoing process, for Europe and North America, and for the world as a whole—that kind of history could be indeed over. And gone with it is the connection of society with history, a connection that consisted not least in widely shared expectations about the future. This was that era's response to experiences of comprehensive change. Today we can have such experiences in far greater measure, but there is no particular interest in the future (or the process that leads to it). That is to say, there is no particular interest in history, however one may conceive of it.

4

One especially striking phenomenon in this connection is the European Union, the more so as it intensifies its efforts to achieve political unification. When nationalities became self-aware in the nineteenth century and strove to found their own states if they did not already have them, they all created a history for themselves, often concocted in dubious ways. This would not be acceptable in the Europe of today. Yet it would have a history to show for itself, also in the framework of world history, the decisive strand of which ran through Europe, as it were. There are many reasons to reflect on this history of Europe, if only for the purpose of registering how amazing the present condition of the world is. It would definitely be a shared history. And as the history of the development of civilizations, democracies, Western values, Western nation states, political culture, and general mores, it has considerable achievements to point to in the political and social spheres (whereby the contribution of the United States should not be forgotten).

The historic dimension of Europe (legitimation and self-determination), however, does not appear to arouse any particular interest in the public, apart from jubilees and perhaps the odd exhibition (generously subsidized). As far as history is concerned, Europeans for the most part seem more familiar with negative statements: No more war! Never again Auschwitz! And, after the expansion to the East, probably also: No more gulags!

Clearly Europeans have a sense of themselves as survivors of a history they have left far behind them; they do not see history as their origin or the foundation on which they stand. History is not something they desire to carry on (in a better way if possible). Hence they feel no gratitude to their forbears for what they achieved with so much labor; on the contrary, they are fixated on all the things they don't understand (and are not making an effort to understand), such as wars, injustice, discrimination against women, slavery, and the like. They feel uncoupled from their history, the seriousness of which they are, generally speaking, less and less able to imagine.

Thus, as far as I can see, the European Union is emerging as the first political entity of the modern era that has no need for its own history and for a historical orientation; it is far from believing that it should "act in full awareness of its recognized historical uniqueness," as Droysen wrote of the nation state, in order to be able to "judge general circumstances from this standpoint and reach decisions" accordingly.[31]

I don't intend this as criticism, but merely to identify symptoms: history is simply no longer an important category. Or does this situation merely reflect the fact that it is not easy to see what kind of future this Europe is aiming at, and so Europe still has no standpoint from which to ascertain its history?

Incidentally, a European sense of history also has a hard time of it in today's world because people no longer like to identify themselves with leading actors in it, but rather with its victims. Europeans also wish to differentiate themselves from other people as little as possible and believe that wanting to make such distinctions is wrong.

5

The same general outline holds for German history as well as for Europe. Of course, both historians and laypeople take an active interest in the Nazi past, one that is even growing rather than abating. We Germans are preoccupied with it, fixated even, like a deer caught in the headlights. But apart from the fact that historical interest is becoming more and more overgrown with expressions of emotion and rituals, those twelve years[32] form a deep gulf between us and our earlier history. The enthusiasm with which Daniel Goldhagen was received in Germany in 1996 clearly resulted particularly from his willingness to certify that the present Germans, now all good democrats, had nothing in common with Germans before the 8th of May 1945. This fit well with his depiction of the latter in the blackest of colors, in a largely unhistorical manner.[33] Thus we encounter a considerable absence of history here as well. This was especially evident in the celebration of German reunification in 1989–1990, when virtually no reference at all was made to any history prior to 1933. The existence of a certain pride in the history of the Federal Republic cannot be overlooked, and young people identify themselves with certain aspects of it. But that does not alter the essentials.

History, it seems—if we discount professionals in the field—has nothing much to tell us any more.

To these five observations more can be added, which explain some of the reasons why awareness of history has receded into the background.

6

The contexts in which we might be prompted to understand ourselves in historical terms are very much weakened today, particularly in Germany. However, Germany just seems to be ahead of most other countries in this respect.

Let us start with the family.[34] To the extent that it still exists, a sense of having a place in a sequence of generations is rapidly shrinking. For personal autobiographies parents still play a role, mainly because they are seen as having done every possible kind of damage to the psyches of their offspring. But who would think to mention grandparents or more remote ancestors today? And what is more, the old model so important for the large and important dynamic class of the upwardly mobile has become obsolete. By this I mean the way small farmers, artisans, and working men and their wives (sometimes in cooperation with siblings) sweated and toiled to provide at least one son with a higher education, who was then grateful to them. Of course, no one would wish the old days back again. But that is not the point.

I would mention, incidentally, that our identities also suffer from the fact that the past is less and less inscribed in them, except in the form of especially stirring, or rather free-floating, memories. In 1955 Hans Freyer was still able to write that "one feature of a personal existence consists of recalling personal experience."[35] Today, however, not only do experiences lose their relevance quickly and to a far greater extent than they used to; it is also questionable whether the rapid pace of life and changing circumstances still permit observations and occurrences to congeal into something like "life experience."

National identity has ceased to be of great moment, and hardly any traces of a class identity remain in Germany. In the fate of a traditional party like the Social Democrats one can observe the extent to which historical consciousness has diminished in political associations within the country, in terms both of obligations felt toward them and hopes for the future. People are correspondingly seldom conscious of the historical trends with which they used to identify themselves—the advance of progress, for example, in which all those who performed productive labor used to feel they were participants. Even those motivated by hope of profits were considered to be contributing to the benefit of society. "In furthering my end, I further the universal, and this in turn furthers my end," as Hegel put it.[36]

Just as children in Germany expect their education and their parents' pensions to be financed from taxes rather than from personal savings or sacrifices, so we—and any group identity we share—are defined far more by the present time than by our origins. And that leads to the next point.

7

Experiencing such rapid and comprehensive change in our daily lives as we do,[37] our living conditions and views are shaped and reshaped so much in our own lifetime that the importance of the remote past pales by comparison. Why should people understand themselves and their background in the context of history, or indeed, is that even still possible today? The transformations of our age extend so far beyond national borders, and are greatly determined by global scientific, technical, organizational, and economic processes and trends, under whose influences the developed nations are growing more and more alike. In a parallel development, the distinctive features of European locales, marks of their historical identity, are being razed or gutted. This has hardly rendered people's historical origins irrelevant; cultural idiosyncrasies of outlook, language, and lifestyle—in the form of good and bad customs— continue to play their role. But they mean less and less. They are fading into the background in comparison with tendencies to make everything alike. Local particularities and unique customs can easily appear provincial nowadays and tend not to be consciously cultivated.

And along with the rapidity of change and the diminution of unique features of our own history, the areas of direct and indirect recollections—such as accounts of grandparents' lives—appear to be thinning out. Such family stories mean less and less, and very few young people take note of and remember them.

8

It has become an open question today whether there is still something we can call "the present"—*one* single "present"—at any given time. Strictly speaking, the present is always a fiction; we create it by agreeing to give that designation to some particular stretch of time—it might last a few years or, at most, a generation—and to ascribe a certain stability to it in the face of many possible kinds of change.[38] People understand, experience, and calculate "the present" differently depending on their age, but the fluid process by which various kinds of "present" slowly shift their position, overlapping and imperceptibly replacing one another, does not disturb the fiction underlying the conventional term, which we appear to need. We would rather conceive of ourselves living in settled conditions than in constant transition (even if we see a need to work on improving those conditions).

These conventions of a "present time" can produce a certain awareness in people living in the same age. And such a shared, self-aware present is certainly capable of relating the past to itself[39] as well as determining its own relationship to the future.

Today, however, the lifetime of generations is growing shorter; many more "generations" coexist than used to be the case (mainly because shorter and shorter spans of years are being identified and labeled as such). Which one should be regarded as predominant, as characterizing the "present," and for how long? Or to rephrase the question: Doesn't this situation mean that our shared reality has already dissolved into a whole collection of different "presents"? The same may hold true, incidentally, for many individuals, depending on the particular circumstances in which they live. The result is that a solid awareness of "the present" can hardly arise any more, particularly in view of the pace of change.

To all these factors we must add the increasing geographical fragmentation of European societies as large numbers of people migrate to different countries, and also the increasing demands for ever more professional specialization. The latter now creates barriers not only between people in different fields, but even between those of different ages within the same field, depending on when they acquired their professional qualifications—or took their last refresher course. I could also mention here the modern tendency for members of very highly trained elites to operate in an international context—just one of the many factors that increase our sense of living in different eras. The columns in which we are marching toward the future are drawing further and further apart, or so it seems, and it is questionable how long we will be able to maintain eye contact. How are we supposed to connect our lives with history under such conditions?

9

The time available to acquire an orientation with regard to history is also shrinking (unless history happens to be one's field of specialization). Thomas Mann, who was born in the nineteenth century, observed seventy years ago: "We of today, preoccupied as we are with tasks that are uniquely new and challenging, have no time and little inclination to deal justly with the epoch that is fading into history behind us."[40] And this applies not only to judging a past epoch fairly, but also for acquiring an awareness of history in general. Not quite thirty years after Thomas Mann's comment, the German historian Alfred Heuss noted: "Pursuing memories and focusing one's thoughts on the past are difficult things to achieve when instead of being free, one's mental powers are demanded by the present environment."[41] And how harmless things were by comparison in his day!

10

Furthermore, history itself is becoming less accessible to us, given the conditions in which people now grow up, live, and think. One of the main reasons for this is the kind of approaches to history currently favored by scholars, and the nuances and increasing complexity that their investigations are bringing to light. Nowadays professional historians tend to stress structures and processes in their scholarly writings and other presentations, and these are far more difficult to grasp than specific actions and events.[42]

In addition, the long, slow processes by which institutions and movements such as Roman law or the Enlightenment developed create difficulties, since they are not easy to convey in an era of instant access to everything. The same holds true for the experience that history forces on us all the time, namely, accepting that for some problems or conflicts there is no quick fix.[43] The present age typically demands everything right away—*tutto e subito*—and we are used to shopping at the history mall, so to speak, for whatever we want. Attitudes and institutions (such as ethnic tolerance or multiparty systems) that once developed slowly over the course of generations are now available ready to wear, pre-sized, and with all the loose ends sewed up. And we are prepared to wear whatever fits. Where people once would have resisted a great many ideas, so as to preserve their own individuality, they are now ready to try on all kinds of opinions as if they were clothes.

We tend to regard any place where things are different, such as the Balkans or the eastern part of Germany, as "backward" or "underdeveloped," even though such "backwardness" means that the inhabitants of these regions still have a history and biographies and, as least as far as the Balkans are concerned, produce real events instead of just staging photo-ops and the like. In such places they still reckon with time—the time that it takes, for instance, for East Germans to turn into what we would find acceptable, namely West Germans. That certain institutions, and even some kinds of knowledge, are simply not transferable is something else again. Here we think: if one thing doesn't work, you have to try another. What else can you do if you don't want to get left behind or give up? Banking on patience and waiting for things to change over the long term is not the answer, at any rate.

But there is also a particular reason why the history of the twentieth century seems to frighten off everyone but hardened professionals. When laypeople want to understand remote events and processes, they tend to draw on ideas that are somehow familiar, perhaps from their early reading, but also from their own experience or the experience of older people that, because it formed part of reality when they were growing up, they have absorbed and made their own. This is the case with ideas connected with war, for example (if a person has fought in or experienced a war, or has heard a great deal about it). Even national policies can become accessible if, let us say, a person identifies himself with his own ruler or government, or with a struggle against them.

But what happens if these events cannot be grasped in their entirety, and the role that this person and people like him played in them strike him as perhaps not bad on the one hand, but on the other as embarrassing, incomprehensible, even one for which he should not be held accountable? What if the historical events in which he participated himself—for instance, the Second World War with all its unfathomable crimes—have made him experience himself and his family in an utterly chilling way, one that continues to haunt him? What if he thus would like to suppress all memory of them (even though pride may get the better of him, so that he loudly defends them or walls himself off from everything that still eats away at him inside)?

In other words, the Second World War, including Auschwitz, the most appalling and disturbing event of twentieth-century history, still casts its baneful spell over us and blocks our path to history. It does so for many reasons, but especially because we have a sense of ourselves and our fellow Germans as unmistakably involved, as perpetrators, but at the same time as blind and helpless, and—as grotesque as it may seem—also as victims. It is indefensible—a dissonance between micro- and macro-history that is virtually impossible to reconcile.

Such feelings need not be conscious, and we are well advised to prevent them from reaching consciousness. By doing that, however, we surround this history (to the extent that it affects us personally or we feel accountable either for the war or our own actions) with a concrete shield to block its radioactivity. Another response is to lay the blame for this history on an entirely different set of people, namely the Germans of that era, who now seem so infinitely distant from us and so incomprehensible. And this has a ripple effect. If one cannot understand oneself or one's own countrymen, the access routes into history become very limited. That makes it difficult, at best, to have any notion of history at all.

And, despite all the enormous differences, we can sense the same mixture of participation and helplessness, of acting and feeling acted upon, in the processes of our own age. We take part in them —sometimes a minimal part, but we still contribute: buying things, investing in corporations, polluting the atmosphere, adding to global warming, knocking down buildings, putting up new ones, despoiling our cities, and failing to pay enough attention to our democracy or our children. But at the same time, if we look at the total effect on society, we are helpless. This, too, tends to be more a vague feeling than a firm awareness. But this feeling gets in the way of reflecting on our situation—and I mean our situation in general, not just with regard to history! As the playwright Botho Strauss has written, "In the past, if a person fainted it was because his or her conscious mind could not master one powerful emotion, while today the consciousness of the *entirety* of the world has fallen into a faint."[44] And we haven't even experienced a particular emotion. No explosions; everything is just imploding.

Both the ability and the need to recognize the context in which an event has occurred, and to assemble such contexts, are rapidly on the decline. Contemporary theater[45] is symptomatic of this, where more and more directors shrink from the effort of creating a context, and where the plays produced look less like events shaped by an author than happenings. Audiences would need to make an effort to understand the former, while they can simply let themselves be amused by the latter (if that is possible). But similar trends can also be observed in the economic sphere: "The ability to see the larger picture is disappearing," one of Germany's leading economists observed not too long ago.[46]

And the fact that this process is accelerating—without our knowing where we are headed, without knowing whether we or our so-called leaders and statesmen, all smiles for their group photo, could ever get a grip on it—makes it that much more unsettling.

Perhaps we ought to approach history from a very different perspective, by asking who can control what in it, for instance, or where control succeeds and where it doesn't, what it takes to control different processes. What role do elites play in such processes, and also political groups and the population as a whole? What responsibility do they bear for what happens, either directly or indirectly? And also: How are the consciousness and situation of ordinary citizens affected?

11

Last: even if we haven't reached the end of history, we may well have reached a point in time when we must ask ourselves if it can be true that all of world history has been staged just for our sake, those of us alive today. It is an almost unimaginable thought: so much ambition, effort, back-breaking labor, struggle, deprivation, suffering, sacrifice, murder, and mayhem—all for us?[47]

The state of history in our society, in Europe and especially in Germany, thus hardly seems auspicious. The numerous historical exhibitions mounted today, historical museums, even staged re-enactments and events, do not argue against this conclusion. For most people they offer only a form of "time travel," led by tour guides from the field of history, as it were. Just like most terrestrial journeys, their destinations tend to be isolated points. Such "time-travel" experiences rarely demonstrate broad historical contexts or a sense of history (nor do they produce the latter in visitors). Perhaps they are intended to compensate for the absence of history in the minds of the general public. Does that mean historians, unless they are addressing professional colleagues or audiences with some special interest in the field, are truly in the same position today as bikini salesmen at a nudist beach?

That conclusion might be a bit hasty, perhaps, for there is one question I haven't asked: Might our current experiences represent just a phase of upheaval, a spurt of acceleration, a transition to something new?[48] Will the situation stabilize again or point us in some discernible direction in a global sense? Will history become relevant again?

Phases of extreme acceleration automatically produce a striking result, namely that the inhabitants of different societies live in different eras, so to speak. The acceleration results from the super-abundance of new possibilities—in our own case the emerging technologies used by the many people who understand how to tap into them: researchers, technicians, computer specialists, investors, planners, and the armies of financial and corporate consultants in Europe and around the world. Their actions affect everyone else, not least because they have sizable unintended side effects, which in turn lead to many other types of change. This means that the more the one group advances, it not only leaves other, now disadvantaged, groups behind; it also creates new problems for the entire society of a kind not easy to master.

If the changes that invade everyday life in this way are large as well as rapid, then as a rule society is unable to deal with them by sorting them into the traditional categories of acceptable and unacceptable, permissible and impermissible, fair and unfair, or even right and wrong. What is happening cannot easily be apprehended and judged on the basis of existing knowledge. Hence a very odd phenomenon occurs: the political sphere, which for much of history changed faster than anything else, suddenly seems extraordinarily slow to react.

But we are confronted not just with unprecedented revolutions in science, technology, and communications. Our orientation in foreign policy and tested approaches for keeping the balance of power stable have also become obsolete after the collapse of the Soviet Union. And as for all the things a single world power without any competition may take it into its head to do—especially with modern resources—we haven't got a clue. We don't know what the future holds for our nation states and our democracy, or if they have a future at all. And finally—to mention one particularly revealing litmus test—we don't know for what kind of life we should be preparing our children.

In sum, the changes that all of us are causing (or a great many of us, at least) find us inadequately equipped. A race against time has begun, a race with the pace of change, but even our categories for measuring change have become uncertain. We don't know when, or if, our knowledge, judgment, and ability to communicate with one another will catch up. Thus for all of us, we who together make up all the societies in the present world, time seems to be running out.

There is a historical precedent for this situation. In 1835, for example, the French political observer Alexis de Tocqueville, disquieted by what he saw, wrote: "The Christian nations of our day appear to me to present a frightening spectacle; the change carrying them along is already powerful enough for it to be impossible to stop yet not swift enough for us to despair of bringing it under control."[49] In his view it would soon be too late to assert control, as there was not enough time left for his age to develop the tools needed for the task.

Tocqueville's entreaty to his contemporaries turned out to be a false alarm. He had observed correctly that a great deal had been thrown into confusion inside the train in which they were all riding because it was accelerating. But he hadn't reckoned with the ability of his fellow passengers, his society, to adapt to a new speed, or even to constant acceleration. It proved possible, through the acquisition of new insights and habits. A generation later Jacob Burckhardt, who tended to be conservative, observed: "the [French] revolution has had results which now completely shape us and constitute an integral part of our feeling for justice and our conscience—things, therefore, that we can no longer separate from ourselves."[50]

What ultimately happens in such phases of upheaval is that people accept many changes in their lives that would have seemed impossible beforehand—and that they certainly had never desired. There is clearly a "normative power of the factual" not only in legal theory but also in everyday attitudes. It is what Max Weber called "*nomological knowledge—i.e.* the knowledge of recurrent causal sequences."[51] This makes it possible for people to adapt to an innovation, and with time they grasp its nature, learn to control it, and use it to make adjustments in other parts of their lives. Once we find our way around in the new conditions and the new speed at which they are occurring, it is quite possible for us to conclude that we are on the right track, in fact, and accept them as legitimate. After acceleration has caused great confusion and anxiety or even panic, the situation can come to look perfectly fine.

Ideally, society would gain control over its own transformation through the political process, as specific issues are debated between progressives and conservatives. We cannot expect that to happen today, however, as we don't have that kind of competency in dealing with the future.

But nothing indicates that we will not succeed in reducing the discrepancy between the speeds again and adapting to the new speeds. The only question is how many people will be left how far behind. All in all, we could regain some ground under our feet in intellectual, social, and political terms, and acquire a better overview, orientation, and conclusions, although the last can certainly vary, and even be diametrically opposed. We may even in the future be able to indulge in the illusion that we have things under control, after we have adjusted our attitudes or, to quote the German sociologist Heinrich Popitz, after we have "learned to want what we ought to want," in many areas of life, "so that in the end we do what we ought to without noticing."[52]

Then new questions could arise, simply because people consider it necessary and possible to find answers for them. As Nietzsche noted: "One hears only those questions to which one is able to find an answer."[53] Establishing new connections could become an interesting challenge again. We might even cease to depend so passively on the visual images that influence so many of our attitudes today, and revert to acquiring our orientation from logical arguments.

Of course, that will be a different society from the one we now have, and a new situation. We must look ahead to it and work toward it with the kind of confidence that Kant declared to be a human duty. It is not out of the question that history will be in demand there and even needed. Perhaps it will even be needed if we are to get there.

Naturally we cannot see where the path of present-day societies is leading. Where, for example, is the history of the political sphere headed and in what direction could or should it be guided? Should we try to preserve or modify the existing nation states, or empty them out and shift their powers to Europe? And what kind of European Union should we aim for? Should it perhaps be a Eurasian or Euro-Mediterranean Union? If power is officially transferred to a higher level, to what extent will new relationships develop among and within nation states that correspond to networks of influence (read: Mafia structures)? Will elite groups, now international in their composition, either find ways to gain a following among the populations of the former nation states or to pacify them by providing space for personal freedom without responsibilities, and set them on a diet of bread and circuses? There is a good deal of evidence to suggest that the term "freedom" is understood today mainly as a form of private leisure time, the individual counterpart to "bread and circuses" in collective terms. And the modern equivalent for "circuses" is probably "entertainment."

But whatever form the future takes, sometime and somewhere we will have to start thinking in entirely new categories about our societies, the world, and the human race. We will have to consider not only what they are, but what they ought to be and how they ought to function—not only about the constraints that affect us, but also about goals and purpose.[54] Sometime, somewhere people will stop trying just to keep up with "developments" and simply adapting to them whether they want to or not. Instead their sense of responsibility will be extended to include what can and should exist. Perhaps this sense of responsibility will even strengthen the democratic processes that give expression to public opinion and the public will, and will in turn receive support from them.

Could this happen in Europe? Maybe we will at some point regain a sense of self and begin to reflect on the remaining features of our lives that are characteristically European, that are homegrown. This process would certainly entail risks, and force us to confront some potentially terrible things—but they also form part of what gave the modern world its stamp, for better or worse. In any case such reflection would promote self-awareness, and it could be the starting point for future self-determination on both the individual and political, collective level.

It is paradoxical, after all, that this Europe, which has contributed so much to the self-determination of individuals and nations, keeps explaining what it is compelled to do to keep from falling behind—and pays no attention to its own foundations, and what it consequently can and should be or, indeed, in what its duty consists.

With the passing of time, then, the question why history matters could well be posed in an entirely new way. On the one hand we might ask about our own roots, if we could reconnect with them; on the other we might ask about history and world history in a general and fundamental way.

Presumably we will have to start over in many areas. People will have to do history differently. It will take on a different appearance in the work of professional historians. And while it will certainly not be a discipline in the vanguard of other branches of scholarship, it might become *ancilla anthropologiae,* a handmaid of anthropology, if questions about humankind become a stronger focus of interest.

Perhaps in the future people will view the great variety of the historical world as a panorama rather than a process,[55] something that may be logical in a time in which all times flow together. It is highly unlikely that the old assumptions will be revived that treat all human history as an upward spiral of progress, or that a major group or class will identify itself with progress. On the other hand, one could well ask what an attempt to extend Kant's *Idea for a Universal History from a Cosmopolitan Point of View* might look like today.

In any event the idea may suggest itself that we can learn from history both on single points and as a whole. According to Polybius, studying history provides the best training not only for an active life, but also for learning how to bear the vicissitudes of fortune.[56] And so historical processes and the peculiarly complicated ways in which human beings are entangled in them—together with the adjustments they make in order to live with and even to identify themselves with such processes—will attract interest. This will become ever more important, as as we must gain an understanding of how we are changing the whole world and ourselves—much more profoundly than ever before—without intending it. And ultimately people might again seek in the contemplation of history that "freedom amidst awareness that we are firmly bound in general and borne along by the current of necessity."

History will become meaningful, even essential, if only because a striving for an overview, for a sense of accountability for our world, must regain ground. It is something that I hold to be a human right and even an important element of human dignity, and I believe it will come to the fore again. Hannah Arendt called understanding "an unending activity by which . . . we come to terms with, reconcile ourselves to reality, that is, to be at home in the world."[57] If this is the aim, then there is no need to worry about the future of history as a field of orientation for the public as well as professionals.

We should be concerned, however, about the question of how history should be done today and in the foreseeable future. And to do this we must start with today's matters and probably make a few prognoses as well. But I don't want to get ahead of myself (even if I will not be able to cover all of the interesting questions in future chapters). However, I must add that if some aspects of history continue to seem anachronistic, that is only right and proper. For only in this way can it serve its own age and future ages.

2

Around 1500

The "European Miracle" and What Made It Possible

"Theme: Our work in this course will consist in linking a number of historical observations and inquiries to a series of half-random trains of thought." These modest, almost playfully defensive, words open the lecture notes Jacob Burckhardt used for his course "On the Study of History," beginning in Basel in the winter of 1868–1869.[1]

Here we will be far less concerned with "a number of observations" than with a series of questions that to a large extent must remain open. Nor will these questions be linked "to a series of half-random trains of thought." Instead, the aim is to shed light from several angles on one problem that we historians face today—especially if we regard history not as a clump of special interests and discourses, but as a field that also aspires to an awareness and understanding of the present.

I would claim that an interest in the present time, or in the key changes in the past that created present conditions, must be the point of departure for every general reflection about the study of history. That remains true even if most people today no longer seem to share historians' interest in the past (and historians for the most part neglect the present). It is no accident that European historiography begins with Herodotus, who was essentially motivated by questions that began with conditions in his day and sought to learn how they had come about, as well as to understand the processes guiding the course of human fate. It also tends to be the case that questions about the present are simultaneously questions about the future.

In view of today's shrinking world and the diversity of historical studies being pursued in different cultures, such an interest in the present has become crucial to human existence. The histories of the world's many countries, empires, and continents are by and large very different, and for most of history they ran their course in almost total isolation from one another. The present day, however, we share to a large degree, and thus we have a common space to which we can refer, and in which the many diverse histories meet, directly or indirectly. There the connections between all the different historical approaches can find solid ground. As a result we are dealing with quite a different set of problems than those Burckhardt faced.

Jacob Burckhardt's reflections took the "three great powers" of the state, religion, and culture as their starting point; he first analyzed the ways in which these institutions interacted, and then considered "the accelerated movements of the whole process of history, the theory of crises and revolutions." He intended to concentrate on "the *recurrent, constant,* and *typical* as echoing in us and intelligible through us." Burckhardt stressed his lack of interest in the "longitudinal sections" that characterized the "philosophy of history current hitherto."

He nonetheless ended up discussing those "longitudinal sections" again and again, as his reference to "the accelerated movements of the whole process of history" indicates. But quite apart from that, it seems to me that a question related to the present is the only possible way to begin a general reflection about history today. This is mainly because most of us approach history as "outsiders," so to speak; the dominant factor in our experience is not historical continuity, but rather constant change and the new situations this change brings about. Burckhardt worried about something completely different, namely a teleological view of history, but this no longer exists—or has not yet come back into fashion. We no longer share the assumptions about universal progress or history as the gradual fulfillment of a grand design that nineteenth-century Europeans "imbibed . . . [from] their infancy,"[2] as Burckhardt put it.

While Jacob Burckhardt could sum up the factors that underlie and give rise to history in his somewhat simplified model of the three powers and their interaction, the historical world and the driving forces behind it look far more complex and numerous to us. We see economics as playing a far larger role; and an anthropological perspective shows many phenomena in a new light. It is also not so easy to divide things up neatly into separate "powers," for they overlap in too many different ways in different epochs. The underlying forces on which a culture—our culture—rests, especially the long-term ones, along with the culture itself, have become urgent problems for us in a wholly new way. We cannot avoid the questions they raise.

Burckhardt ended his introduction by saying, "we are often rudely reminded of the general and individual shortcomings of our capacity for knowledge."[3] His reminder remains valid for this discussion, and in a heightened sense. One reason is that the kinds of questions we are dealing with here are not accessible to the usual methods employed by historians. And although it is possible to describe the methods one would need—essentially they boil down to comparisons—individuals are limited in what they can achieve by using them. Nor has collaboration produced much in the way of results, unfortunately.

The aspect of our present situation that I wish to address here is the European special path. I say "special path" because European culture clearly was not simply one culture among others. It followed a path from Athens to Auschwitz that not only differed in fundamental respects from all others, but has also transformed the world profoundly.[4] In this process Europe was seconded over time and in increasing measure by its most important offshoot, the United States, which ultimately outstripped it.

As soon as you go back some distance in any other part of world history, it immediately becomes obvious that the question of the European special path is central to an understanding of the present there: for without that path the present in this other part of the world does not appear self-evident in any respect at all; rather, it stands out against a backdrop of epochs determined in a very different manner, and the part of history that gave rise to the wide gap between then and now becomes a problem. It turns out to consist primarily of the history of the people who promoted change all around the world—the Europeans, or perhaps one should say "the West." It would be possible just to document European intervention in the many separate histories of the world and leave it at that. But we won't understand the larger picture until we ask why this intervention occurred and what caused it to be successful. At the same time this question is part of a contemplation of the mixtures and symbioses into which the various cultures of the world entered when they adopted elements of European and American culture, either willingly or unwillingly, under diverse kinds of pressure—in a process that continues to the present day.

Moreover, the question of the European special path is central to Europe's understanding of itself—as well as to the way it is perceived from the outside.

This question is not regarded as urgent in European societies. Nor is it a simple one, once it leaves the domain of scholarship, for it poses several dangers. One is the naive pride (stronger in America than in Europe of course) in some of the results of this history, which are understood as positive, exemplary, as setting a standard. They include mass prosperity, many types of freedom, and, last but not least, the Western concept of human rights. Not that this pride is unjustified! However, its transformation into a kind of general pride, and consequently a sense of superiority and entitlement, *is* highly problematic. The arrogance that goes with it could produce unpleasant results. Such an attitude leads to the overhasty conclusion that the whole world ought to become like the West. People can mean well when they say this; it can be plausibly argued with a good conscience, by taking what is Western to be universal. Yet it overlooks the fact that others see in the universalist attitudes of the rich countries mainly a sense of their own superiority and ambitions to dominate, and that is not based on subjective impressions alone. One quality on which Europe prides itself is tolerance, and with a certain justification, but often it does not extend as far as some might like to believe.

On the other hand, there is a sense of embarrassment about all the harm Europe has done,[5] and perhaps also a fear that Europeans will be reminded of their own obligations. And finally there has been the effect, fed from many sources, of Europeans' sense of uncertainty about themselves and their own idiosyncracies, which they enjoy indulging but dislike being reminded of. Not without reason has the tendency grown in the West to accept—or claim—that all peoples and cultures are equal, and that no cultural idiosyncracies are superior to any other. At least it makes unpleasant thoughts superfluous; for otherwise the suspicion of racism surfaces all too quickly.

If I am not mistaken, Europe's potential self-confidence is hemmed in by a web of ambition and self-righteousness, but also by bad conscience, anxiety, and a great deal of hypocrisy. Europeans tend to consider themselves something special, but then again they want to be like everyone else.

We don't seem sufficiently able to distinguish between what Europe once was and meant for the world, for both good and evil, and what it is—and its potential in an altered world. An additional difficulty consists in the fact that although we are sitting in one boat with the United States and sailing under a Western flag, we have almost no influence on the course that is set. How can one think about European uniqueness in such circumstances?

Nevertheless, there has been such debate among historians, and it has grown livelier in the past few years, not least because of the much-discussed book by E. L. Jones entitled *The European Miracle*.[6] I would like to sum up some of the insights of this discussion here, and then present my own somewhat different perspective.

One can date the beginning of the "European miracle" from different points: the Industrial Revolution, the rise of modern capitalism, or the scientific revolution. Or one can start with the question of how it happened that Europeans set sail from home, discovered and surveyed the world, set up bases around it, and settled some parts and conquered others—first the Portuguese and Spanish, followed quickly by the French, Dutch, and English. All of them exploited their territories and in the long run imposed European law upon them. In other words, the question becomes why was it Europe that did this, and not China, for instance, or the empire of the great moguls in India or the Ottoman Empire? And why was it that these empires did little to hinder European expansion? (It must be noted, however, that China and for a time Japan offered resistance to the Europeans and were able to close themselves off from European incursions to some extent. For their part, the Ottomans advanced to the outskirts of Vienna and ruled considerable parts of Hungary, the Balkans, and the Mediterranean for a long time.)

But whatever date one chooses as the starting point of the "European miracle," one must go back to a relatively distant point in history. The modern era did not begin overnight, and it gained in breadth and lasting influence only gradually. The recent debate on the subject has been dominated by economic historians or those who tend to pay particular attention to economic factors, and they have important predecessors, such as Karl Marx and Max Weber. While the debate gives priority to economic conditions and their immediate basis in geography, technology, and science, it also includes a wide variety of other factors in European success, such as political organization and religion. Virtually everyone is in agreement, however, that the origins and shaping influences of Europe are to be sought no earlier than the Middle Ages or at most, roughly speaking, the year 1000 C.E. Max Weber alluded to antiquity, but only in passing, in order to define the medieval city; he was more interested in a comparative and typological point of view than in assessing any continuing influence (in contrast to Marx). Weber recognized only a few minor exceptions, such as what he called "the day of Antioch," when Jews and Gentiles shared a meal, which he considered decisive for the history of Christianity and the West.[7]

This means that the search for the reasons behind the success and superiority of Europe, its victory, has become separated over the last few decades from another view that for a long time was so prevalent as to be considered almost self-evident. It held that the West had its origins in antiquity and descended from the Greeks, the Romans, and Christianity, whose roots lay in large measure in Judaism. It is very odd how this view has simply disappeared from the discussion. Perhaps people saw it as too closely connected with the old, blinkered view that world history essentially consisted of the history of Europe or the West. No historian denies these origins categorically of course, but they no longer seem to play a role in the development of the European special path. Instead, that path passes through the stages of "expansion," "the Scientific Revolution," and "the Industrial Revolution," with all their proximate and more remote preconditions, side effects, and consequences.

My own question—to come straight to the point—is whether antiquity did not play a significant role after all in the development of Europe and its special path. Was it perhaps a necessary condition, or did the special path actually begin in antiquity? I would like to approach these questions from two angles. The first is from our own vantage point, looking back from the modern era. For this approach I have chosen the year 1500 as a starting point, the beginning of European expansion in the world together with all the more or less contemporaneous, far-reaching changes that expansion wrought within Europe. (Of course, the Europeans had already embarked before that time on some of the paths on which they made advances, and in the first decades of the sixteenth century the further direction was still entirely open, as was the question of whether it would eventually lead to success.)

In the next chapter we will look at the question from the second angle, going back to antiquity and asking what experiences and achievements continued to have an important effect in later ages.

One might say that my question leads to a search for what is European, and my sense is that Europe begins with antiquity, not with the diverse collection of Germanic, Latin, Slavic, Finno-Ugrian, and other peoples who inhabited Europe after the decline of ancient cultures.

I should like to add at once, however, that my own "capacity for knowledge" (in Burckhardt's phrase)—and, as far as I know, that of historians in general—is not nearly sufficient to prove this hypothesis or even supply enough evidence to make it appear probable. Therefore, I propose to pursue questions that must essentially remain open.

There is one thing about which I am quite sure, however: we must ask what created the preconditions that made Europe's special path possible; there is no way around it. If the question exceeds our abilities to answer it for the present, and if the answers will presumably always remain a subject for debate, that is no reason not to ask it. Even historical questions that aim too high can have their purpose. They are justified if the subject being investigated is important, or if they sharpen our awareness of different components of more general problems, such as what constitutes history or in our particular case, how does history give rise to culture? At the same time formulating such questions makes it clear what a challenge they present.

In order to find answers, one certainly ought to have a far better and more precise understanding of high cultures outside Europe, particularly their strengths and potential (which are usually somewhat obscure to European eyes). But we also need to understand their limitations and to what extent these were defining and constitutive, that is, to what extent they made it impossible for the members of such a society to go beyond them in any permanent way. And one would also need to know many areas of European history very much better than I do. Nevertheless, someone must make a start by risking some comparisons.

At the present moment the problem can be tackled only if we see ourselves as architects constructing a false vault: we must start to build from two sides, hoping to meet in the middle. One point must be clear from the start: I am not proposing that we return to the old construction of history, the one that concentrated exclusively on Europe. This Eurocentric approach began in essence with the Greeks and Romans and saw them as models, proceeded through the Middle Ages, and finally arrived at the modern era with its striving for ever greater heights. Whatever the merits may have been of past arguments for this approach, such narrow-mindedness is not possible now.

This construction—in its typical form—not only overlooked the Eastern sources for much in Greek and Roman culture, but also rested on arrogant assumptions about the rest of humanity. Intelligent observers, some of whom took their cue from Nietzsche, began to distance themselves from such a view of superior European culture after the First World War. That conflict "demonstrated to all of us in one monstrous mass experiment," wrote the Austrian author Robert Musil, "how easily human beings"—he meant "Europeans"—"can move to the most radical extremes and back again without experiencing any basic change. They change—but what changes is not the *self.*" Musil also observed generally, without any distinction as to culture or "races," that the human being "is every bit as capable of cannibalism as of *The Critique of Pure Reason.* We should stop thinking that this creature *does* what it *is;* rather it be-comes, for God knows what reason, what it does."[8]

In view of such experiences, which have increased horrifically in the interim, the humanistic ideals of the old model of European his-tory do not take one very far. And that has certainly contributed to its being quietly jettisoned (even if word hasn't yet reached some scholars of ancient history). We know how many Europeans have failed to live up to those ideals, even if their education stressed them, and also that non-Europeans could master what we took to be "our" culture, achieving more with it than a great many Europe-ans with whom they found themselves in competition.

Nevertheless, the question regarding differences among cultures remains relevant. Internal cultural patterns and forms of replication are more resistant to change than are individuals. And cultures used to change even more slowly before the differences between them had been worn down so much. They needed a very long time and many specific conditions in order to develop, each in its own way. And in this sense it may very well be the case that we—without ar-rogance, without any humanistic narrow-mindedness—have good cause to inquire into how the culture of Greek and Roman antiq-uity contributed to the identity of Europe. And that we in doing so must go beyond the rather narrow radius of the economic histori-ans' approach.

Europe is more than geographical expansion, modern capitalism, rationalization, and the Industrial Revolution—or at least it used to be. Its history can accordingly not be viewed solely from these and related vantage points.

How, we may then ask, did Europe come to pursue a special path in the modern era?[9] I will first try to summarize the usual arguments, and follow them with my own questions. A part of the explanation is usually sought in geography: the characteristics of the continent, the soil, and climate. There is generally a rather moderate climate, but with cold winters—especially north of the Alps—so that many sources of diseases are at least greatly weakened. To be sure, there are also epidemics, to which human beings are particularly susceptible, but very few large-scale natural disasters in comparison with other parts of the world.

In Europe the soil is relatively well suited to agriculture, without any need for major technology such as the regulation of rivers. Once land has been cleared of trees, no special skill is required to cultivate it (although skill helps). Thus all kinds of people can live in small groups, without depending on the creation of large realms or political entities for their survival. If wars inflict damage, people can start over relatively quickly in the same place. There is plenty of room for private initiative. In general there is sufficient water, apart from occasional periods of drought, and some important minerals are available in the ground, especially iron, with enough forestation to provide charcoal for smelting.

In this spacious landscape the population was unequally distributed, especially north of the Alps. Therefore, over time a trade in bulk goods became a necessity—in grain, for example. Other basic commodities were also unevenly distributed, such as salt. Fishing developed on a large scale, and the catch was distributed by means of long-distance trade routes. A series of coastal waterways and rivers facilitated trade.

Since not all the land was needed for cultivating grain, a great deal of it could be used for grazing cattle. This was advantageous in providing a diet rich in protein as well as fertilizer for crops. As a result the average European grew taller and heavier than the inhabitants of India and China.

Furthermore, the terrain is divided by mountain ranges and hills in a way that facilitated the growth of a number of separate political entities. And, finally, eastern Europe served as a buffer zone, protecting western and central Europe from the repeated incursions of nomadic peoples from the interior of Asia.

Arguments of this type, of which further examples could easily be produced, suffer, however, from a general weakness: they underestimate the ability of human beings to use very different strategies to adapt to different environments and make them productive. Scholars like to argue, for instance, that the Aegean region of Greece was highly suited to the development of small, independent city-states after 1000 B.C. However, the same region had clearly been able to produce and sustain relatively large realms (and palace cultures) during the earlier Mycenaean age. Similarly, central Europe easily permitted political entities of varying sizes to flourish over the centuries; later growth was not due solely to improved transportation and communication networks, which evolved slowly.

It is fairly certain that the natural contours of the terrain did not suggest regulating the flow of rivers. Nevertheless, it was possible for very different political and economic structures to develop. The geographical conditions left considerable freedom to inhabitants and rulers.

Furthermore, the fact that Mongolian and Turkic peoples (in contrast to the Hungarians, for example) made their forays chiefly into China and southward toward India, Persia, and Asia Minor can probably be explained by the wealth and advanced cultures that they found there, in contrast to the relatively primitive development of Europe.

Some scholars have pointed out the relatively low population density in earliest times, which then grew rapidly—through the creation of settlements, among other things. In this argument momentum resulted from a need to catch up. There is also a calculation according to which west of a line drawn from St. Petersburg to Trieste the population married later on average than in the East, and had fewer children, a trend that worked against overpopulation. Apart, however, from the questionable accuracy of many such calculations for earlier periods, don't such claims or results demand an explanation in their own right rather than provide one?

As far as the protein content of the European diet goes (to the extent that it can be determined in comparison to the diets of other peoples), it is hard to know what conclusions to draw. It did not give Europeans a clear overall advantage, it would appear. In any case it is clear that particular features of ethnic groups do not explain anything by themselves, because everything we are able to detect about such characteristics (apart from skin color and other external features, perhaps) suggests that they are determined by historical influences as much as they determine history. Maybe the genetic investigations of the Icelandic and Estonian populations will teach us otherwise, but as long as that has not occurred, we should be cautious in drawing conclusions.

A series of other factors, which historians mention again and again in the context of Europe's unique development, provoke considerable doubt as soon as one learns that these same factors were also present and at work in the societies of India, China, the Islamic world, and elsewhere—to the same extent or perhaps more so than in Europe—without creating the sort of dynamics that characterize the European special path. Any desire to stress the importance of the German plow or three-field crop rotation techniques vanishes as soon as one thinks of the sophisticated agricultural methods devised in China. Or do important differences exist on specific points?

With all due respect for the industriousness and skills of medieval European craftsmen and the courage and wealth of medieval merchants, as soon as one looks toward India, China, and the Muslim world it becomes impossible to maintain that such qualities are specifically European. Of course, we encounter certain requirements and methods unique to each culture. But do the recognizable elements of a capacity for production and trade in Europe justify identifying this capacity as a special driving force toward modern capitalism and the decisive role played by Europe in world affairs for such a long time? Max Weber suggested the appropriate answer long ago.[10]

It is equally unlikely that "the invention of invention" in the me-

dieval period represents something specifically European. David
Landes has noted the invention in the West of the water wheel,
spectacles, the mechanical clock, and printing with movable type,
for instance.[11] But if one compares the excellent processes for smelting iron that the Chinese developed, and their invention of the mag-
netic compass, paper, and printing with movable type (in the eleventh century!), the astronomical clocks that they could build, or
their wonderful system of artificial canals, is medieval Europe really
ahead by more than a nose? Europeans figured out how to make
gunpowder more effective by granulating it, but it was the Chinese
who invented it. It is true that eyeglasses and clocks made labor
more effective in a smaller population, but how much did that contribute to giving Europe an edge? There is also some evidence, incidentally, that Chinese emperors tried to stimulate inventions by offering rewards.[12]

It is correct to say that fishermen in the Atlantic had developed
vessels far more seaworthy than the typical Mediterranean ship
long before the time of Columbus. However, could Columbus's car-
avel have competed with the ships that the Chinese had built a short
time earlier? The largest presumably had a water displacement of
1,500 tons, whereas the figure for Vasco da Gama's flagship is 300.
The Chinese ships had more cannons, far larger crews and loading
capacity, and undertook voyages as far as Madagascar. Around
1420 the Chinese fleet consisted of 3,800 vessels; 1,350 of them
were warships, including 400 "floating fortresses."

When the famous expedition to South Africa led by Admiral
Cheng Ho set sail in 1405, it consisted of 317 vessels with 28,000
men on board. Whole forests had been cut down to build the ships,
and new settlements created to house the workers: hundreds of
ship's carpenters, smiths, sail makers, drivers, rope makers, and
even men whose job was to measure the passage of time. The shipbuilding techniques were extremely refined and sophisticated.[13] Columbus, by contrast, had three caravels when he set out for the

West Indies; his undertaking was undoubtedly much more daring and adventurous, for his route led him out into the open ocean. The willingness and competence to undertake such a voyage may express some specifically European quality. But one could reach such a conclusion only if it could be proved that such a quality was lacking elsewhere. Possibly it was more important that Columbus's first expedition, like several that followed it, had found sufficient support from national and city governments such as Genoa. And in any case this alone did not guarantee that the Europeans would win the race, or that they would ultimately be the only ones to cover the greatest distances, even penetrating into Siberia. And we should not overlook the outstanding achievements of the Chinese in navigation, as well as the Polynesians in their trade across the South Pacific.

But if one then notices that the Chinese failed to develop or exploit numerous inventions, that, for example, the great astronomical clock in Beijing was not set going again when it became clogged, that the smelting of iron was suddenly reduced, that even the magnificent fleet was allowed to rot after Cheng Ho's voyage—then it is hard to resist the impression that what was missing was not ability in the most varied forms, but the possibilities to make use of it in ways that would keep leading to new inventions. Thus while many different impulses to invent, discover, and venture might arise, it was possible to put a stop to them—and that was even the express intention.

Clearly political power in China was so finely balanced that significant changes—perhaps especially those stemming from private initiative—were regarded in many circles as deeply unsettling. Such an attitude would have corresponded relatively well to the teachings of Confucius, which were full of mistrust toward merchants and trade (but also, it should be noted, toward the military). Burckhardt speaks of the kind of nation that closes itself off, saying it has cost "so much to bring the state into tolerable order that people expect no good to come from the outside world, but only trouble."[14] In China the order was so well established in people's minds that ultimately it imposed limits on individual enterprise. The argument has even been made that the majority of the merchants and manufacturers, who had come up with so many innovations, ultimately proved willing to submit to the system, even if a minority undercut it by smuggling and bribing officials.[15] Uprisings did occur, but only in protest against particular officials, or specific grievances; they never intended, or at least never succeeded, in instituting new rights and freedoms, let alone creating the "confraternities" of citizens in medieval European cities that Max Weber discussed.[16]

Thus China—and presumably other highly developed cultures— seem to prove something that Thucydides took to be self-evident, namely, that human beings continually strive to improve their situation if they are not hindered by external circumstances. Thucydides was thinking about the dangers of trade voyages during the early period of Greek history, not the least of which was piracy.[17] But the intentions of a particular political order can apparently produce the same result, if it is an order that preserves itself through the exercise of power, permits no alternative to itself, and has a framework so clearly established that no escape from the system that foresees a given space for each group is possible, or in which open conflicts between diverging ambitions are largely suppressed. The question is only whether in addition to external factors more profound barriers exist based on particular mentalities or outlooks, barriers that prevent the unfolding of significant private initiatives or cut them off at the roots in the way children are educated and socialized.

Any reasonably solid conclusions will have to be based on comprehensive cross-cultural studies. When one notes that international trade flourished among Muslim merchants,[18] however, it seems likely that a great deal of freedom existed in that society for the development of private initiative. Yet the breadth and intensity of Islamic receptivity to ancient learning in the early Middle Ages, and the enrichment of it by Muslim scholars through their own research, prompt the question of why—despite its great libraries, many institutions comparable to universities, and notable scholarship—the culture did not advance beyond a certain point. Was there a window of opportunity that would have allowed it to embark on the same course as that later pursued by Christian Europe? And if this failed to happen, was the cause perhaps simply that the "essential strength of Asia" had been "permanently and forever broken by the two periods of Mongol rule"? It was conceivable, Jacob Burckhardt thought, that Asia was "dead" as a threat to Europe.[19] But perhaps the latitude given to trade and research had relatively little influence on the development of early Muslim empires because these activities had little or no effect on political structures. Was this because no disposition toward profound change was present in their populations (or even just parts of them)? Or because resources were not in such short supply in relation to demand that great efforts had to be made again and again to mobilize new energies? Because the potential for innovation that existed in Muslim empires remained limited to scholarship, technology, and trade?

Max Weber pointed out various factors unique to Europe, such as the special character of the medieval European city, particularly its autonomy.[20] Thanks to the tradition of Roman law, inhabitants enjoyed security in legal matters, rational trial procedures, a right to participate in local government, and appropriate institutions. All this presupposed a particular conception of citizenship, which developed only in the West. In such cities people had relative freedom to strive to get ahead or not; it was worth their while to work hard, to engage in trade. A type of active entrepreneur developed, and specialization and competition could grow, with far-reaching consequences. And all of this led in turn to many lasting changes that created important foundations for modern capitalism.

In addition to the city, many scholars have correctly pointed out that an important, peculiarly European driving force was the existence of multiple and diverse political entities in competition with one another. This rivalry contributed to the cities' independence and the possibilities for initiative they offered. It guaranteed, for instance, that while censorship could be practiced in one place or another, it could never be total. The potential offered by the invention of movable type could be exploited to the full. It was also usually possible for minorities, especially capable and innovative ones (including Jews and Huguenots, among others), to escape and settle elsewhere if they were rejected, persecuted, or barred from getting ahead. In the new surroundings they were enabled to carry on their old activities to the benefit and stimulus of the economy or to undertake new ones.

In general the competition between political entities contributed in many ways to increasing civic activity and furthering research and crafts, in part by keeping taxes down.

From the beginning medieval Europe offered considerable diversity in terms not only of terrain, but also historical traditions, in places as different as Italy, where many ancient practices lived on, although in diluted form; the areas of the former Roman Empire in Gaul, in which still less of Roman civilization lived on; and the regions east of the Rhine, the newly occupied lands in the German East, Bohemia, Hungary, and Scandinavia. In addition, many important stimuli and impulses—along with pillage and destruction—came from the Normans, who also served as intermediaries for Arab culture, then far more advanced than Europe's.

Did medieval Europe take shape as it did because single regions or nations took the lead at different times, producing innovations that benefited the entire continent? Spain began the process in the sixteenth century, followed by the Netherlands in the seventeenth century, and then France and England. Each led in a different way and for a limited time until the resources feeding its particular momentum had been used up (or so it seems), or until other skills and visions (which had been nurtured in other places) promised and delivered greater success.

In an odd way Europeans of this era started over again and

again. Every new invention, every new theological or philosophical school, every new style in architecture (such as Romanesque, Gothic, and baroque) was developed to a certain peak in a relatively short time. Each dominated for a while; its repertoire expanded into "late forms," only to be replaced by another. Did parallels exist in other cultures, even if they differ in details?

Was this fondness for innovation a result of competition, where it was permitted—competition in a great variety of fields? Did it result from the participation of so many people in so many different countries? For it should not be overlooked that although this world consisted of many separate political entities, the regions had close cultural ties. Scholars and their universities, artists, and merchants were in communication with their counterparts all over Europe, using the shared language of Latin (and in many cases open to ideas and contacts even in the Arab world). The links grew stronger over time with the founding of national academies, which corresponded with one another. Despite all the obstructions devised by governments and the Church, the relatively autonomous and occasionally privileged system of learning, at universities organized as self-governing bodies, repeatedly prevailed and registered great successes, as did the arts.

Overall, in any case, much suggests that already in the Middle Ages and early modern period Europe was characterized on a relatively broad scale by differentiation, dynamics, and a keen interest in making new discoveries. This was due only in part to expansion overseas. There was a cumulative tendency to the advances, countered by relatively little opposition.

Were the forces of preservation weaker than in other cultures? Were the hierarchies less firmly established and anchored, so that people could be more open to innovations of many different kinds? Were the differences—and communication—simply so strong between the various regions of Europe that the sheer number of approaches to solving problems created momentum toward ever-increasing change? Or did particular features of the Christian faith and its theology or special qualities of the European city play a role, and perhaps tip the scales?

Of course, the explanations presented above are very sketchy, and many riddles remain, such as the constant replacement of one style by another. But no matter how all these factors may have played out, no matter what further explanations of this sort could be proposed, do they really explain Europe's special capacity to act? Don't they demand their own explanation in turn? I mean this not just in the sense that historians can never stop seeking forerunners or trying to trace causes further and further back in the past. My question is rather whether a real understanding of anything does not require a certain degree of depth.

Can one simply assume that the plurality of political entities was a geographical given for medieval—and modern—society in particular? I doubt it! The conditions and influences that shaped them probably lie in specific features of history, not of geography, especially in late antiquity, which established the patterns for the times that followed.

The Germanic kings and groups of allied tribes who advanced into the Roman Empire in that era and established their rule both within the empire and along its border areas, under strong Roman influence, were themselves at a fairly early stage of cultural development. They found themselves confronted with a disintegrating empire that controlled a vast area. As a result the dimensions of their territories, and their frontiers, were more or less predetermined, but at the same time the existence of a certain connection beyond them was a given, too.

Strong rulers were able to establish large realms. Charlemagne's empire stretched from the Pyrenees to the Elbe River and deep into Austria and Italy. Yet it could not survive. And the power accumulated by the great emperors of the following period proved to be ephemeral. A shifting number of states existing side by side remained the norm, although lasting rule was established in some places on a relatively modest scale.

But this meant that, despite all the achievements of the German tribes, and their considerable ability to learn, they had also inherited a weakness: they were not nearly so quickly able to establish lasting superior power in a central location, that is, to institutionalize their rule in the grand style and with staying power, to cement it in functioning administrative bodies, and anchor it in the outlook of their members (especially the nobility).

The question arises whether the relative weakness (not only in terms of large numbers and rivalry) of the European political entities provided a legacy from the very start that would force monarchs over the centuries, no matter what they might try to accomplish, to make a good many concessions to the aristocrats among their followers, and also to the cities. And this was just as true for the Church, whose support the monarchs urgently needed for many reasons. Far from submitting to secular rulers, the Church always existed as a separate center of power, confronting lay authority when not actively combating it. Subjects thus were able to acquire and retain many liberties, not just as privileges granted to them individually, but often as members of a group that could negotiate collectively. Over time these constellations could have been subject to a particular dynamic.

Perhaps one could make the claim (or demonstrate) that in this Europe—in one place or another—relatively large amounts of unrest and discontent were at work. Is it correct to say that resources were not nearly sufficient to meet demand, and that demands in excess of the possibilities could be absorbed (and effectively limited) in some places, perhaps, but never suppressed everywhere at once by an all-embracing system? The Germanic kings' ambitions centered on the emperor's crown and other goals connected with it that in the last analysis were not achievable. Can we then say that forces were always at work *somewhere* that aimed, consciously or unconsciously, at more than just small adjustments in the existing social order? Did they keep the entire system in motion and alter it further (giving rise to still more change)? And thus it was not simply a zero-sum game that was being played, and the rise of one force did not simply correspond to the decline of another?

Was this not the reason why more possibilities existed here than just a little free space opening up now and then? Why significant economic developments could take place, with many overlapping interests and conflicts that resulted in even greater changes? Above all, possibilities opened up for princes, the Church, and cities to create lasting institutions to secure their own power, although many setbacks occurred. Uprisings could sometimes lead to the creation of new social orders. It became possible for people to conceive of alternatives to existing institutions, at first on a small scale, but later also on a large one, over and over again. Members of the estates and early parliaments developed ideas and ambitions that made later constitutions possible, and the founding of democracies and republics. The exercise of autonomous powers was ultimately extended from the nobility, cities, and sometimes even peasants to all the citizens of a nation (although in most cases a phase of absolutism intervened).

But here we should inquire not only about particular constellations that were determined by antiquity, but also about legacies from that period, which later peoples soon took over and made their own.

Roman traditions continued to dominate much in Italy, of course. Medieval cities were based on them in many respects, such as their concept of citizenship, the *coniurationes* (oath-bound fraternities), and the city constitutions that were established following ancient models—including the offices of consul and tribune of the people, for instance—thanks to a knowledge of institutions acquired from Roman historians.

Rome had also handed down a legacy to the Church, the spiritual power that was always something of a countervailing force to political authority. The Church was the heir of antiquity in three ways:

1. through the Gospels, the teachings of Christ, which came from Hellenistic Palestine, that is, from the Jewish tradition but also the Greek, in ways hard to define precisely. In any event the Gospels were passed on in the Greek language.

2. through its theology, principally the patriarchs, who were strongly influenced by Greek and Roman thought; and also through the necessities of apologetics.

3. through the institutions of the western Church, in which Roman influence extended all the way to terminology; in addition, the papacy drew on the myth of Rome.

The confrontation of worldly and spiritual power gave rise to fruitful tensions on many levels, even within the minds of individuals. But the interplay between these two forces also created free spaces. As a result the basis on which European monarchies were founded lacked certain important elements usually present elsewhere.

Discrepancies between the teachings of the Gospels and the institutions of the Church were the reason for many renewal movements, which extended into the political sphere. The tension between "the imperatives of a supra-mundane God" and the normal activities of "a creaturely world" was virulent in many ways.[21] The tradition of the monastic orders, which multiplied rapidly and also developed their own rivalries, gave rise to a counterculture that turned its back on the world; nevertheless, such world-renouncing orders could suddenly find themselves confronted with political, economic, and educational tasks, and for some of them they found interesting solutions. Ascetics were sent into the hustle and bustle of cities—another form of tension that had a profound effect on medieval society, for the monastic orders played a significant role in the organization and division of time.

On the other hand, the Church—whose members were all but indispensable as administrative, political, and even military leaders for centuries during the Holy Roman Empire in particular—preserved and passed on much from antiquity to the Middle Ages: writing, language, technology, texts (chiefly in the monasteries), and not least Roman law, which the Europeans of the Middle Ages encountered mainly in the form of canon law. Starting in Bologna in the eleventh century, however, Roman law was studied independently of the Church; other universities soon followed, keeping the tradition alive. Roman law, which would become a foundation of the modern state and its economy, had taken centuries to develop under very specific conditions. Would it have been possible to create any equivalent for it quickly if it hadn't already existed? Does the claim that a society is capable of producing what it needs extend to an entire body of law?[22] If it does, then one would have to ask next how a society could develop legal institutions without a great many university-trained jurists, who existed in medieval society and soon exerted a widespread influence. Of course, that claim is a bit reckless in any case.

The modern state is the only type constructed in such a way that it could live on without monarchy. This became essential after the French Revolution abolished it. For the same reason it also offered many favorable conditions even earlier for the needs of science (scholarship), trade, manufacturing, and for the spread of Roman law throughout society (however imperfectly the latter may have occurred). The modern state is based on a rational conception—would it have been possible without Roman law, or Greek philosophy, for that matter, and Greek political thought? What gave it the ability to survive all the profound changes that occurred and live on into the future, if not the fact that these elements formed part of its foundations?

For further fertilization of European society by antiquity with enormously far-reaching consequences, one need think only of the

Renaissance (or renaissances, from the Carolingian to the Italian of the fifteenth century and beyond). Then consider how much was adopted, sometimes from the Arabs of course, but most particularly absorbed from antiquity, almost without conscious awareness, through the medium of language, and Church theology.

The scientific community is a feature of both medieval and modern times; so are the universities, and so is the splendid combination of competition and cooperation that became characteristic of their relationship with one another.[23] Even if freedom of inquiry was not permitted everywhere on an ongoing basis, opportunities for it arose again and again, in a great variety of places; scholars could count on being able to report publicly the outcome of their research. Occasionally a patron would want to keep those results secret, but such attempts usually failed. This community could lay claim to extensive autonomy; prestige and reputation depended on achievement, which had to be demonstrated and confirmed in an international forum. All of this contributed significantly to the advance of science. But the question is: Could this learning and the respect that it enjoyed have developed without ancient models?

The natural sciences are a modern phenomenon; their precursors, such as nominalism, the natural philosophy of the fourteenth century, originated in the Middle Ages. But would medieval philosophical debates—such as those between the nominalists and realists, or the Dominican and Benedictine orders—have been possible without the legacy of antiquity? It was this legacy, revitalized in the Middle Ages, that proved so fruitful in the Renaissance and the age of Reformation, and in connection with the discoveries that promoted the development of modern international law, starting in Spain.

Corresponding evidence can be found for the economy, which grew so strong in Europe, and also for the high value attached to labor, trade, and crafts; and for the dynamics of change.[24] None of this was characteristic of antiquity; in fact, such values ran directly counter to much that determined important aspects of ancient Greek and Roman society. Nevertheless, it remains possible that—

mediated by cities, law, the citizens' freedoms, and monasticism—
essential foundations for them stemmed from antiquity. After all,
every act of receiving can give a totally new meaning and potential
to what is received.

In short, couldn't it be the case that even today, precisely under
today's scientific ambitions, antiquity ought to be considered as the
conditio sine qua non of medieval, early modern, and thus modern
and postmodern Europe, at least hypothetically/theoretically? Because the Roman Empire determined the original constellations,
further through Roman law and also precisely through the Greeks,
who through intense questioning of the political order, the gods,
and the world contributed so uncommonly much to rationalization,
down to fundamental questions of society—with many continued
effects in the Middle Ages and modern period?

But I would like to add two questions:

1. If one is seeking the conditions that made the European special
path possible, might one not have to include one rather odd fact,
namely that in antiquity (and thus, as a direct but mostly indirect
consequence, in medieval and early modern Europe as well) people
did not become so dependent, psychologically or otherwise, on a
given order of things that they were unable to imagine an alternative? In other words, didn't people maintain a sense of personal independence (and personal property!), a certain distance from the
ruling order that could turn into a virulent disaffection? And by
maintaining this distance, didn't Europeans (or, more typically, minorities within the population) also retain a potential for freedom?

2. Didn't Europe (in the sense of what was and is distinctively European) actually begin in Athens, with an entirely new freedom and
the opening of broad latitudes for the mind and imagination? And
this freedom began in the political sphere, in the discovery of the
citizen, although it had virtually no impact on the economic sphere.
Didn't this potential enable people to reach far beyond traditional
categories—with results that made the West dramatically different?

Many questions, but that is after all a good old Socratic, European tradition; or rather a characteristic way of life in which tradition is just what returns, in that it always begins anew and aims further than one can actually go.

If, however, one might think to raise the objection to these ideas that they are Europe-centric (perhaps even a lapse into old classicisms), then I would like to counter whether the view that leaves antiquity out of consideration is not far more Europe-centered—in that it takes a great deal for granted that has come down to us from antiquity and been shaped by it, and that is anything but a matter of course when seen against the background of non-European cultures.

3

Athens and Rome

The Origins of Europe's Special Path

How did Europe come to set out on its special path? We will look at this question now with respect to the Greeks and Romans: What role did they play, to what extent did they first make it possible? Are there reasons to believe that this path, and thus Europe, began in antiquity, because some defining quality of European culture took shape then? That would mean that antiquity constitutes not the "pre-history" of Europe but the "early phase" of its history, suggesting in turn that European history is primarily the history of a culture and less a history of the various ethnic groups or peoples who inhabited the continent in the Middle Ages.

The supposition that the special European path began in antiquity is not an easy or comfortable one, in view of all the self-doubt that Europeans have good reason to feel, and also because several prominent features of ancient society arouse disapprobation today, such as the existence of slavery and extreme discrimination against women.

And the supposition is not without its difficulties. After all, in late antiquity not only did the Western Roman Empire vanish but also, increasingly as time passed, the social foundations on which ancient culture had reproduced itself for centuries (although never evenly). In the East, many Roman traditions lived on for almost a millennium in the Byzantine Empire, which thus continued in a quasi-

61

permanent state of "late antiquity," as it were. While this Eastern realm influenced European history, it also suffered under it, so the Byzantine Empire can hardly be regarded as a part of Europe, save as a museum and conservator of ancient, mostly Greek, traditions until they blossomed again, chiefly in Italy, during the Renaissance.

In trying to identify the aftereffects of antiquity, we must therefore distinguish between two fundamental kinds of influence. First, antiquity laid the groundwork for developments such as the rise of the German kingdoms in late antiquity, which in turn led to so many later consequences. And, secondly, there were the direct lessons to be learned from antiquity, in other words all that it handed down as a legacy.

It is true that the modes in which any legacy is adopted are determined by the situation of the recipients, by their needs and their understanding of what the legacy means.[1] In this particular case, however, the process may have extended far beyond the adoption of a few particular features, and consisted instead of something far more comprehensive, namely, a continuation of the special path already begun in antiquity. This could have happened either through a consistent stream of tradition, either conscious or unconscious, or through frequent recourse to ancient culture to borrow or revive specific aspects of it, as occurred especially during the great renaissances but also at other times.

How a culture arises and the conditions required for it are not easy to determine. Our concrete questions here are: Could Europe emerge from ancient culture having incorporated not just a random set of characteristics, but precisely those that would prove definitive (which remain to be identified)? And, if so, how?

In the last chapter our central question was: How strongly was Europe determined from the outset by conditions at the end of antiquity? Now the time has come to ask what made the development of Greek and Roman cultures extraordinary. One can make the case for a whole series of features that distinguish them from all other cultures, and then infer what the consequences were for further development. My hypothesis is: what distinguished antiquity was the *conditio sine qua non* for Europe. Modern Europe could not have resulted from any other path. Yet that must remain a hypothesis, for the reason alone that in order to judge one would have to know the potential of other cultures (i.e., what they did not produce but could have produced to attain a similar path). I would add that the special features of antiquity that are distinguishable also seem to me to suggest that it is here that the actual early phase of European history took place.

The cultures of the Greeks and Romans were very different. As we consider the formation of a culture, the Greeks will be our primary focus of interest. Of course, the Romans developed their law and forms of political organization, along with an empire that enabled them to inscribe them profoundly on the memory of the Mediterranean world and beyond, giving Rome mythic status. Apart from this, their contribution lies more in the reception, preservation, completion, and geographical and historical extension of Greek culture (no mean thing in itself), until finally Christianity began to prepare a new world on the foundation of both, negating many aspects of them, to be sure, but also adopting a great deal.

First of all then, the Greeks![2] The process by which they formed their culture differs in certain essential points from everything else we know—from Egypt and Mesopotamia to India, China, Central America, and also, to a degree, sub-Saharan Africa. That is to say, this culture already represents a special path, in that it occurred without the shaping force of a monarchy. Instead, Greek culture emerged from the center of society, with the aristocracy at first playing the principal role. Connected with this is the fact that in its initial phase, political power almost never acquired a significance worth mentioning. Not much opportunity existed for the conscious planning and shaping of instruments of power, relatively speaking, especially because in the early centuries, when important trends were established, the developing culture was shared by a large number of independent city-states. There was no thought of a coterminous culture and empire, as was the rule elsewhere. The separation of these polities from one another by the sea may have played a role.

The initial phase in the first half of the last pre-Christian millennium, chiefly in the eighth, seventh, and sixth centuries, was then followed by a second decisive phase in which the Greeks were forcibly separated from many of their own traditions at various places. The further development of their culture became concentrated in one city, Athens, where a fresh start was made in many respects, a way that enabled the culture to have an important impact on world history. At this point change was most emphatically politically inspired—in its dynamic, experience, social identity, in its sacrilegious component, and questioning of tradition. Once again, however, change was not dominated by a monarchy, but took place within a democracy. This means far more than we normally tend to think, especially in an era that is weary of hearing democracy discussed.

Incidentally, the cultural development that occurred in ancient Israel (and probably also in the Phoenician cities in its vicinity)[3] also lacked the strong shaping force of a kingdom, although the form of society was monarchical. We know virtually nothing, however, about the distinctive features of the Phoenicians, and, as far as we can see, their role in world history was limited to exploring the Mediterranean. One effect of this was to draw the Greeks into a broad exchange with Eastern cultures, which perhaps provided models for founding cities and affected life in the city-state, not to forget written language, which the Greeks borrowed from the Phoenicians and adapted to fit their own needs. Israel proved strikingly able to resist strong influences from its surroundings, but politically was quickly exhausted.[4] It had to withdraw into itself with all the magnificence of its God and the ways in which it related to

Him, and exerted a significant influence beyond its own borders only when mediated through the Greek language. This occurred through the Jewish scholars in Alexandria who wrote in Greek, but chiefly through the Christians.

The significance of a powerful (and not declining) monarchy in placing its stamp on developing cultures is reflected in the fact that non-European high cultures, as far as I can see, never conceived of any alternative to monarchy but chaos (except at a very late stage, and then under European influence). Even if an empire that achieved unity later disintegrated, the fragments were ruled by princes (or governors), and often it was one of them who restored the lost unity under his scepter.

Although each case differed in its details, the determining factor must have been that, over the course of cultural development, not only the apparatus of political power but also religion (including cult and hierarchy), myths, literature, architecture, art, science, and outlook were shaped by the monarchy, and in relation to it, in a process that made breaking out of established patterns of thought nearly impossible. Where self-administered districts existed, it was only on the scale of villages and clans, as in China. And while some societies may have possessed an ideal conception of order (such as *Ma'at* in Egypt) that allowed people to assess the rule of a particular king and criticize it, it was only so that he might be induced to obey the rules or be followed by someone who would. People could become outraged, but only by specific persons or measures, not against the social order in general. In one instance, when the pharaoh Akhenaton tried to free himself from many customs, he succeeded for the period of his own reign, but his reforms barely outlasted him, and his successors strove to erase all memory of him. Tradition was stronger.

Jacob Burckhardt suspected that "individuality tried to raise its head wherever it could" among the Assyrians, Babylonians, and Persians, but succumbed "to civil and religious restrictions, caste institutions, etc., leaving not a trace behind."[5] That may well be true. In China attempts of this kind are documented, and traces of them remain. Almost all of them are found in the surviving records, however, not in social reality. And scope for individuality obviously existed within narrow limits, never even approaching a challenge to the traditional order. Whatever initiatives may have arisen in a wider sector of the Chinese population were stifled relatively quickly. Most initiative remained limited to the private sphere, so that the static nature of the whole was not disrupted.

And how could alternatives to the traditional ways of doing things have taken shape in view of the strength of castes in India, clans in China, the hierarchical structure of their societies, and the size of their empires? The difficulty of communication would have prevented any opposition to authority from spreading to large segments of the population—let alone the kind of cooperation that would amount to "horizontal solidarity."[6] By this I mean a willingness among citizens, as equals, to disregard their individual and small-group interests (and existing ties to people in positions of power, who represented the best chance of achieving them) and to join forces in a broad coalition to pursue change in the whole society.

How was it possible that culture developed so very differently among the Greeks, namely, a people who had to go back to the beginning and start over, so to speak, after Mycenaean culture collapsed? What Mycenae represented, namely, a palace culture influenced by Cretan and more distant Eastern models, was soon left behind. The Greeks even gave up writing because they no longer needed it. Nevertheless, certain memories of the great bygone age survived independently and were handed down in a rich tradition of epic poetry. New generations were delighted by new versions of old tales of conflict and struggle, of the strengths and weaknesses of great heroes, their vulnerability and tragic fates. In the *Iliad,* the culmination of this tradition (probably from the second half of the eighth century), the heroes developed, as Karl Reinhardt expressed it, from superhuman figures to flawed human beings, a step that characterizes the Homeric epic.[7] The process of composing and editing the *Iliad* occurred in an age when the Greeks on the Aegean were beginning to break out of the narrow confines of their traditional world, both geographically and in their philosophical understanding of human fate and the universe. It was a step that opened up further imaginative horizons and entirely new possibilities for action and adaptation.

How this came about can no longer be discerned. It is clear, however, that in the eighth century new problems within the Greek world were demanding new responses, while at the same time more frequent contacts with Eastern high cultures provided strong impulses for change.

It is probably not wrong to say that the East acted as godparent to the development of Greek culture. The Greeks borrowed many kinds of knowledge from the East—technologies, arts, myths, and images; they imported specialists, and ambitions as well. But they were not compelled to imitate the Eastern empires' political and social structure. These empires were too far away to exercise influence in the Aegean—or to force the Greeks to join ranks to defend themselves. The contacts between West and East remained limited to trade and, on the Greek side, learning.

Those who profited from such contacts, both financially and otherwise, were not monarchs, but rather large sections of the influential class among the Greeks (roughly speaking, the aristocracy). And this in turn accounts for the Greeks' ability to solve the biggest problem facing them, namely, the pressures of overpopulation, by undertaking large-scale ventures abroad. They founded many new cities in the northern Aegean, in Sicily, on the Italian mainland, and elsewhere. Vast opportunities for planning and establishing colonies opened up, incidentally offering many occasions for people to reflect on the conditions under which they were living. The

Mediterranean between southern France and Cyprus became a Greek sea.

But one thing did not change: the *polis*, the city-state. As so much was being transformed, the *polis* remained the most important form of political organization among the Greeks, especially those who lived on the coast and acted as the driving force behind the expansion. They wanted to live in small, politically independent cities, surrounded by their agricultural territory; anything else was out of the question. They waged many wars then and in the following period, and viewed themselves largely as warriors. But the Greeks rarely conquered foreign cities, and if they did, they almost never considered incorporating the citizenry of such places into their own. Hence it was difficult for any one city to acquire more power than the others. Greek kings had never been strong, and once their subjects began to trade overseas and found colonies, most of them were far too weak to take over the operations and seize for themselves the associated gains in money, glory, and scope for action. The aristocracy was thus able to solidify its control in a sphere to which it had always attached great value.

It was characteristic of the Greeks to strive for the greatest possible autonomy as owners of largely agrarian territories.[8] They wanted to be versatile, ready to face all kinds of challenges; only on the fringes of these societies was there room for specialization. And they wanted to hand over as little as possible to the polity and its government. Like the Romans later, they held that paying taxes was unworthy of a free citizen. Citizens performed military service themselves, like the Romans in the Republic, and paid expenses out of their own pockets. Men elected to office also bore most of the costs associated with their position. The Greeks (in contrast to the Romans) wanted officials to have very little power. In short, the polity was not supposed to become more than the sum of its parts.

Accordingly, Greek aristocrats did not want to be dependent little fish in a big pond, but big fish in small ones, as big as a few can be if they make up a whole. Such a system contained a certain inevitable tendency toward equality. A further corollary, given the scale of the Greek city-states, was that public space in the literal sense played a significant role. Citizens met, debated, engaged in politics, and resolved lawsuits and other kinds of disputes in public places, face to face.[9] Those able to afford it essentially lived a form of communal life, in conversation and politics, at festivals, sports events, and symposia. The public sphere was clearly distinguished from the domestic sphere (and the life of women), just as leisure was distinguished from work, and myth from ritual. It was a sphere of freedom.

Although we don't know when this way of life started, it flourished in many cities, creating considerable latitude for action, speculative thought, and the imagination. And what counted in these public spheres was excelling, achieving prominence; power mattered less. Probably nowhere else have the aims of a well-rounded education and competition played such a role, both within the citizenry of a city and in its relationships with other cities. Membership in these small polities was clearly limited, but people moved far beyond their own circles; a certain larger public sphere linking the cities definitely existed, not limited to the great athletic competitions, where rivalries were played out in the grand style.

Perhaps it was not very unusual that in the beginning the Greeks wanted to live autonomously, relatively unfettered, and unconstrained by rulers or government, and succeeded in doing so. Or to put it another way: possibly the truly singular aspect of their cultural development was not that they had this desire, but that they retained it, modifying some things here and there but generally strengthening the tendency rather than abandoning it. Popular assemblies have existed in the early phases of various cultures, for example, but the Greeks are exceptional in not losing them over the course of further development.

To a certain extent the culture that the Greeks founded under these circumstances represented a unified phenomenon, although the different cities and regions gave it their own stamp, particularly in the centers of transportation and trade. And the conditions existing at the outset determined the further course of cultural development, when value continued to be placed on autonomy, freedom, and a well-rounded life. This meant that few openings existed for establishing instruments of power, obligations, or restrictions in either the political or religious sphere. When the excesses of the aristocracy had to be curbed, the members of this class had to come to an agreement among themselves as far as was possible, since there was no superior power that could have imposed limits. Hence certain "primal" traits, if one may so describe them, such as uncurbed lust for revenge (the opposite side of the great nobles' sense of self-importance) and enormous arrogance persisted; neither laws nor education ever succeeded in truly suppressing them. The best that could be achieved was to tone them down and try to contain them within certain arenas, in ever new variations of cooperation and rivalry.

Over time, of course, this brought many problems with it: feuds, and occasionally usurpations of power by rulers referred to as "tyrants," as well as social conflicts resulting from the exploitation, impoverishment, and enslavement of peasants.

It is striking, however, that it was almost always impossible to establish lasting tyranny, for the tyrants could do little to institutionalize their power. Instead, another way out of the conflicts was found, another possibility for restraining the power of the aristocracy and ultimately reducing it.

New attitudes arose, at various places and in various ways, and they also spread—in a lengthy process of finding alternative answers to the challenges of the age. This is easiest to grasp in the political sphere, where a political way of thinking developed.[10] Although the inspiration came in part from Egypt and the Middle East, the process soon led to solutions specific to Greece.

Again and again knotty controversies arose that threatened civil war. The clearer it became that no side could come up with an acceptable solution by itself (and simply seizing power was not acceptable), the more people turned to men with particular intellectual ability, hoping that they would be able to restore order. Such men were given special authority to negotiate. Their first task was to remove the causes of the conflict, and as a rule this involved helping the weaker side, to prevent its adherents from resorting to civil insurrection. Averting uprisings by means of negotiation was a revolutionary step compared with what existed in other cultures, but the method developed naturally in Greece. The next step was to find a sustainable form of order, as no one wanted a monarchy. But creating an equilibrium, or at least some counterbalance to the aristocracy, was no easy matter. To achieve this the problem solvers needed an understanding of causality, particularly the reasons why some problems kept recurring. These reasons would be hard to find unless events were assumed to be governed by a certain logic. This in turn raised a more general question: Were there logical principles governing the whole world?

In the political sphere the Greeks sought and found what they took to be the proper order as intended by Zeus. But if a fundamental order of things applied to cities, then it also should extend to the world as a whole, the cosmos. Thus it was no accident that Anaximander grasped Solon's political concepts philosophically in terms of an autonomous order existing among the heavenly bodies.[11] Everything suggests that early Greek philosophy, with its unprecedented inquiry into connections and causes, its striving to explain fundamental natural phenomena in rational terms, grew out of—and was made possible by—attempts to solve social problems. What other societies found in central monarchies, namely a guarantee of order, the Greeks sought philosophically, through recourse to general laws. They could take the knowledge of astronomy acquired in Babylon, for instance, and apply it most fruitfully to their own questions about laws of nature. These loosely structured, free cities adopted astronomy and made it their own, because they now needed a more precise order.

A further aspect joined the mix. *Metron ariston,* runs a Greek proverb: "the right measure is best." Solon reckoned "with an invisible measure of knowledge that holds the ends of all things; it was the hardest of all to find."[12] This measure, and the numbers and numerical relationships in which it could be expressed, was sought by the Greeks in mathematics, in architecture, in city planning, and in art. It was important to them as a correlative of freedom. For if individuals were to be as unrestricted as possible in their freedom and talents (which were developed and needed in the shared public sphere), then any limits imposed on them had to be established by a shared understanding based on universal principles. People needed to anchor their freedom in something objective.

Over time, however, very concrete factors brought about a considerable extension or modification of the political order, at least in some of the more turbulent cities. There a broad class of citizens pressed for the right to participate in government. As they became more knowledgeable, they raised new demands based on a belief in justice (represented by Zeus in the pantheon of gods) and an awareness of their responsibility for the city. In contrast to the prophets of Israel, the Greeks believed that if the community fared badly not only were its citizens personally responsible, but also that they could—and should—change their approach. Moreover, the aristocracy's traditional domination of the public sphere added to the attraction of political activity for the rest of the citizenry. Thus during the sixth century precursors of democracy came into existence; known as isonomies, they were systems in which aristocrats still were in charge of political life, but a broad class of ordinary citizens now had a voice.

This archaic culture of Greece produced many works to delight the eye, ear, and imagination, works that captured their feelings in words, depicted how they saw themselves—whatever was suited to manifest their skill in the aesthetic sphere. The Greeks of this period created great poetry, both epics and the lyric poems that could give expression to all the bold longings and aspirations of individuals in a turbulent, unstructured society. (The latter type of poetry was appreciated, even though writing it was not exactly advantageous for a political career. However, the political sphere was not highly developed.) The early Greeks created the *Kouroi* and *Kourae* (statues of naked young men and women), and paintings, but they also cultivated conviviality in its higher forms, sports, and not least wisdom and philosophy.

Perhaps the most important aspect of early culture for the following period—the fifth century, the century of classical Greece—was that it left many avenues open. The political institutions created in this period had relatively little power, except in Sparta, the great exception, and in a few smaller cities, which merely proved the rule. In particular, neither religious beliefs nor cult practices were organized in such a way as to allow rulers to exploit them as instruments of political domination.

Thus the early stages of cultural development in Greece (up to about 500 B.C.E.) are quite distinctive. In many areas the Greeks had not advanced very far—no comparison with what had taken place elsewhere! But presumably never before had such a relatively large population established and preserved so much freedom and autonomy in the early stages of a high culture, by which I mean the development of all the ways, including an early philosophy, in which the Greeks organized their communal life on a relatively high level, offering individuals many forms of interaction with one another, but at the same time a sense of inner balance. And probably no earlier culture had expressed itself so little in the material sphere, in engineering or monuments. It had not been necessary to regulate rivers, and rulers could—indeed, had to—make do without colossal palaces and temples. Finding the right proportions and style was more important than scale in architecture, as was cultivating the strength and grace of the human body.[13]

Of course, the Greeks bore the imprint of their culture; to this extent they—as a society—had long since acquired an established pattern. (What holds for whole societies is always different than what holds for individuals.) What characterized this societal pattern, however, was that citizens were neither subjects of a powerful monarch nor adherents of a religion that prescribed and enforced answers to important questions. Essentially they enjoyed great freedom of action and latitude for philosophical speculation. (There was one great exception: military factors and foreign policy enabled a tyrant to establish a relatively firm and lasting rule in Syracuse.)

Hence the Greeks were relatively open, often perplexed, and strongly disposed to question things. They asked questions about correct proportions and laws, about the proper order for their cities and the order of the world. And these tendencies were not limited to a small circle, nor were the questions sporadic impulses that produced no results. Instead, inquiry was typical of this society, because virtually no predetermined answers existed, and no ingrained beliefs barred the way. Or at least that is my surmise. Its degree of accuracy could only be tested by detailed comparison of ancient Greece with China and India, let us say, or Arab culture at its height.

Where else do we find a society in which political entities—in this case city-states—were generally understood as nothing more, or very little more, than its citizens taken together? Where do we find that citizens wanted to be a part only of a whole that they created themselves, as far as possible in direct debate with one another? Where else did citizens succeed in such an endeavor, replacing many traditional answers, which they no longer found sufficient, with a form of rationality that declared their entire system of government open to discussion, along with the meaning of human life and the structure of the universe?

It is hard to say what would have happened to this culture if conflict had not arisen with the Persian Empire, the great power to the east, or if the Persians had won instead of the Greeks. Perhaps Greek civilization would have faded into oblivion, or survived in traces that only archeologists could find. But this is not how it turned out.

The victory over the Persians altered Aegean Greece with a stroke, and further changes followed in ever quicker succession. Greek culture (which in many respects was still in a process of development) became concentrated in one place—with immense consequences. In Athens, in the fifth and fourth centuries, the Greeks wrote a profound, if not ineradicable, chapter of world history. It is hard to grasp now what occurred in these decades, largely because generations of classicists, schoolteachers, and amateurs have lavished so much love and care on the story and made it so familiar that awareness of how truly extraordinary it was has nearly been lost.

The great majority of what the West has, with good reason, come to consider the literary legacy of ancient Greece—the tragedies, historiography, philosophy, and rhetoric, almost the entire literature apart from Homer, Hesiod, and the early lyric poets—was written in or for one city within a few decades.[14] While it was not only Athenians who produced these works, the others lived there or were strongly influenced by what was happening in the city.

It would be strange indeed if the extraordinary cultural achievements of the fifth (and early fourth) century were not very closely connected with Athens' history during this period. We are dealing with one of the most exciting centuries in all of history, and it would be a mistake not to expect highly unusual developments:

1. A city with approximately 40,000 adult male citizens is transformed almost overnight from a small polity into a world power. It must now develop corresponding policies, without being in the least prepared for it.

2. Athens soon dominates the alliance between Greek city-states so overwhelmingly that it brings the whole area effectively under its rule. Very few Greek cities had ever attempted to acquire power far beyond their individual limits, and none have achieved it before now, or will afterward. (The exceptions are Sparta and Syracuse, where very particular conditions applied). Now Athens acquires such a realm overnight, so to speak, all of it territory separated from Athens by the sea, and retains it for decades.

3. Athenian citizens immerse themselves in public and political life to a degree most uncharacteristic of earlier Greeks. By under-taking and accomplishing a tremendous amount together, they greatly extend the borders of their city-state, and consequently the *polis* demands much of their attention. This must have seemed very strange to the rest of Greece (again with the exception of Sparta). The intensification of all areas of life makes Athens powerful and arouses seemingly boundless energy; as a result Athenians push the envelope, testing many kinds of limits.

4. For the first time citizens can decide under what kind of system they want to live, and are given a choice between the most radical alternatives conceivable: *either* experienced aristocrats, supported by the authority of a council of their peers, will decide policy with the assistance of the Assembly of the People, *or* policies will be voted on by ordinary citizens without a parallel aristocratic group imposing limits on them.

5. Athens creates a radical democracy. The principle that the group of people affected by decisions should also make them goes into effect, in an extreme form, for the first time on this large a scale. The most important decisions are in fact made in the Assem-bly of the People. Citizens are no longer the objects of aristocrats' leadership but initiators of their own policies—with all the respon-sibility, problems, and sleepless nights that can entail.

6. For the first time people are serious about the equality of all citizens: even the poorest are included. It is hard to imagine the

fears that such a step must have aroused—it becomes possible for completely uneducated and ignorant people to form a majority and determine the policies of a world power (even though an individual figure like Pericles may speak with great authority in the Assembly and sway it with relative ease).

7. As all this is taking place, Athens experiences a burst of progress in technology and the arts, as new methods are discovered in crafts and trades, farming, and rhetoric. Some innovations are introduced by immigrants and visitors. Athenians become proudly conscious of their know-how and skills.

8. They also become aware that in their new and dramatically altered situation the traditional attitudes and ways of thinking are inadequate; the old moral and ethical guidelines (and limits) no longer suffice. They have to make decisions and take action in ways unfamiliar to earlier generations of Greeks. Facing a new set of highly political problems, and wielding new power, they need new rules. Their "nomological" knowledge—their familiarity with the causes of things that happen frequently—ceases to be useful, although it is essential in a democracy for people to have a shared basis on which to judge what is just or unjust, right or wrong, possible or impossible. Now it transpires that many things that have always appeared impossible or wrong are possible or right, and vice versa. What is lawful or unlawful may be easier to determine, but what happens if you cannot always act justly? What happens if you come to realize, for example, as the Athenians do, that your own rule over others is tyrannical?

9. When people cannot continue in their traditional ways, yet there is also no possibility for new ways of doing things to evolve gradually, logical argument must replace experience, and rational inquiry must take the place of business as usual. This becomes an urgent requirement in Athens, because everything is changing so rapidly. Although the members of the Assembly of the People must have been at first quite unsophisticated, speeches addressed to them

must now be made up of clear reasoning. The political order must be consciously reshaped on new principles or, if you will, placed on a rational basis.

Presumably, in view of such deep ruptures and the disappearance of tradition, everything important was questioned—except for certain fundamentals that characterized Athenian society and that citizens wished to retain: the political sphere would remain separated from the domestic sphere (meaning the economy), and great value would continue to be attached to independence and participation, but these would be limited to free men, who were typically masters of slaves, and exclude women and slaves.

Still, the questioning of the traditional order—the attempts to understand the new experiences and the consequences resulting from them, through the application of logic—extended far beyond politics in the narrower sense. That is, the political sphere was so central for these citizens that questions about it affected their entire worldview. New questions were raised about law and justice, about what it meant to be human, about the gods and the order of the world. And the Athenians obviously registered this clearly and took on the entire set of challenges.

When I say "the Athenians," I mean the poets and dramatists, sculptors and architects, intellectuals and philosophers whose works have come down to us, as well as many figures unknown to posterity. Although they were an elite, what they produced—their tragedies, comedies, and public buildings—were in many cases intended for the entire citizenry. Plays were performed in their midst; the philosophers lectured in public, and Socrates posed his questions there. The works of creative artists and thinkers were motivated and inspired by the experiences of these same citizens, by the issues that their existential connection with the *polis* more or less forced them to consider, and the positions they took on them.

Jacob Burckhardt once described this time as one when "education was characteristic of all—and hence the interest in art, poetry, etc."[15] I find I must disagree with him, for this does not seem to get to the heart of the matter. I would not say that all Athenian citizens were educated; rather, they were all affected by the practical and painful decisions they had to make and be accountable for. This is what was "characteristic of all," and accounts for why they did not merely *take an interest in* art and literature; they *needed* them. Their reasons can be inferred if one takes a look at this "art, poetry, etc."

They needed the arts as orientation, because traditional customs, the things they took for granted, could no longer sustain them. They needed help in keeping pace with the acceleration of change; they had no sense of firm ground under their feet. This could be experienced as an intoxicating rush, in which new vistas of action and insight opened up, capturing the imagination of ordinary citizens and philosophers, artists and politicians. We can obtain some sense of this experience from the classical and highly sophisticated design of the buildings on the Acropolis and in Eleusis (where religious mysteries were celebrated). But none of this could have existed if Athenians had not faced the risks and the terrors such experience inspired and accepted them as a challenge, over and over again. We can hardly gauge the extent to which Athenians' self-confidence had to seek a balance against uncertainty, failure, and repression. Tonio Hölscher has described the classical age of Greece as a daring venture,[16] precisely because it originated in taking many kinds of risks. Jacob Burckhardt even wrote of "all that was reckless and unbalanced in Athenian life, which actually moved in a continuous crisis with continuous terrorism."[17]

One answer to the question, "What is a human being?," was provided by classical Greek sculpture—on the basis of many theoretical considerations, incidentally. But the same question is at the core of Greek historiography, tragedy, early epistemology, and philosophy.

The question about human identity was closely tied to questions about the gods, in that it was concerned with what they would allow human beings to be, do, and achieve. What were the gods' intentions toward humankind? Was everything that people believed that they knew about the gods perhaps wrong, or merely inadequate? Did they exist at all? Was there any way to tell? And what divine laws governed the world? Should people still accept the old ideas, or revise them in the light of new experience? These questions could not be separated from questions of human law and justice.

How these questions were asked, how people dealt with them, and the areas of life to which they extended are illustrated by the Attic tragedies. The responses were conceived and expressed in terms of myths, which the dramatists often reinterpreted and reshaped, giving them a new intensity. The questions were posed in such universal terms that the plays remain deeply moving to this day.

Let me give you some examples: Athens is growing enormously powerful. Will this arouse the envy of the gods? It is known that they can strike down the mighty. Or will this happen only if powerful people also act unjustly? Athens has been trampling on many traditional Greek rules and attitudes, arrogantly pursuing its own self-interest. What will be the consequences, what is being lost in the process, for Athens as well as others?

Athenians undertook much that had been previously considered beyond the scope of human ability. This prompted the question: To what extent can human beings act without the approval of the gods, or in opposition to them? Are very successful people perhaps subject to a dangerous kind of blindness, a delusion sent by the gods that will cause them to make precisely the wrong decisions and bring about their own ruin? This is the situation in Sophocles' *Antigone,* where Creon believes like an "enlightened" Greek that rulers of a city have the power to do as they see fit, while Antigone, in opposing him, invokes unwritten laws. If the ideal is to find a reasonable solution for every problem, what happens if people have a ruler who becomes caught up in a process of "pathological learning"? A human being considers himself great but proves to be pitifully weak, and at the mercy of greater forces. He wants to flaunt his power but makes himself extremely vulnerable for that very reason.

In short, Greek tragedies played out versions of all the issues that must have preoccupied Athenians on a deeper level, given their new accomplishments, experiences, and the decisions they had to make.[18] They can't have had our modern reactions—either taking these issues for granted, or feeling apathetic or at a complete loss. They had no practice or settled routines in dealing with such questions, and so might have reacted with resignation or even despair. But the Athenians were ambitious: they wanted to know where they stood, and what the gods intended; they wanted to find meaning in what was happening.[19] And they succeeded, not only politically and militarily, but also in learning to see and understand the world in new ways. Bolstered by their success, they became able to endure the uncertainty and ambiguity of the world. Thus Jacob Burckhardt concluded: "It was only in a *Greek* cosmos that all the powers of the individual, released from his bonds, reached that pitch of sensitiveness and strength which made it possible to achieve the highest in every sphere of life."[20]

All this must sound highly exaggerated. Nevertheless, the sum of it must be correct. For we face a choice: either we regard the entire legacy of this century as a complete accident, or we attempt to understand the unique nature of the conditions that, taken together, made it possible.

The history of tragedy from Aeschylus through Sophocles to Euripides and their artistic development show how the questions, the problems, and the ambitions gradually changed, with regard to justice, for example, or self-confidence. They also show how the Athenians discovered the ambivalence of greatness, of "tragic greatness," and how their expectations of finding meaning and their conceptions of freedom reached new heights. And, finally, the plays reveal the opposite side of the coin as well: how they became aware of the spread of pettiness and failure, of their lack of orientation and helplessness as order and meaning slipped away, and of the malicious jokes the gods played on human beings—an awareness that was possible only if one had high expectations and demands. The Athenian dramatists were capable of capturing even the last degree of the breakdown of meaning in images and myths, since some of the later tragedies used earlier ones as a foil, to show how disappointed people could become cynical manipulators. There has probably never been a tragedy that plays over an abyss to the same extent as Euripides' *Bacchae,* the last work of the youngest of the three dramatists.

Some parallels can be found in the work of Greek historians, but also a great deal that was conceived from a very different vantage point. Historians sought to get along without the traditional framework of meaning, by restricting themselves to what could be demonstrated empirically and trying to grasp the uncertainty to which all actions and plans are subject. The enormous possibilities for change led the Sophists to the radical conclusion that everything was relative, and every order merely a set of conventions, so that human beings should seek firm and secure principles in nature. They soon found, however, that natural phenomena were susceptible to very different interpretations. While all human beings were equal by nature, nature also demonstrated that lions and hares were definitely *not* equal.

So the Sophists became mired in doubts and philosophical *aporiae* on the one hand, but could make effective use of them in rhetorically dazzling lectures on the other. If everything was relative, it opened up the possibility that their students could employ their rhetorical skills—and perhaps questionable means now and then—to acquire political power. Others were made profoundly uneasy by these possibilities.

Since reasons for doubt could be provided for so many views on specific questions, Socrates sought to find solid ground by asking about general concepts and categories: What is just? If someone has declared that a particular thing is just, what makes it so? In what do beauty, piety, or virtue consist? Traditionally the word *arete*, which we translate as "virtue," also meant "success." Hence whatever seemed to promise success and whatever was virtuous tended all too easily to flow into one another (just as in *politike techne* the dividing line between ethical methods and those promising success easily became blurred). Socrates proposed a contrasting concept of virtue, in which virtuous conduct was not simply the path to success, but was instead based on justice. According to Socrates, it was better to suffer injustice than to commit it. Yet he became more and more enmeshed in his questions, ultimately reaching the conclusion that he "knew nothing, so to speak," where human wisdom was concerned. No one else knew anything either; in fact, they knew far less than Socrates, for at least he was aware of how little he knew. And in spite of everything, on many occasions Socrates heard an important small voice inside himself, which he called his *daimonion*, that warned him when he was in danger of committing an unjust act.

Plato took up not only Socrates' questions but also most of the problems dealt with in Greek—and sometimes even Egyptian—wisdom literature. Plato's discussions of these fundamental questions laid the foundations of Western philosophy: How is it possible to know something? What makes human beings capable of acquiring knowledge? Can we rely on sensory perceptions and on opinions, which are exposed in random ways to the flow of events in the world and thus constantly subject to disturbance? Must knowledge not strive for a firm basis, the immutable and eternal foundation that ultimately sustains all existence?

Looking at the political life of his city, Plato said that it made him feel "dizzy," or at least that remark stands in a letter attributed to him.[21] This prompted him to begin thinking about the world in a new way, in order to gain a firmer footing, philosophically speaking. He investigated questions—about the city-state, about justice, forms of virtue, language, about the soul and its share in existence, its immortality, and finally the cosmos—with a radicalness and openness that led to the most remote corners and many *aporiae*. He developed (or borrowed from Socrates) an art to formulating questions that made problems vivid and immediate, made them get under your skin. Whatever we may think of his answers—many of them intended ironically or only hinted at—the way Plato put his questions has had an enormous influence ever since. As definitive answers to them are not easy to come by, all philosophies, and some theologies, have taken them as their point of departure again and again, either directly or indirectly. The loss of certainty in all spheres of life made it necessary to reflect anew on the world from the ground up; the Greeks' own experiences and vulnerability required them to ask questions of a universal kind. Greek was only the outward clothing, in which a general logic or *ratio*, a spirit of scientific inquiry, was working.

In developing his philosophy Plato abandoned a great deal that was specifically Greek, or even disavowed it, such as the city-state of free and equal citizens, and probably even politics as such. Yet the way he did so, which grew directly out of Athenian political experience, and the radical formulation of his questions have proved extremely fruitful for later thinkers.

The first of these successors was Aristotle, who by opposing his teacher Plato, or at least distinguishing himself from him, in a certain sense placed Greek political life on a new foundation. More than that, however, he collected and summed up all the fields of knowledge of his day, ordering them philosophically and advancing them further, not least because he sought truth in observation and rigorous analysis of empirical facts rather than searching for the principles behind them. Aristotle progressed so far that his work was still used as the foundation for a whole variety of fields when scholars began to pursue science again during the Middle Ages.

Thus what reveals itself here, all in all, is a population of citizens that enjoys enormous success, changes with enormous rapidity, and is willing to face up to all the resulting problems that offer themselves to their thinking and judgment—and probably also to their imagination and feelings—freely, openly, and in a spirit of adventure. And the Athenians drew the whole world of Aegean Greece into this process of transformation, cruelly and harshly, out of a love for power, admittedly, but also fascinatingly. A new way of being in the world arose, and an entirely new way of asking about the world.

In this context it is important to keep in mind the special development that the Greeks, particularly the Athenians, fostered in the political sphere. By making the role of citizen central to their lives (if not the only truly interesting part) and pursuing it with extreme intensity, they created a situation in which they had to make difficult choices. But this meant in turn that everything significant that happened or changed resulted from conscious decisions rather than processes that ran their course automatically, as it were. Emphasizing the political sphere made a pair of opposites the central theme of the culture: the possibility for powerful people to make plans, coupled with the unpredictability of chance—in other words, everything that makes human beings simultaneously the lords of creation and the playthings of fate. And all this played out in a polity where people knew each other, where it was still possible to have a sense of the whole. We seem to have an explanation here, in the way the political life of Athens could touch upon even the ultimate questions of human existence and make them come alive, for the ability of Greek culture to touch people ever since, to "get to us," as the expression goes.

As long as the success and momentum lasted, as long as the Athenians retained a certain bravado—much like a tightrope walker, one might say, able not to look down—they could go on confronting the really important questions. People could bear the search for profound answers, rather than insisting on simple ones right away.

This must be what has made their works of art inexhaustible up to the present day, up to and including the artistic depiction of life as meaningless.

Max Weber would have recognized this as a process of growing rationality, one both carried by the broad mass of citizens and extending into the basic questions of human existence. It began in the political sphere and moved outward from there, barely touching on the economic sphere. For this reason Greek culture began with the experiences of freedom, self-determination, and a highly active sense of responsibility, and it was advanced by the Athenians' certainty that they would be able to understand the world in matters both large and small. Ultimately they arrived at the insight that they knew nothing, and would have to start over, asking even more profound questions. This belongs to the best of the tradition that would determine developments in early modern Europe, and hence the West.

Yes, the Greeks ran their economy on slave labor and excluded women from the public sphere (even denying their ability to reason, to some extent). Yes, democracy and the hubris of power occasionally got out of hand. The latter problem was discussed and criticized in public—in tragedies, in Thucydides' "Melian Dialogue," and elsewhere. While the discussions didn't succeed in changing anything, they did provide the first great stimulus for the development of Plato's philosophy. But despite all the limitations apparent to us, isn't this already Europe in some sense? Isn't it the first culture to be based not on domination, but on freedom as a standard or model, at least for some? Doesn't it represent a whole new way of relating to the world, offering radically open-ended possibilities for action, for observing the world, and for making decisions, which have to be preceded by questions and discussions? While we cannot today accept the Greeks' shortcomings, their crimes, and false hypotheses, aren't the positive aspects of the culture—the dynamic, forward-looking, and challenging elements—ultimately more important?

Much from the Greek cultural tradition can be used and enjoyed in a number of ways, some of which may well seem narrow-minded and smug. But presumably the answers the Greeks found are less central than the questions they posed, to which people have returned ever since.

After the decisive defeat of Athens in the great Peloponnesian War, with its enormous losses, the great age of the city-state came to an end, in the sense that with the loss of political power the strong engagement of the citizens in the areas that we today define as culture faded away. But while the great momentum diminished, much continued. Philosophy was only then approaching its peak, even though it was forced to retreat into ever-narrower circles.

Rhetoric, language, and the culture of discussion remained lively and developed further, as did art. Historiography expanded into universal history; the scholarly disciplines flourished. A great deal of work was done that continued to have an influence into the modern era. The schools of philosophy, especially the Stoa, had some importance in this respect, although the succeeding Hellenistic age proved even more important.

The rulers of this period attached great importance to the cultivation of Greek literature and scholarship as a way of legitimizing themselves; hence they founded great libraries and research centers, such as the famous Museum in Alexandria. This was all the more remarkable because their interest in practical knowledge was slight at best. What conferred prestige (and thus interested the monarchs) was theory, the abstract philosophical knowledge that in the Greek view represented the highest achievement of which human beings are capable. Mathematics and astronomy experienced boom times, although geography, mechanics, medicine, and many other fields made significant progress as well. And not unimportantly, people studied literary texts and accomplished a great deal for their preservation. Perhaps the most significant events in this period, however, were the conquests of Alexander the Great and the enormous geographical expansion of Greek culture that was achieved along with them.

After Athens had virtually ruled the Aegean in the fifth century, the question of predominance was not settled with Athens' defeat in the Peloponnesian War. What replaced Athens in the long run, however, was not one of the city-states that had brought Athens down, but the Macedonian monarchy to the north.

Although ethnic groups of the northern Aegean spoke dialect forms of Greek, the Greeks nevertheless regarded them as barbarians. The peoples in the North shared very little of southern culture, and the style of life typical of the city-state was unknown to them. On the other hand, they represented a considerable military potential, if someone could manage to unite, organize, and make use of their forces. The man who succeeded in doing this on a grand scale was Philip II, although he must have been aided by some guidance from the Greeks, and most likely by their support as well. He was able to extend his hegemony to Greece, and it appears to have been part of his expansionist policy to wrest control of at least parts of Asia Minor and to liberate the Greek colonies there.

According to Aristotle, who had served as tutor to Philip's son Alexander, the Greeks united two qualities that were found separately in other peoples: a courageous spirit and intellectual ability. The combination would have made them politically supreme had they been able to unite. Aristotle, who formulated this proposition, apparently considered it only theoretical, since such a consolidation was inconceivable in reality.

From the perspective of a king who, although he had received a Greek education, was practicing an entirely "un-Greek" form of rule on the northern coast, things may have looked a bit different. Alexander may have shared his teacher's high opinion of the Greeks, but he was in control of Macedonia. He was young, had already proved his mettle as a military commander, and counted Hercules and Achilles among his ancestors. Why shouldn't it be possible to seize the Greek empire from the Persians?

And so the goal that Greeks would never have been able to achieve by themselves became a reality under Macedonian leadership: a great conquest, although influenced in many ways by the Greeks themselves. One might even ask whether Attic Greek culture of the fifth century was really a necessary precondition for Alexander's military campaign and empire to succeed.

In any event, in the aftermath Greek culture spread far to the East, all the way to present-day Uzbekistan. Numerous Greek cities were founded, and while they may have represented only isolated islands surrounded by foreign civilizations, they nevertheless exerted a certain radiating influence and attraction on the non-Greek populations in their vicinity. At the same time the Greeks absorbed many people and ideas from the East. The result was an ecumenical development that made Greek the most important language and the medium of communication for the whole eastern Mediterranean region and beyond. The number of people who adopted Greek culture and handed it down grew exponentially. Certainly the achievements of the Greeks in the fifth and fourth centuries, particularly in Athens, would not have been easily forgotten. But now the soil in which they could continue to propagate had grown vastly more extensive.

In the same fifth and fourth centuries new forces were also stirring in the western Mediterranean, on the frontiers of the Greek sphere of influence. They differed significantly from the forces at work in Macedonia, although certain parallels existed. Here, too, much had been set in motion by the Greeks. Ultimately this was the beginning of something entirely new in the history of the ancient world and the Mediterranean. It was a new, land-based power, and while it was also intent on expansion, it appeared not to need much indigenous culture—at least at the start.

We do not know precisely what caused the city of Rome to try to extend its power beyond its own immediate surroundings. But after Rome made its first successful conquests, whenever conflicts arose in the vicinity, it became customary for one side to call upon Rome for help. And once the Romans arrived, they stayed. As soon as they gained a foothold somewhere, they felt it necessary to secure their influence over the adjoining area. They did so within the area they now controlled by establishing Roman settlements or building roads, and on the periphery of these territories by entering into a new set of alliances. In the short or long term this led to contact with new, more distant, powers, and new conflicts. As the Romans hardly ever lost a war, their empire continued to grow until it finally extended across the entire Mediterranean region.

Rome itself was governed by a small and contentious but nevertheless highly self-disciplined aristocracy, using an unwritten constitution that had evolved over time. Government was based essentially on precedents and a number of institutions so widely accepted that they came to be taken for granted. The citizenry tended to be divided up into clienteles of aristocrats, who offered them a certain amount of protection and advanced their interests in exchange for their votes in the popular assembly. This system remained in place for centuries. Naturally Rome was familiar with institutionalized opposition (possibly from observing the Greeks); it took the form of officials called tribunes, who represented the common people. If we look at the broader picture, however, it becomes evident that the conflicts between aristocrats and tribunes of the people actually served to cement the power of the aristocracy, by imposing enough limitations on the aristocrats' power to prevent uprisings. Maintaining the stability of the Roman Republic was made easier by its great conquests abroad.

The military component of these conquests was the legions: superbly drilled and brave troops, ready to give their all. They were supported and promoted politically by Rome's continual extension of its client networks; at least indirectly they represented the interests of allies and even conquered peoples, and Rome was also generous in its awards of Roman citizenship. While Rome was never a democracy, and citizens remained largely dependent on the Roman aristocracy, citizenship nevertheless conveyed a number of rights and liberties.

To a certain extent, then, Rome had a developed political and diplomatic culture. It also began early on to develop its own legal culture, which in time gave rise to an important tradition of jurisprudence—the only ancient field of scholarship discovered not by the Greeks but by the Romans, through their own practice. This tradition was based on the authority of praetors (elected magistrates whose office was part of the unwritten Roman constitution) and the decision of senators and members of the order of knights to specialize in the area of law. The interest of the latter lay primarily in developing and refining the legal system as a whole; their concern must have been connected with the great importance aristocrats attached to looking after the interests of their clients. With the passage of time Greek philosophy came to exercise an influence on Roman jurisprudence as well.

In general, however, the Romans' cultural needs remained in rather narrow channels. They never made continuation of the existing order the subject of discussion, or challenged an entire tradition of rules and attitudes. Nor did they feel a need to reflect from an entirely new standpoint about gods and men—until the late Republic, in the last pre-Christian century. But even then, when the old system had begun to fail at every turn, it was not seriously placed in doubt. A number of questions and uncertainties did surface, however, and turned Romans' attention to the Greeks.

Romans had already developed some admiration for Greek culture in the early days of conquest. They soon learned Greek, and during the late Republic began to rethink their political domination in terms suggested by the Stoic philosophers. Other areas of philosophy tended to be dealt with only academically, but in their country villas wealthy Romans displayed the cultivated lifestyle of the Greeks—along with a great deal of booty and looted artifacts.

(They took care to act conspicuously Roman in the city, however.) They collected art and assembled libraries, which they also used. And Roman governors enjoyed being worshiped like deities, following the example of Greek monarchs. When Augustus finally erected his monarchy on the ruins of the Republic, cleverly adhering to Roman tradition, he sought to create a unified language of artistic and architectural form[22]—after a wild profusion of styles had sprouted during the late Republic. A Roman school developed that drew heavily on classical Greece. At the same time Roman poetry flourished; it was inspired and enriched by Greek models but responded in entirely new ways to the destruction, dangers, and challenges of the current era.

And thus the empire initiated a Greco-Roman symbiosis that, despite the gulf that continued to divide the Greek East from the Roman West, made each better acquainted with the other. Romans in particular became more familiar with Greeks and Greek culture. Greek art and education, knowledge, and philosophy spread through a new region and gained adherents, although they lost ground in the East during this period, beyond the frontier of the Roman Empire. The Roman role in the culture of the empire consisted at first in securing peace, continuing to develop the law—for the true flowering of jurisprudence occurred in imperial Rome— and in establishing orderly government and administration on a generous scale. Beyond that the Romans had amazing success in civilizing regions in the western part of their empire by founding, constructing, and organizing countless towns. They built roads and harbors, temples, theaters, thermal baths, and public squares; they created tract after tract of new settlements. And this is not to forget the great works of poetry, history, and philosophy produced by Romans during the same era.

Rome demonstrated an extraordinary power to assimilate the peoples in the regions it acquired. Soon everyone in the western part of the empire spoke Latin, and as time went by the right to Roman citizenship was extended to the entire empire. The upper echelons of Roman society gradually admitted aristocrats from ever more distant parts of the world into their circles.

The new empire Augustus had founded also had a run of good luck. For more than two hundred years few serious opponents existed on its enormously long frontiers. Consequently, relatively small armies were sufficient to defend them, and that in turn kept taxes low. In retrospect this period looks like a kind of Indian summer, in which civic culture could flourish.

Then, however, difficulties began to arise. Trying to hold the Roman Empire together proved an increasingly difficult task; there were heavy military losses and setbacks, and it often had to be subdivided. The eastern half managed to survive until 1453, although in more and more truncated fashion. Because the decline was slow, however, many Greek manuscripts were saved from destruction, and a great deal of literature and philosophy was preserved.

When Germanic kings finally became the rulers of the western part of the Roman Empire—often as governors of the Roman emperor to start with, at least in name—the Roman tradition did not cease altogether, but it became heavily diluted. Many institutions could not be maintained. Nevertheless, the language remained, even if it largely splintered into various dialects, which later developed into distinct languages. Latin was successfully restored to a certain extent during the Carolingian Renaissance. And in addition to much else, people retained the memory of a great world empire, its victorious armies, and its splendor. Rome and the empire became a myth that endured through all the interruptions.

And the Church remained, which had gradually spread and begun to organize under the protection of the empire. It had absorbed enormous amounts of Greek and Roman thinking, and would pass it on.

Historians used to see the rise and ultimate victory of the Christian religion as the cause—or one of the major causes—of the decline of the ancient world, and some still do. Paul Veyne speaks of the "massive violence of Christianization" within ancient culture.[23] Yet in another sense Christianity was also the offspring of classical antiquity, and at the end even a need.

To be sure, the religion came from outside, from Palestine, or more precisely, from Galilee, where Jesus had gathered a group of disciples around him and taught. And the main elements of these teachings were on the whole foreign to Greek and Roman antiquity: that the last days were near, for example; that God was loving and forgiving but also jealous; that God had a son who took complete possession of his followers, as indicated in the Christian Scriptures. "Whoever comes to me and does not hate father and mother, wife and children, brothers and sisters, yes, and even life itself, cannot be my disciple."[24] Where would one find the like in classical antiquity, or a commandment to love one's neighbor?

Max Weber stressed that "one of the most significant intellectual achievements of the Pauline mission was that it preserved and transferred this sacred book of the Jews to Christianity as one of its own sacred books . . . In order to assess the significance of this act one need merely conceive what would have happened without it. Without the adoption of the *Old Testament* as a sacred book by Christianity, gnostic sects and mysteries of the cult of Kyrios Christos would have existed on the soil of Hellenism, but providing no basis for a Christian church or a Christian ethic of workaday life."[25]

Yet the teachings spread, mainly among the Greeks, but later also among the Romans. Greek was the language of the Gospels. It was in Greek that the Apostle Paul wrote his letters. Greek and Latin remained the most important languages of the Church. Rather oddly, the new religion produced a whole series of theologians as early as the second century who strove to acquire a scholarly understanding of it, and debated with the "heathen." Through them and their scholarship, a great deal of Greek and Roman thinking entered Christianity and was passed on in this now altered form.

The main reason why this religion finally achieved such broad influence after 150 years of struggle was that the forms and public sphere of ancient society had lost their ability to sustain people; it was becoming more and more difficult to reproduce them from generation to generation and fill them with life. Consequently, Christianity's promises of salvation, the extraordinary potential for faith, and the intensive communal life practiced by adherents grew more attractive by comparison.

On the other hand, no one would have been able to interpret Christian texts, derive theological positions from them, debate with other theologians at synods, or participate in written exchanges without a good classical education. One of the Christians' main strengths probably lay in their ability to offer philosophical answers to questions from contemporaries; these added a further dimension to their religion. Ancient philosophy was a renewed focus of interest at the time, in broad circles both inside and outside the Church. Hence Christianity also exerted a positive influence on ancient philosophy. At the same time the new religion became the subject of numerous intellectual debates. Many people were drawn to the Old and New Testaments and found them fascinating reading.

But Christianity could not become the official religion of the empire until after the crisis of the third century, when wider segments of the population were attracted to it. The persecutions ordered by some emperors ultimately made it stronger. Thousands of martyrs proved that it could not be defeated by such tactics. But as an official religion Christianity necessarily acquired a political dimension, in ways that classical antiquity, and the Roman Empire in particular, had prefigured.

Thus Christianity absorbed much of classical antiquity, borrowing elements of it for its exegesis, theology, and the organization of the Church, all the way down to vocabulary and concepts. And by drawing new populations to the religion it also continued the process of Hellenization and Romanization. Last but not least, Christianity also shared the need to ask questions and the willingness to do so, and it passed all of this legacy on to later generations. In the West people continued to embrace it in many ways and obviously made use of it.

We can now return to the question of Europe's special path, and when we do, one thing is impossible to overlook: antiquity is an indispensable part of Europe's pre-history.

The next question is more difficult, namely, whether antiquity was not a necessary condition for Europe. Here we must ask, for example, whether what Christianity, Roman law, and ancient philosophy made possible and set in motion in Europe could have been realized without these initial advantages.[26] Could chancelleries have developed similar practices? Could the medieval and modern bourgeoisie have developed, or the intellectual struggles, or competing political entities? Would nation states have formed in similar ways? And what about the sphere of civil law? Would it have been able to develop along the same lines without a pre-history that included the rule of law and democracy in relatively large geographical areas (which other cultures did not produce)?

Would it have been possible to work all of this out by virtue of intellect alone, in all the different conditions people found themselves in, without this advantageous tradition? Could people have achieved the same or similar results just with good communication? Or would people never have arrived at many of these situations, because they grew out of practices that would not have existed without antiquity?

We should recall that it is far more difficult for a large class of people (such as the bourgeoisie) to establish a basis for effective political activity than it is for monarchs. Both need forces to establish and secure their rule; however, a monarch can gather and organize a sufficient quantity of such forces far more easily and rapidly than can citizens, particularly in polities that cover a large area. In medieval Europe citizens could achieve shared rule only in geographically limited domains, namely cities—but what would the cities have been like without the legacy of antiquity? How could people have developed a common will on a lasting basis without the head start conferred by antiquity? How could a sense of solidarity have been created in broad sections of society, how could democracy finally be established across extensive territories, without the processes of education and the acquisition of knowledge, without awareness of the possibility of democracy, without the manifold prerequisites for it, including the requirement that the members of a society see themselves as citizens and regard the governing of society as their own concern?

Questions of this kind pose difficulties for us, because we tend to think that we have every imaginable kind of knowledge at our fingertips, so to speak. We assume many people are ready to acquire the information they need as soon as they need it (and that it is usually available in handy, pre-packaged form). It is hard for us to conceive of the societal and cultural barriers that once inhibited this kind of attitude and have now fallen away. Who among us today can imagine how hard people worked to acquire this knowledge and fought to have it accepted? If we want to examine how much can be created or invented on the spot, as a situation requires, without pre-existing knowledge or tradition, we might need a greater familiarity with other cultures. Yet it seems rather unlikely that they could provide much information about the ability of people to acquire civil rights and successfully defend them. Presumably, we must try to expand our current potential for understanding. But until then antiquity appears, or so I would claim, to be an indispensable prerequisite for Western development.

Finally: Did the European special path perhaps begin with the Greeks? Does antiquity represent, in a manner of speaking, the early phase of the history of Europe? Paul Veyne dismissed the question of whether Rome was the foundation of modern Western

Europe, observing, "Historians have better things to do than to perpetuate the genealogical fantasies of *parvenus.*"[27] He is no doubt correct about that, but the question is precisely whether Europe was—and is—a parvenu. Veyne himself, we should note, takes no interest at all in this genealogy.

Yet let us consider what emerged from our discussion of the Greeks: Wasn't there something about them that was already European, especially since it occurs nowhere else? It goes without saying that the Greeks, Romans, and early Christians were completely different from us. The same, however, can probably be said of small children, charming as they usually are, in comparison with the quite different (and often revolting) adults that they grow into. It is probably a very important step for our understanding of the Roman and Greeks that we realize how alien they are. But isn't this also true of the Middle Ages, and even of most of the modern period? Even for all history, especially since we ourselves are changing so rapidly?

Even though the ancients are largely lacking in experimental science, technology, capitalism, human rights, and particularly in the constant development of new forms and styles, once they had found classical solutions in art, isn't it significant that the Greeks discovered the political process and the Romans jurisprudence (and a noble conception of humanity, even if it was applied only to limited circles at first)? Isn't it significant that they achieved self-determination and acquired an ambition to understand the world in terms of predictable laws, and that these elements formed part of an entire tradition?

I would claim that in antiquity something wholly new entered world history, and that it not only created the foundations for what would then come to constitute Europe, but that Europe itself actually then began. For the first time a culture arose that was free of domination, free of the hardships that repression brings for the mass of the population. It was full of uncertainty, but also ready to face the experience of great philosophical latitude, to ask questions and to accept that they might shake the foundations of their own lives. This was a new form of human existence, and autonomy, freedom, civic responsibility, equality, and democracy represent only one side of it. Over the centuries the surviving works of Greek philosophy, art, and literature have probably played an even greater role in enabling the people in Europe to accomplish a great deal of which they would otherwise not have been capable, in forming and educating them. Rome's legal tradition, its republic, its rule, and its culture were also necessary, and finally the new religion of the Christians.

The inheritance was and is risky. It also led to Auschwitz. Whether one should be grateful for it is an entirely different question. But that is not the point I want to make here. It might have been better for the world if the Chinese or Indians had conquered it, either directly or indirectly.[28] But they didn't, and presumably they would not have been able to, or wanted to. The fact that Europe could and did was not suggested by antiquity. How it was shaped by antiquity, however, must have made a decisive contribution— through the groundwork laid at the end of the Roman Empire, through a legacy imparted from the beginning, and through what Europe could make out of it.

Burckhardt once noted that historians should pay attention "not only to material, but more especially to spiritual causes and their visible transformation into material effects."[29] Here one could observe an instance of that.

Ultimately, of course, we (in Europe) must decide ourselves whether we want to accept antiquity as our early history. Historians can say only whether it is possible in scholarly terms. And I believe there is good reason to claim that it is.

To say that ancient civilization perished in late antiquity is not a valid objection, for it is characteristic of European history that new beginnings have been undertaken over and over again. Since antiquity European culture has been daring, options have remained open, and movements that place everything at risk have not been blocked in the end. And competition does its part. Culture is not a house with foundations that are laid once and for all, so that everything else can be built on top of them. It also presents no guarantee against barbarism.

In this sense the acceptance of Christianity in the Roman Empire and among the Germanic tribes (in the western part of the empire) is just such a new beginning and a thoroughly European phenomenon. It had an effect on political life far beyond the religious sphere, as did the rediscovery of antiquity later.

Antiquity, especially its Greek component, has always been effective as a latent potential. The important thing was that knowledge of it did not disappear altogether. But achievements of the fifth and fourth centuries have been in the air ever since. It would not have been easy to forget them. And even if that were possible, the spread of information about them to the Hellenistic East and then the Roman Empire prevented a total loss from occurring, until the Christians (and Byzantium) absorbed them in different ways and passed them on.

It is possible again today that—despite all our knowledge—we face the necessity of a radical new beginning. Are we facing the end of Christianity, the nation state, democracy, the ambition to grasp what is happening in the world?

But the ability to begin over again—might it not be that herein lies the special character of European culture since the time of the Greeks? It cannot consist of some narrow-minded definition of "cultivation"—that, as Nietzsche observed, is something for philistines.

It was Goethe who said that freedom and life cannot be owned; rather, they must be won anew each day. And the same applies to culture. It can be magnificent, but also monstrous. It can also be present only on the surface. And it has its limits.

In some circumstances it can go off the tracks, as the long series of European crimes shows, from ancient Greece to Caesar's military campaigns and the crusades, from the extermination of native peoples in North and South America (the "American Holocaust") to Auschwitz, Hiroshima, and Nagasaki. It was again Nietzsche who expressed amazement that people could consider the ancients *humane*.[30]

Whether things are headed off the tracks today is the next question that will concern us. Historians can discuss some aspects of it, such as how historical change occurs in the short term or—now that we have twice discussed whole eras—in the medium term. We can also discuss how historical change can get completely out of control. More of that in the next century.

4

Deeds and Contingencies, Politics and Processes

Where History Takes Place,
and Who Is Responsible for It

We are experiencing historical change on a scale previously unknown, and also driving it forward faster and on more fronts than
ever before. All around us the conditions of our lives and our world
are changing, be it in the world of work, transportation, communications, the ways we spend our time, gender relationships, life ex-
pectancy, climate, and medicine—including the new gene technologies (and soon probably human cloning as well). I could add beliefs
and values, personality structures, family, society, and government,
and no doubt everyone could make their own contributions to the
list.

And whether we want to or not, most of us participate actively
in these processes of transformation. Chiefly, of course, they are
driven by institutions and the people who work for them, such as
scientists in the research laboratories that now exist in unprecedented numbers all around the world. Consultants, corporate leaders, and media moguls play a large role, not to overlook those who
manage huge sums of money. But none of these people would get
very far without the rest of us—all the consumers, people who seek
health (and a long life), who travel and follow fashions, who don't
want to be left behind, who accept newspeak uncritically. Or with-

out the Internet users, businesspeople, artisans, scholars, and politicians, all of whom strive to master these new possibilities, continually adapting to innovations, *making use* of them, and thus driving the process still further.

The number of new discoveries and inventions increases considerably from year to year. Reports of these breakthroughs are passed around the world, and people immediately begin to apply them, come up with new combinations, and develop them further. No theoretical discovery must wait long to be converted into some practical tool with far-reaching consequences—or to be surpassed. Not so long ago it was the case that the daily activities of most people amounted mainly to reproducing the familiar, the tried-and-true, or, at best, improving it slightly. Today the innovative or experimental component of even everyday work is incomparably greater.

All these activities, taken by themselves, usually have quite limited goals (despite what appear to be some geneticists' fantasies of omnipotence), although some of them may seem splendid, of course, especially in comparison with what was considered possible only a few years or decades ago. One person wants to research a particular subject for the sake of career advancement, while another enjoys experimenting, a third is a hacker, and a fourth is seeking new techniques for curing a disease; perhaps they want to outshine their competitors; all of them want to raise money, or earn it, or manage large sums so that they grow even larger. Both our everyday experience and expectations suggest that innovation is advantageous everywhere.

As people engage in all these activities, very few of them are thinking of how their actions may affect life in other places, or maybe even all over the world—but together they bring about change, or, more precisely, together *we* bring about change. We do so through the unintended side effects of our actions. Often we are not even aware of them, but they enter into the great processes of change in the age and drive them onward. And so it comes about that what things do of their own accord is change, and not, as it used to be, stay the same. Of course, some changes lead only to variations; others prove to be dead ends, but a great many seem to leave their mark in the conditions of our lives and in us, too.

Thus, collectively, we have enormous capabilities and ever-increasing means, including the power to destroy life on earth. We have brought ever greater portions of nature under our control—but will we be able to do the same with the process of change?

As far as we can tell, the institutions that have been created over long periods to conduct public affairs—the nation states, parliaments, governments, and all the associations that they have formed such as the European Union and the United Nations (including the World Climate Conference)—can promote or retard developments slightly here and there, and perhaps channel them in certain directions. On the whole, however, institutions appear to be lagging quite far behind the many developments that emerge on their own. The best they can do is create laws for managing new trends, and otherwise try to use them to advance their own region or agenda.

The greater the mutual dependencies become, that is, the longer the chains of interdependency,[1] in a world in which boundaries are also breaking down and distances shrinking, the less these institutions are able to control. And as less and less can be decided politically, less serious and sustained political debate takes place, and the more democracy suffers. Politics becomes more and more irrelevant—or at least that is the norm—and so less and less happens there, or, more accurately, citizens take less and less interest in political events, unless they are presented as entertainment.

In sum, if I may borrow a formulation that has served well in studying the late Roman Republic: we are dealing with a yawning divide between the enormous amount of transformation that is occurring in society and the small amount that can actually be affected through debate in political institutions. Elsewhere I have described this phenomenon as a discrepancy between social mutability and controversiality.[2] When it occurs in politics, the consequences are potentially catastrophic.

The consequences are hard to appraise. But certainly changes that are proceeding according to their own independent dynamics are far ahead of the political process, meaning the arena where societies put the problems of their era (both domestic and international) on the agenda and debate them. This is one way of getting a grip on such problems and bringing them under control, but only in a certain limited sense, because politics itself is affected by many other processes running on their own more or less autonomous course.

Is this an unusual situation? Is it perhaps only a reflection of the special burst of acceleration in the rate of change that is occurring in our own time? How do social mutability and controversiality relate to each other in other epochs of history? And what is the relationship between politics and the processes of change?

We might ask these questions, or we could take a step back and ask far more general ones, such as: How do the changes that together constitute history come about? Can we distinguish particular forms or ways in which people participate in them, depending on their power or position? How do the transactions in which we all take part—including our conversations, perhaps, our thoughts, and the things we don't think about—become history? What are the possible places that people have in it, what possible roles do they play? And that simultaneously implies: What responsibility do they bear? For if you participate in something, you have to accept a certain responsibility for it, don't you? Or does that rule not apply to history? And this question suggests another: If we have such a responsibility, how do we deal with it? What conscious and unconscious mechanisms do we develop to be able to endure it? In what follows I would like to discuss these questions in relation to different historical epochs, in order to see if we can distinguish different specific forms in which history occurs.

The German historian Reinhart Koselleck writes: "We should guard against completely rejecting the modern turn of phrase concerning the makeability of history. Men are responsible for the histories they are involved in, whether or not they are guilty of the consequences of their action. Men have to be accountable for the incommensurability of intention and outcome, and this lends a background of real meaning concerning the making of history."[3]

People are responsible for their histories, in the plural, Koselleck says, not for history, but that is already problematic enough. It is generally agreed that one is indeed responsible for one's own actions, and sometimes one can be legally responsible for things one - *doesn't* do. In both cases the boundaries of responsibility are drawn relatively close around the individual.

Nevertheless, there are situations in which responsibility is understood in a somewhat wider sense with regard both to acting or failing to act. They include the family sphere, for instance, how parents treat their children, or how teachers treat their students. It matters how soldiers act toward other members of their company; how railroads maintain their rails and corporations their fleet of cars. Magistrates, civil servants, and elected officials all have extended spheres of responsibility. It is a long way from there to speaking of responsibility for all of Europe, or humanity—but isn't it perhaps necessary to do so in this day and age? In all cases mentioned above the responsibility extends beyond the present into the future. The Latin word *providentia* (from which *prudentia,* "sound judgment," "discretion," is derived) means both "foresight" and "precaution." It is a quality of God ("divine providence") and was also thought to be possessed by Roman emperors and statesmen. Thus far everything is clear, if one disregards for the moment the question of how such responsibility is apportioned among, let us say, all the inhabitants of a town or all the soldiers of an army. But can an individual be responsible for history/histories? Koselleck speaks of the "incommensurability of intention and outcome," meaning that they must be measured by different yardsticks, and that is true on both the small and the large scale. In the old days people expressed this idea with the saying, "der Mensch denkt, Gott lenkt"—man proposes, God disposes (and when the teacher asked little Johnny to change the proverb into the past tense, he said, "Der Mensch dachte, Gott lachte"—man proposed, God laughed).[4]

Since written history came into existence in the fifth century B.C.E., we have known that historical events result from the interplay of many forces, in ways in which chance can play a large role.[5] It was precisely this insight that made analytical historical scholarship both possible and necessary; it is no accident that the Greeks came up with it. But we must then ask how, if events are determined by so many factors, can individuals—or cities, or armies, or governments—be responsible for them? Koselleck says they must be answerable, they must be held accountable, but even if one can accuse them of specific mistakes and attribute specific crimes to them, they did not really have history on either a small or a large scale under their control. Certainly they could not know ahead of time about many things that would happen and to which they contributed.

In the nineteenth century a new sense of self-assurance arose, partly as a consequence of the French Revolution. (Was this self-confidence modern and bourgeois?) People were keenly aware of the problematical relationship between human responsibility and history. When the German dramatist Georg Büchner studied the Revolution, he saw "an inescapable force" in the human condition, "granted to all and to no one. The individual is merely foam on the waves, greatness sheer chance, the mastery of genius a puppet play, a ludicrous struggle against an iron law: to recognize it is our utmost achievement, to control it is impossible."[6] In 1890 Friedrich

Engels offered his own impressive formulation of human impotence in history: "There are countless intersecting forces, an endless group of parallelograms, from which one result emerges—the historical outcome. This itself can then be regarded as the product of a power that, taken as a whole, has neither consciousness nor will."[7] Lorenz von Stein observed: "The grander the scale of world history, the less influence the individual has in it, and not only the individual, but ultimately all individuals taken together."[8] But the more difficult the situation became, the more hopes to which it gave rise. Engels had written in 1878: "The objective free forces that used to dominate history up to now are coming under human beings' control. Only from this point on will people make history themselves with full awareness . . . It is humanity's leap from the realm of necessity into the realm of freedom." A "planned and conscious organization" of the future appeared as a possibility, although only for brief moments.[9]

Great statesmen have always stressed the discrepancy between their ability to make policies and what actually results from them. "The wisdom and vision of men have definite limits beyond which they can see nothing, God alone being able to see the final objective of things," wrote Richelieu. "It suffices often to know that projects which one undertakes are just and possible in order to embark upon them with good reason."[10] Bismarck saw the historical development of a country as too strong and wide a current "for an individual . . . to be able to set its course. It is not possible at all to shape world history." "We just do our duty in the present . . . Whether what we do will last is in God's hands."[11]

At the other end of the spectrum is a man like Hitler, who spoke repeatedly about his desire to make history. "In the end," he said in a speech delivered on January 4, 1933, "it makes no difference what percentage of the German *Volk* makes history. The only important thing is that we are the last ones who make history in Germany!"[12] Hitler always saw himself as engaged in a dialogue with history. In Vienna he declared on March 15, 1938, "As the Führer and Chancellor of the German nation and the Reich, I now report to history that my homeland has joined the German Reich."[13] It was described as the greatest statement of a successful "mission accomplished" in his life.[14] The crowd responded with cheers. A Bavarian police official reported dryly that at first the occupation of Austria was greeted with "dismay" and "uneasiness," but then, he went on, "in view of the historic nature of the event, and the fact it went off so smoothly and without any bloodshed, people are not taking it so tragically."[15]

Hitler demonstrated the absurdity of the proposition that "men make history" in his own unique way. And incidentally, the German historian Heinrich von Treitschke, who coined the aphorism, did not intend it as it is usually understood. With all due respect to great men, he meant only that history is not ruled by laws (like nature), but instead governed by free will, because men—one could also say human beings—are active agents in it.[16] This still leaves room for the idea that a great deal of history is not "made," but rather "happens." (The phrase is often used in such a way that "history" serves as a stand-in for "politics" or "policy." "To make policy" is a common expression, not at all wrong, and "history" can easily be substituted, in view of the fact that the two concepts converged for a time in certain places. "Policy" is often understood in such cases in the sense of particularly far-reaching or momentous aims, of exactly the kind great men are thought to pursue. So if these—apparently—great men make "historic decisions," one could assign them a correspondingly large amount of responsibility.[17] Ordinarily, however, policies produce more modest results.)

If, however, we distinguish between policies/politics and history, and declare that responsibility must be taken for the former (as far as humanly possible) but not for the latter, only one higher authority remains to whom we can assign responsibility for events as a whole, namely God. Many people—both historians and statesmen

—have been content to do just that—or at least they give little indication that they thought otherwise.

Often, of course, "God" was merely an expression that could only too easily have been replaced by terms such as "providence," "destiny," or—when things went badly—"doom." For instance, *Versagen und Verhängnis* ("Failure and Doom") is the title of the book in which Alfred Heuss discussed the "Ruin of German History and Its Understanding."[18] Again and again, in dealing with the Germans of the National Socialist era, writers have spoken of "seduction," "doom," "fate," or "fatal entanglement." Sometimes people speak of "history" as having intended something (or not), thus making history responsible for itself, in a sense. A great deal can be explained by history's superior power. People appeal to it, often in order to claim that they couldn't help that things turned out the way they did.

Strictly speaking, historians may not use divine providence to explain the phenomena they are studying (unless perhaps they want to regard the fact that so many mediocre politicians have not brought about even more catastrophes over the course of time as in itself proof of the existence of God). Instead, they must abide by Marx's famous dictum: "Men make their own history, but they do not make it just as they please in circumstances they choose for themselves; rather they make it in present circumstances, given and inherited."[19] To this I would add only that a good part of what they do contributes to the circumstances that confront them—or the next generation—later on. The sum of past actions can grow into enormous forces that then present themselves as "fate."

Let us now return to our earlier question: How does history, or historical change, come about? The simplest element involved is action—political actions performed by politicians and nations. Politicians and countries are virtually never alone on their playing field, however. As a rule they run into other players and conflicts arise.

How these turn out is then often enough determined in some part by circumstance—the weather conditions during a battle, for instance, or during the transmission of information, the fortuitous interplay, that is to say, of all the different factors making up a particular situation. Actions are thus inescapably bound up with events. Even if one army or navy is far superior to its opponent, let us say, the conditions for asserting that superiority will still involve unforeseen events, although they will play a subordinate role. Thus what gives rise to political (and military) history is a succession of actions and events.[20]

Herodotus, in the fifth century B.C.E., was the first to try to grasp a period of history by tracing actions and events through two or three generations. He wanted to understand how, after many years of peace between Greeks and barbarians, great hostility could arise between them and lead to the outbreak of the Persian War. The usual answers that were offered did not satisfy him, and so he investigated and described first the growth of the Persian Empire over several generations and then the course of the war.

It would be very appealing to go in detail into the reasons why war broke out. But I must content myself with pointing out that this way of looking at history, which seems elementary to us—and also very old-fashioned—represented a significant innovation at the time. For one thing, it was unprecedented for a private person without any official standing to venture to ask questions about the course of history, to realize that studying the original sources was essential, and to publish his results. All in all it was an extraordinary undertaking.

This last step, publication, was unknown at least in the high cultures of Egypt and Mesopotamia or in the neighboring empires. There, information about historical events was not the concern of curious individuals, but under the control of government officials, in particular the kings. And they were less interested in acquiring information than in disseminating it. As a rule what kings made public was not events, but great deeds—namely, their own, and nearly always only those that had turned out well. If they permitted or encouraged interpretation of any extended period of time, they did so in relation to themselves, the aim being to present what happened as mainly their achievement or victory. Enemies served as a foil, for a victor needs someone to play the role of the vanquished. When mention was made, rarely, of things going wrong—as occasionally happens in Hittite accounts—the setback was understood as divine punishment for previous offenses.[21] In other words, what occurred had been meted out to the king, and by extension to his kingdom, by a higher power. Their suffering was deserved. Military defeats were not the result of conflicts, which could be empirically traced, among several agents under conditions that could include unforeseen events. Chronicles focused on the person of the ruler, not events.

And, despite all the differences in the details, the same can be said of the accounts of the Israelites, who were not attacked by the powerful king of the Assyrians for political reasons—never mind what their leaders may have thought at the time. And they were defeated not because his military forces were far superior, but because Jahwe wanted to punish them for worshiping foreign gods. Or at least that is what the prevailing version, written later, reports. In this case the account suggests that it was the people of Israel as a whole, not just a ruler, who deserved to be chastised.

There is no doubt that ancient monarchs in this region were capable of grasping short-term sequences of events, battles, diplomatic missions, and the like in terms of multiple agents, as a meeting of many actors under particular conditions that were subject to contingency. But clearly they were not interested in or capable of reconstructing multigenerational processes from this perspective or—at the very least—not interested in making such accounts public. I suspect that it would have run counter to their ambitions for lasting rule and stability in their empires; perhaps it would have contradicted the meaning that they themselves gave to events. Given the contemporary standard of public documents, a great deal of uncertainty could have arisen, and much slipped out of the rulers' control.

The fact that Herodotus and the Greeks took a very different approach has a number of causes. Instead of being kept secret, policy was a public matter in their homeland, a task for citizens—especially in Athens, but to a lesser degree in other parts of Greece as well. And the conduct of war was an area in which citizens were particularly involved. They were well aware of the difference between intention and outcome. Of course, they, too, had a tendency to view what occurred in terms of reward or punishment, or some other expression of a god's will toward them. Herodotus cites numerous examples from the accounts on which he based his work. Nowhere, however, did they strike him as sufficient. Political history, he found (and as the Greeks had cause to know), was more complicated than that. For this reason, and because he was already committed to the requirement of early Greek science that told him to limit himself to empirically established facts, Herodotus conceived the plan of reconstructing the great impact of the Persian War on the world he was familiar with in terms of history, that is, by following the course of political and military developments as far back as his sources reached.

What had occurred was not only what someone had deserved or had been meted out to him, but rather what had resulted from action and reaction over long stretches of time, with chance occurrences added to the mix.

Such political history was and remained *the* Greek form of seeing history, that is, tracing processes that took place over an extended period of time and affected the public at large. It was and remained the essential content of their histories. We have known for more than two hundred years that "history" represents a far more comprehensive process of change than this, but the Greeks didn't know it. This is not to say that they had failed to observe change taking place outside the realm of politics and military conflict. A fifth-century tradition held that human beings had first developed agriculture and animal husbandry, and then cities, from very primitive beginnings. The Greeks developed a whole theory of culture, in fact, but it dealt only with its origins in the distant past. Only Thucydides went beyond it, by tracing a history of conflict on an increasing scale of magnitude up to his own time, because he needed a basis for asserting that no previous war had been as great as the one he wanted to describe.

The Greeks also knew that philosophy was a recent development and that a succession of philosophers had reached distinct conclusions. Tragedy had changed. Many things had been invented. But all of this information was considered to belong to specific branches of knowledge: the history of tragedy to poetics, the history of philosophy to metaphysics, and so on. No one had thought to include them in a more comprehensive form of history.[22] No occasion had yet arisen to suggest the existence of social or economic history, so the ability to recognize and reconstruct them was lacking.

Of course, in a fast-moving century like the fifth, people were aware of many changes within their own lifetime. They realized that many traditional ideas were becoming obsolete, and that if they were going to keep abreast they needed to raise their children differently and find new ways to seek success. But these insights also remained outside the recognized boundaries of "history," and remained a matter of scattered observations, although they sometimes found their way into accounts, as when a historian might interrupt his narrative of the past to remark on some phenomena that made their first appearance in that era.

This kind of history, although limited, corresponded to reality at that time. Political and military deeds were the true content of Greeks' lives, both within their own city-states and in interactions between them. They were first and foremost citizens. (We are now aware, of course, that not all of them *were* citizens. Slaves, foreigners, and women were excluded from this status, but for this reason they also did not play a role in perceptions of public life at the time.) The city-state, the *polis,* was the focus of their interest and their existence, and they were accustomed to devoting enormous amounts of time, attention, and energy to it. Their home life, or possible occupation, was of interest only to themselves, but insignificant in terms of the whole. A man's rank was essentially determined by the role he played in the public life of his *polis.* No matter if one regarded holding political office as good or bad, Aristotle observed, if citizens were equals, then they ought to hold office equally, that is, in rotation.[23] Their relationship to one another was expressed in the holding of office. For the lower classes, as time passed this responsibility may have come to play less of a role in their lives than securing their material existence, but for the upper classes it was and remained of great importance. In this society, participating in the public life of the *polis* and in politics was far more a goal in itself than a means to something else.

Accordingly, the pursuit of other goals (of an economic or financial kind, for instance) was kept out of politics. If the Athenian economy flourished, this was an incidental result of politics, much like festivals, public buildings, and tragedies. While we might consider the latter part of "culture," at the time they all belonged to public political life. In such a world political deeds and the circumstances that influenced their outcome were central—in neighborhoods, in cities, and in relationships between cities. Macro- and micro-history were closely linked. Comparatively speaking, the Greeks neglected everything else that in a different society might have directed attention toward social and economic conditions.

As a rule, what was perceived as happening consisted solely of political disputes and conflicts. And also, as a rule, perceived changes were restricted to political conditions. These shifted as a result of struggles won or lost, resolutions passed or defeated, or decisions on the field of battle. Everything was fought out directly by the participants. And the effects were not felt much beyond the political and military spheres.

The wars may well have involved considerable loss of life. In the Peloponnesian War—which was highly exceptional in its length and scope—there was waste on a larger scale as well; agricultural resources were lost and moral leadership eroded. Like most wars, it also consumed a great deal of timber for shipbuilding. But overall people could assume that their world would remain essentially the same: the social order, the structure of the economy, slavery, the limitation of the public sphere largely to men, and even the continued existence of independent city-states as the dominant political entities. Change occurred only when one *polis* became stronger than the others for a period of time. Of course, we can see evidence of a long-term historical process in the defeat of the Greeks by Macedonia and ensuing developments. But it is quite doubtful that at the time the Greeks themselves could have perceived more than variations in the relationships of the city-states to one another. After the Athenians finally lost their independence at the battle of Chaironea in 338, Demosthenes, who had argued in favor of war, was awarded a wreath, because the defense of freedom was seen as an honorable cause. That counted for more than the defeat Athens had suffered.

In this world the main focus of interest internally was the political order of the city and the relationship between its various parts; externally it was the rank of the city within the Greek world and beyond. This was especially true in Athens, and especially during the democratic era. Against this background we can see how and in what way the problem of responsibility appeared to the Greeks (to the extent that it went beyond the family or private circles).

Democracy and its forerunner isonomy became possible because of the many abuses and weaknesses of rule by aristocrats. As the push toward democracy took place and arguments were put forward to legitimize it, one issue that stands out is the degree of responsibility of the bulk of the population for the *polis* (and for running it). The Attic statesman Solon, who—as far as we know—was the first to take important steps on the path that finally led to isonomy, is said to have complained that citizens liked whatever took care of itself (admittedly, this is according to a later source).[24] In other words, they were accustomed to letting matters run their course. He must have been referring to the feuds among the nobility that often involved murder, vengeance, and retaliation by the initiating side. Such running feuds could affect the entire population, and it was not easy to put a stop to them. Solon attempted to involve the citizenry, and in the long run his plan succeeded.

The result was what the Greeks called "placing matters in the hands of the citizens." Such issues, they concluded, ought to be the subject of public discussion and the outcome should be decided by vote. In Greek democracies all matters of any significance were resolved by political decisions, and this on a previously unknown scale. Responsibility was given chiefly to holders of political office, so that accountability played an extraordinary role.

But responsibility was also assigned to people who had advised a particular course, and the Assembly of the People could be faulted for having voted in favor of a measure. The view that prevailed in each case grew out of the debate. What happened overall was under the citizens' control to the extent that the subject had been debated openly in their midst and put to a vote. The fact that the citizenry did not always keep itself under control, especially in the fifth century, was a different problem. Partisanship was in many cases rather extreme. Constitutions themselves could be partisan to the extent that they granted power to the few (in an oligarchy) or to the many (in a democracy), so that major changes were often possible only by overthrowing the constitution. This was often brought about by riots. There were also highly destructive processes of "pathological learning," which were interpreted as fits of "blindness" or "delusion." The people's ability to reason might be suspended, or prove inadequate. That was part of the bargain, and if someone wanted to prevent it from happening, he would have to design an entirely different, non-Greek system, as Plato did in his *Republic*.

Matters stood on a different basis only in foreign policy, especially in war. There neither debate nor the passing of resolutions signified; what counted were tests of arms and victory or defeat in battle. The outcome was understood to depend on many factors. One could ask whether the gods had "meted out the same fate" to both sides. If that proved to be the case, then responsibility could extend only to one's own city, army, or fleet. The citizens of Athens, however, were so extreme (in their delusion of superiority?) that they sentenced defeated commanders to banishment or death. For a while the Athenians believed themselves capable of planning a very large war on the basis of their own superior strength (although they failed to win it). Athenian policy in the early period of its maritime league after 480 was dictated by a sense of its responsibility for Greek freedom beyond the limits of Athens' own territory in the face of the threat posed by the Persians.

That wars occurred over and over again was considered more or less natural (although great powers might feel the necessity of offering justifications for starting one). When attempts were made in the fourth century to establish a general peace, citizens again looked beyond their own cities, claiming a responsibility for all the Greeks if that meshed with their interest in furthering their own power.

For everything that remained the same or continually reproduced itself, that is, for virtually everything outside the sphere of politics, the question of responsibility did not even arise.

Almost two thousand years later Kant reacted with "a certain indignation" to the kind of history I have just described, what he called "men's actions on the great world stage." Though conceding that "wisdom . . . appears here and there among individuals," he regarded the bulk of this history as "woven together from folly, childish vanity, even from childish malice and destructiveness." But even if one could not assume that the participants' intentions were reasonable, he continued, a philosopher could at least "try to see if he can discover a natural purpose in this idiotic course of things human."[25] Kant presumed that all the forms of human conflict served an end of nature, namely, continual development for the better.

This assumption transformed a great deal of what the Greeks took for granted about politics and conflict into a problem, something that required drastic change. Kant viewed politics (and war) from a distance as an outsider, as a member of a bourgeois society that had entirely different values from the "political" society of antiquity (and was dependent on peace in an entirely different way), and as a son of the Enlightenment.

Most important, Kant adopted a view of human action in history that was entirely foreign to antiquity and developed it still further. To the ancient world, there was a straight line, so to speak, between intentions and outcomes, and its direction could be altered only by the possibly contrary intentions of others and contingent circumstances. In Kant's view, by contrast, direct intentions and their consequences were accompanied on a grand scale by indirect, unintentional consequences, side effects operating as impulses within larger, long-term processes. Opponents, even enemies at war with one another, might potentially be working toward the same end without knowing it,[26] insofar as their struggle and competition, and the defeat of one side, would ultimately lead to a new way of thinking and an alliance of nations.[27]

The Greeks believed that the gods could deceive individuals and convince them that wrong was right—for that is the definition of *ate*, "delusion." They intervened, that is to say, in the actions of individuals, or certain armies or city-states. In Kant's view nature does not directly influence the actions of individuals, but it has ordered things so that in the end its intentions are realized. Nature uses human conflict as a lever for this purpose.

This premise exists within a broader philosophical context. "Nature" in Kant is roughly equivalent to Adam Smith's "invisible hand," which directs the actions of the many so that they serve the good of the whole, and also to Schelling's "unconscious necessity" and Hegel's "cunning of reason" *(List der Vernunft)*. Adam Ferguson states that "nations stumble upon establishments, which are indeed the result of human action but not the execution of any human design."[28] Giambattista Vico reached a similar conclusion.

Thus we find a number of people expressing amazement over the fact that human beings have devised all kinds of institutions that prove highly beneficial to future ages, even though they presumably could not anticipate what the future would bring. They act blindly, but still produce what later generations seem to require. At the same time these philosophers perceive a great difference between individuals' intentions and the overall outcome.[29] The horizon within which individuals act, satisfy their needs, and conduct their dealings is very narrow, as are the selfish goals that motivate them. But what emerges as the sum of these activities is prodigious: goods are produced in great quantities; affluence increases across a broad spectrum; the division of labor and relationships of exchange in the marketplace facilitate processes of economic improvement on a scale never dreamed of before. One can make the same claim for politics, as Kant does. He sees in the interplay of even the most foolish or despicable intentions the workings of a process that will produce in the end the best political result.

There is the same discrepancy between the moral quality of individuals' intentions, which are often more than dubious, and the thoroughly positive effects of their activity on the general good. "Private vices, public virtues," as the British philosopher Bernard Mandeville observed. By producing general affluence, all the wretched selfishness of people engaged in business turns out in the aggregate to look like virtue. Albert O. Hirschman illuminates the context in which this discovery occurred in his book *The Passions and the Interests*.[30] This is the precise opposite of the view that predominated in antiquity. Back then it was thought that every citizen needed to possess virtue (and insight), because the *polis* could not thrive otherwise. A member of the community without these qualities would cause harm to the whole; there would be something rotten in the state of the citizenry. If you did not believe, let us say, that the Athenian people (*demos*) possessed sufficient virtue and insight to lead the *polis* properly,[31] then you would logically have to curtail their rights and, in the extreme case, make philosophers into kings and vice versa. Partisan groups of all kinds were also considered highly dangerous, so theorists devised ways and means to eliminate possible points of conflict. The alternatives were political divisions, the risk of an overthrow of the constitution, and possibly even civil war.

By contrast, in Mandeville's time, the eighteenth century, we find the leader of the British party out of power referring to it as His Majesty's opposition. (Only later, in the nineteenth century, would it come to be known as the sovereign's "most loyal opposition.") And not many years later Adam Ferguson pointed out the usefulness to the nation of opposing political parties and their debates.[32]

What had happened to put the opinions of this period so at odds not only from the predominant view of antiquity, but also from that of the preceding century or two? I would like to offer just a few observations.

In Great Britain at least (where many of the remarks cited originated), a nation state existed, providing a framework within which even passionate disputes could be tolerated. Such controversies could not tear the state apart as easily as they might a *polis*, which consisted of a relatively small number of citizens. The country had both a monarch, who existed on a plane above the parties, and a parliament to which debates could be relegated and confined.

It also had a society—strictly speaking, for the first time,[33] since in antiquity neither a state nor society existed as such, but only a body of citizens and a group of fellow residents without political rights. This society was increasingly dominated by one class, the bourgeoisie (roughly speaking). This was also a new development, for it was essentially an urban class with its own values, advantages, and abilities; many of its members, not just its leaders, had a university education. It offered a possibility for something to develop and flourish that had never had any significance for a person's standing in antiquity, namely, specialization. Specialized skills had become prized in medieval cities, corresponding to the other new form of specialization of which they were a part, namely, the division between town and country. In cities landowners did not dominate the hierarchy of social standing, or did so with only rare exceptions. The early modern period brought inhabitants of different cities into many forms of contact with one another, creating connections across long distances and giving this class an entirely new significance.

With such contacts came new products and new possibilities for manufacture and trade. Again, this occurred first in Great Britain, chiefly in England—a process that could be well observed from Scotland by men such as Adam Smith and Adam Ferguson. Within only a short time people realized that the truly important factor in acquiring wealth, producing goods, and making profits was not nature, but labor. This required a new justification for wealth, because it was now understood to be derived from the work of many people. Simultaneously, advances in science led to the doctrine that nature should and could be subdued and exploited for the benefit of mankind (the goal of labor). Bourgeois society developed from all this, and the Enlightenment.

The bourgeoisie of the modern era attracted the attention of observers, who realized that they could not describe how modern society really functioned using the traditional categories and theories of antiquity. As noticed first in Great Britain, more processes seemed to be operating on their own, without direction from above. Precisely by being able to invest their efforts freely, people were able to increase production, trade, and wealth considerably, and all this benefited the modern state, which needed and demanded extraordinarily large sums of money.

For the first time, in sum, one large class of people had produced significant changes across large sections of Europe and North America, merely by going about their daily lives, and largely in order to satisfy their own needs. In some cases this had been achieved through the pursuit of extremely selfish goals—a form of behavior that had previously been despised. This development went hand in hand with scientific discoveries and an enormous expansion of knowledge and education, which created a public sphere shared by the entire bourgeoisie.

It became inevitable that another kind of history would be discovered in addition to the familiar history of political events: the history of processes of long-term change. Many factors at that time encouraged people to assume that a guiding power lay behind the sum of changes being brought about by so many. It was thought to operate in a roundabout way, with cunning, or, like Kant's nature, on the basis of a long-term arrangement. This was a new dynamic, determined not by individuals but most likely by society as a whole, which people came to understand as "history" or "progress." History thus became the product of itself, the result of its own processes.

The dynamic that first emerged from the side effects of many individuals' actions could also be driven forward consciously, with a sense that one was setting sail for new shores. Yet it did not depend on that. The notion of progress that took shape around 1800 was not limited to the economy, society, and science, but extended at the same time to general education, culture, morality, and law. However, such an extended definition worked only if the whole spectrum of society benefited and was advanced.

The Greek movement toward democracy, by contrast, arose not from side effects, but rather from the immediate actions and learning processes of the citizens themselves: guided by political philosophers and others, they had to recognize the problems, disseminate their insights, learn from one another, and move forward step by step. They certainly knew nothing about the possibility of democracy until they created one. What drove them forward were a desire to escape their predicament and concerns about justice, about more rights, and a voice in political decisions. But each of these steps was striven for and achieved consciously, by persuading the Assembly of the People to pass the corresponding resolutions. It was easy to understand that the people had to acquire rights of their own if they were to defend themselves against the nobility. Economic security was naturally a prerequisite for citizen involvement, but many efforts to achieve it had been undertaken through the political process as well.

All this took place in a common assembly consisting of a few thousand men—on a human scale, in other words. And history consisted, as we noted before, of human actions and their contingent circumstances; it was understood as "occurrences," in the plural. The term "history" was applied only to a written work that placed a chronological series of these occurrences in a larger context.[34]

Since the eighteenth century, by contrast, major long-term developments have been measured by two entirely different yardsticks: one for the process as a whole and one for the tiny increments from which it is assembled. (A huge gap has also existed between the insights and ideals of intellectual elites, which often anticipate actual developments, and the possibilities for pursuing or actually realizing them throughout society.)

How did the eighteenth century view the matter of responsibility? Ideas about specific institutions such as the family and the state (and the system of states) presumably remained much the same, although more attention tended to be directed toward the future, as was generally the case at the time. New goals came into view, such as making work easier, creating more leisure and more freedom for more people—increasingly so in the nineteenth and twentieth centuries. But to my knowledge no mention was made of a responsibility toward history. The discrepancy between human action and the totality of historical development was too great. After all, the upshot of Kant's "Idea for a Universal History from a Cosmopolitan Point of View" is that history is an "end of nature,"[35] and all one can do is work in such a way as to support and further it.

Very soon, of course, capitalism and industrialization brought new problems and appalling social conditions that called out for reform and regulation, from prohibiting child labor to bettering public health and creating social insurance. The entire infrastructure of society needed work. Improving education and schools was no less important than road and railroad construction and a myriad other tasks.

These developments opened up broad new fields of responsibility not only for governments and civil servants, but also for the political movements that now began to take shape (both progressive and conservative) and in the long term led to the founding of political parties (and trade unions). At about the same time another set of problems suggested other goals: the expansion of the rule of law and the creation of representative governments—and ultimately democracy.

The nation states of Europe faced enormous challenges and acquired large new obligations, but also power. They benefited, that is to say, from the many different processes at work in attempts to improve conditions. And simultaneously it became evident to governments that they could decide to promote, impede, or channel broad social and economic trends not only in their own nations but also in distant parts of the world. Tariff policies, for example, could counter the effects of globalization.

Major changes—soon taken for granted—helped alleviate many of the worst conditions. How a particular problem ought to be handled, however, became the subject of debate among political parties within the various nations. It was "captured," so to speak, and contained in the area between the parties' different positions. Alternatives to tradition took shape first in the liberal bourgeoisie, then among the Social Democratic voters of the proletariat. These groups pursued their own interests on a large scale while incorporating many smaller particular interests; at the same time they adopted conceptions of entirely new social orders and strove for their realization. Political parties always have the potential, at any given moment, to act as brokers or negotiators between the changes taking place over time and the status quo. All in all they performed this function very well in the late nineteenth century, and by following political debates the members of European societies could acquire information about the problems they faced.

In essence the role played by politics in attempting to find solutions for problems caused by progress remained very large for a long time (and, correspondingly, the political history of this era remains important). Much had to be regulated politically, including the field of education, and improvements were made, even though many of the changes were far from spectacular. With time the bourgeoisie (and ultimately also the proletariat) acquired a far better grasp of their situation and came to understand that the new insights and ideals put forward by intellectuals could be recast as specific political aims. The traditional domain for which statesmen had been responsible grew in size, because self-perpetuating processes required them to make more and more decisions about the structure of the state and society.

Progress brought many benefits with it, in some respects for society as a whole, in others for individuals (if only that, let us say, fewer people had to suffer from toothaches). This made accepting responsibility easier, especially for proponents of innovation. Conservatives, on the other hand, had a harder time of it; frequently, they were forced to revise their goals and transfer certain innovations that they had resisted, usually in vain, to the column of "institutions worth preserving" (so that they could go on and fight other innovations).

Both groups, progressives and conservatives, saw themselves in relation to history and continued to do so well into the twentieth century: for the former, history pointed the way to a better future, while the latter appealed to history in arguing for slower development, and thus a different mode of proceeding. Overall the feeling prevailed for a long time that progress could bring positive innovation without too great a loss of old traditions. Johann Gustav Droysen, for example, believed that "every insight, once gained, is retained in human consciousness; that the community . . . feels itself united and preserves the knowledge it has acquired, in order to build on it further."[36] And he certainly did not mean to say that most of this knowledge belonged in museums.

In any case, progress led to palpable and lasting relief from mass poverty, hunger, crowding, and ignorance, and created defenses against natural disasters. It was to be expected that forces were always present urging society toward the future.

Societies bring about structural change in different degrees, and have different ways of dealing with it. As far as the latter is concerned, a society can control change, or at least debate it as part of the political process, or at the very least be aware of what is occurring. In terms of causing change, the spectrum begins at one end with the state or the political process essentially in sole control of the types of change that are allowed to occur. Further along are cases in which self-perpetuating processes exist but are beneficial for much of the population, and thus do not need much control; governments can encourage promising developments and try to keep negative side effects to a minimum, in part by ensuring that most of the changes are made the subject of discussion and negotiation among political parties. The same possibility continues to exist even if we advance to a stage where much of the self-regulating change is not welcomed by large segments of the population. Negotiation still represents a kind of control exerted by the society as a whole.[37] Finally, however, we approach the other end of the spectrum, and the possibility that the autonomous processes of change now exceed the ability of the political process to "capture" and limit them; beyond that lies the situation in which it is not even possible to keep abreast of all the kinds of change that are taking place.

In the first half of the twentieth century people began to feel ambivalent about progress; from the First World War to Auschwitz, Hiroshima, and Nagasaki, its negative side became evident—not to mention all the crimes perpetrated against colonial peoples, some of them committed in the name of progress. It became apparent that while useful new tools had become available, they could also be used in the most terrible ways, for a means of controlling them responsibly had not developed in tandem with the technology. In addition, they gave rise to new ambitions in the social and political spheres, such as government plans to sterilize groups of citizens in the name of "national health." Erroneous notions of responsibility and historical mission gained ground, even dictating policy at the highest levels for a certain period.

"But how do matters stand today?" we may well ask. We are confronted daily with an unceasing stream of innovations, and around the globe processes of change are being set in motion, many of them self-perpetuating, for a whole range of reasons. No overall direction is apparent; no class of society appears to identify itself with a particular kind of future—instead, countless individuals of all social and national origins are making efforts to seize the possibilities open to them for improving their lives. There does not appear to be an entire class, a bourgeoisie or proletariat, attempting to develop new theories about the world on the basis of its shared experience, and then to devise policies and mobilize their forces in support of them. "Conservative" and "progressive" positions seem to have become fluid to a large extent, and even disputes about fundamental principles do not contribute to clarity. History, in any event, no longer appears to be moving in one identifiable direction, in the traditional sense of a process moving from the past via the present into the future in some generally accepted fashion. And, finally, neither nature nor any kind of secularized expectation of God can provide us with a sense of certainty about the path we ought to follow, or even the illusion of one.

Despite all the great and welcome innovations of the age, do we have any assurance that they will be exploited only in ways beneficial to us? States, criminal organizations, and sects can acquire tremendous potential for destruction at very affordable prices (aided by spies and traitors if need be). We can be immunized, but bacteria and viruses can mutate. We have an increasing capacity for breeding human beings, keeping them under observation, exerting pressure on them, and destroying their backbone (or preventing them from developing one in the first place), not to mention their human dignity. Could it be that, since society can no longer be changed, some people are trying to change human beings instead? But what kind of New Man would that be? And, in the meantime, what about the frustrations of all those people who cannot keep up with the pace of change and can no longer be easily "captured" by any kind of political process?

We must also ask what it means that we and our children are exposed to enormous change not only in the circumstances of our lives (leaving aside all question of intentional manipulation) but also in our convictions (to the extent that we still have any), values, and ideals. It is not just that we are compelled to learn a great many new things; that is all to the good. What is more problematic is the necessity to unlearn so much and absorb new information in its place, over and over again.[38] In a process that runs parallel to the exponential increase in new knowledge, the information and skills we have become obsolete—along, perhaps, with the certainty that we ought to acquire and keep strong convictions about anything. Although it may strike us that some of the changes are not really taking us anywhere new (like an exercise wheel going round and round in a hamster's cage), others bring real shifts—even if only to a place where old attitudes and convictions become untenable.

In short, we are caught up inescapably in ever-accelerating historical processes in many aspects of our lives. At the same time we seem to have no particular need to turn to history for orientation or guidance. Why should that be so?

First of all, of course, the idea does not normally suggest itself to experience one's own time as history. We do the things we want and have to do, depending on our occupations and the circumstances of our lives, perhaps with a perspective that involves the future. But none of this becomes history until later, when it lies behind us and has perhaps acquired a place in a sequence of past experiences. That is not the case with great events, where the outcome is uncertain, and any decision that is made can have far-reaching consequences. These are rare today, however, and have been largely replaced by polls, media campaigns, and entertainment, to which the foregoing does not apply. How, then, should we be able to see ourselves, our daily actions, and experiences in historical terms—especially since what is likely to matter for history are the unintended side effects of our actions rather than the quite different ends we had in mind?

On the other hand, it could occur to us to ask whether, in such a new situation, we might need comparison with earlier eras in order to acquire some sense of orientation from the past about what the future might hold in store.[39] As Niccolò Machiavelli wrote, "he who wants to see what is to come should observe what has already happened."[40] But any predictions about the future, the opposite of the past in the historical continuum, are rendered exceedingly difficult because so much is caught up in the process of change. And perhaps this process has advanced so far by now that people no longer want to know—at least not about the conditions that future societies, and the whole world, will have to face.

Then the question becomes: Is the reason we don't want to know because we can't imagine them, or because we can't do anything about them in any case? Because we cannot see how developments are to be brought under control? Or, even if we were to try, the tack we should take? Have people given up trying to understand the whole process? Or is the *real* question one we don't dare to address: namely, how to take responsibility for the processes of change?

At this point an example from a different era may be useful in clarifying the set of problems involved.[41]

In the history of the Roman Republic we can observe how, from a certain point onward, the same kinds of actions and pursuit of the same goals that had enabled Rome to become a great power, and preserve itself and its form of government for centuries, promoted a process leading to the Republic's demise. In this end phase the struggle against external enemies had grown more difficult, and Rome needed outstanding military commanders. The army no longer consisted of the peasants with whom Rome had fought its earlier wars; now the soldiers were landless men, and it soon became customary after they had fought campaigns to demand grants of land where they could settle. The Senate was firmly opposed to this, however, because the commanders who demanded and received land for their troops won their lasting loyalty—thereby becoming major political players who could call upon their troops' support in political disputes.

Several vicious circles resulted: the greater the need for uncommonly talented men as commanders in the field, the more dominant these men became if they succeeded; although nominally of the same standing as other senators, their prestige and political power increased enormously. When they demanded that their soldiers be settled on land of their own, they came into conflict with the Senate. If the representatives of the people sponsored bills in an effort to push through the commanders' demands, the Senate tried to veto them. The sponsors of the resolutions then used force to prevent a veto or ignored one if it passed. As a result the disputes served to undermine the constitution of the Republic, even though that was no one's primary intention.

And the same thing occurred in many other areas. Rome's exploitation of its provinces resulted in many forms of corruption. And the more Romans became accustomed to luxury, the more their motivation to squeeze the provinces economically increased. Officially, efforts were made to counter this trend and reduce corruption by establishing new courts and imposing harsher penalties for breaking the law. The main effect, however, of these measures was to raise exploitation to even greater heights, because people simply added the judges of the new courts to the list of officials it was necessary to bribe. At the same time, moreover, the norms according to which children were educated grew narrower, so that on average each generation of senators was less and less equipped to master the worsening situation. No one was aiming to bring down the Republic; the Senate's express intention was to defend it, but the combined effect of all the parties' efforts was its destruction. It was Livy who observed that while in the end the Republic could not survive the abuses, neither could it survive the attempts to correct them.[42]

If I may sum this up in a more general formulation: the burdens placed on traditional institutions and on the traditional form of education, among many other things, proved too great. And there were no countervailing forces to create new institutions—or new rules for raising a new generation of leaders, for that matter, who could have placed the problem of the overtaxed republican constitution on the agenda, against the wishes of the traditionalists, and "captured" the destructive phenomenon in their debates. There was no way for an alternative to tradition to take shape. The great military commanders had no cause with which they could have associated themselves that would have led to a strengthening of the Senate and republican institutions. In a nutshell, all the powerful people, even all those with the potential to become powerful, were satisfied (or could be satisfied from time to time), while all the dissatisfied people were powerless. The latter class included especially the inhabitants of the provinces from which Rome extracted so much money to satisfy the many demands of its own citizens—not always successfully of course, but acceptably for the most part. As the Republic as a whole had no way of getting a grip on the situation,[43] it slid into a prolonged period of civil wars.

The lesson is that the side effects of actions designed to satisfy accepted needs or enable everyday business to be conducted depend not on the actions themselves, but on the constellation of circumstances in which they take place. A pleasurable act of procreation, for example, will have no great effect on a static population, while if there is an upward demographic curve it can contribute to a population explosion. A bribe paid to a judge will have no side effects if it occurs in isolation, but in a different context it will contribute to a pernicious process of spreading corruption. Thus whether a given act has side effects depends on the number of people engaging in it—whether it be begetting children, bribing judges, engaging in scientific research, or inventing things and making discoveries. The principle remains the same when the matter at stake is the number of times the constitution is infringed and the gravity of the infringements, or the number of ways the traditional standards of education fail or political systems become overburdened.

The reference to the downfall of the Roman Republic is not intended to draw any kind of parallel to present-day circumstances, but only to point out a possible structural problem of a general kind: we know of cases when problems have arisen that a society could not master within the framework of its traditional institutions, of cases when a society could not cope—among other things —with the great changes it was undergoing (usually in the form of unintended side effects of its own actions). As a consequence this society ended up at the mercy of their cumulative impact. We know of cases in which societies simply did not know enough, were unable to "keep up"—a situation not reflective of the amount of knowledge available but rather the relevance of that knowledge to the specific problems they faced. Societies can lose their ability to articulate opposing positions and work through the various possible outcomes; they may not be able to give up certain customs or bad habits until they have led to massive problems.

And so my conclusion would be: when some observers describe our own era as "the end of history," it would be nonsense to take them literally. But if it is true that today we are all more or less adrift; if one regards the present condition of European political parties as reflective of larger trends; if there are good reasons why governments are withdrawing from more and more areas—might it not be that "history" is taking on a new shape? It may well be the case that politicians and the political process are failing increasingly to address the overarching processes of change—meaning that an entirely new kind of "invisible hand" is at work, which we cannot define, and whose effects we cannot anticipate. In any event, it seems likely that a large shift in the relationship between social change and the ability of the political process to "capture" and debate it (mutability and controversiality) might be underway right now.

As in ancient Rome, there is no lack of underprivileged and disadvantaged people today, especially in Africa, Latin America, and Asia. But unless I am mistaken, they are unlikely to be in a position soon to question the existing world order (and the distribution of material goods), that is, to place the problem of a future order on the political agenda. Yet their situation will certainly have an effect in many ways—like so many other problems that are not easily addressed through politics.

Or does this simply represent once again a conservative point of view, which regards everything new as suspect because it does not yet fall into the category of what should be preserved, although by tomorrow it may seem worth defending? Should we place our bets on progress, like Kant? It would be an interesting experiment to envision what a history "based on the principle of world citizenship" might look like. But the real questions are: Can we bet that progress is automatically headed in the right direction—so that our task is only to understand the process and further it? And most important: Can we believe that the political tools we have at our disposal in the forms of national governments and international organizations are sufficient to keep unpleasant or dangerous "developments" from occurring?[44]

When people by and large "do only what happens," to quote Robert Musil once again, and do it in the company of billions of others—on a gigantic scale and completely removed from decision-making processes of every kind—it is nearly impossible to take responsibility for it, especially since what is "happening" occurs both with and without our intervention, and to a large extent in the form of side effects.

Nevertheless, many new movements, which often take the form of nongovernmental organizations, attest to the ways in which people can make attempts independently of all governments and "regular" political institutions to assume responsibility for humanity and the state of nature on the planet. One of the questions prompted by such activities is how they will affect the existing systems for making decisions and whether humanity—or at least significant portions of it—can regain control of processes it has set in motion. Or is it rather the case that, as soon as such organizations have achieved greater success, they will threaten dangers of their own? In any event, the relationship between individuals and the entities to which they belong (and through which they have the best chance of influencing developments) on the one hand, and the amount that is changing (i.e., the process that would most likely require intervention) on the other, has been utterly transformed.

If, in view of all this, people would rather not think about the question of responsibility for all the processes to which they are contributing (and for which their children and grandchildren may have to pay), that is only too understandable. It has consequences, however, notably the postmodern understanding of freedom, which frivolously concentrates on personal free space in matters both great and small, on little niches in a world that was itself turned into a set of niches long ago by the travel and leisure industry.

Thus it is likely that people of today have arrived at an entirely new place in history. The Greeks, if they needed to take their bearings, took them from the history of their own city-state and its relationships with others. From the eighteenth century on, Europeans and North Americans understood themselves in distinctly historical terms, identifying themselves as participants in a movement of forward progress (which of course could be resisted). And once they got used to progress as a good thing, they rather arrogantly claimed that their own nations represented it. But now, after all this, something is coming into existence that defies definition in traditional categories.

But be that as it may, if my remarks on history can help us to analyze our present situation more successfully—by drawing comparisons, for instance—then I will have succeeded in demonstrating that history can definitely still be of interest today. That would, in its turn, bestow a new and uncomfortable responsibility, but potentially a very fruitful one, on historians.

5

Auschwitz

Following earlier usage (and because I know of no better term), I will let "Auschwitz," the name of the largest death camp, stand here for the entire policy of extermination that National Socialist Germany employed above all against Jews, but also against gypsies, the mentally ill, Polish intellectuals, Russian prisoners of war, homosexuals, and others.

Auschwitz in this sense presents an enormous challenge for historians, especially if they are not just plowing their special fields, but contemplating history more generally from the vantage point of their own time (and the history of Europe and its special path in particular). And if, I would add further, they believe that their obligations as historians extend not only to the principles and methods of their craft but also to their contemporaries.

Probably no other event in history offers such radical resistance to every attempt to uncover some meaning in it. Indeed, every attempt to discern meaning can seem like an after-the-fact insult to the millions of victims. I would include in this category even the interpretations that run, "At least Auschwitz led to the founding of the state of Israel," or "the human race needed Auschwitz as a lesson, so that nothing of the kind could ever occur again." The latter result is by no means guaranteed.

Wilhelm von Humboldt once observed, "The historian worthy of the name must depict every occurrence as part of a larger whole, or show the form of history in general with respect to each, which amounts to the same thing."[1] But what does it mean to "show the form of history in general" with respect to Auschwitz? Or to comprehend Auschwitz as part of a whole? If it forms part of a whole, how does it affect our view of other parts of that whole, such as events from antiquity? Or does Auschwitz represent a break with civilization that may perhaps shed an entirely new light on the shaky and dubious grounds of all historical study and interpretation?

What kind of framework could possibly include Athens and Auschwitz? What kind of a whole? Or are such questions too ambitious? Should one content oneself with more modest ones?

Nietzsche once referred to the "retrospective force" that he saw every great individual as exerting: "for his sake all of history is put on the scale and weighed again; a thousand secrets of the past creep out of their hiding places . . . There is no telling what may yet become a part of history."[2] If a "great individual" can exert such a force, must not an event such as Auschwitz do so to a far greater extent? What could one then discover about the past, or humankind?

It is for this reason, I think—without wishing to intrude on the territory of contemporary historians—that reflections on Auschwitz appropriately also belong to the tasks of historians specializing in other eras. We cannot ignore the fundamental questions that arise from it in our research, interpretations, and descriptions.

The sum of the crimes involved has with good reason been called unparalleled, unique,[3] even though human history has no lack of mass murders (particularly if earlier crimes are regarded in terms of contemporaneous population figures). The complex for which the name Auschwitz stands consists of an attempt by a national government to kill an entire "race," which it had defined especially for this purpose. The definition extended to all the members of a religious community that had existed for millennia, including those who had renounced it or whose ancestors had done so, including the elderly and infants, without exception, as far as they could be identified and detained. Their extermination was conducted for the most part in assembly-line fashion, as if they had no right to be considered part of humanity, no right to be murdered in their own clothes or in any clothing at all. The victims' gold teeth were given to the Reich bank; the women's hair was cut off and rolled into large balls for industrial processing and reuse. Nothing of the kind had ever occurred before, not even under Stalin. And what is more, this extermination policy was directed overwhelmingly at people who had shown no hostility to the Germans—on the contrary!

It exceeds all comprehension. Night after night, it still haunts the people who survived the camps. All reason must resist accepting such an event as within the scope of human possibility. As the political scientist and journalist Dolf Sternberger (1907–1989) wrote, "A person trying to understand what the realization of this plan actually means would lose his mind. And if he does not lose his mind over it, he has not truly perceived the phenomenon of Auschwitz. (I realize this is paradoxical, but there is no other way to express it.)"[4]

Elsewhere Sternberger declared, "The process that is Auschwitz also consists not only of the crime of methodically exterminating human beings, but also the million-fold inaudible scream of the innocent victims. There is nothing to 'understand' about that scream, as it could not make itself heard." Is that correct? Is there "nothing to 'understand'"?[5] Sternberger goes one step further: "Those who would try not just to present the process that is Auschwitz, but also to understand it, would take historical identification to the point where it turns into virtual complicity."[6]

I must say that I find his position both well founded and quite persuasive. Sternberger's radical formulation makes clear what a challenge historians face in this case. Anyone who wants to talk about "understanding" in history can—and must—test it in this specific instance, since it illustrates the way in which Auschwitz has changed *everything*. And nevertheless—can we really accept that in the case of Auschwitz "understanding" is impossible?

And as far as depicting it is concerned, can we take Martin Broszat's observation and leave it at that? He wrote: "No matter which history book one opens, when the Third Reich begins, authors take a step back. Any empathetic attitude toward the historical past ceases abruptly, as does the pleasure in relating a historical narrative."[7] It is as if such authors are speaking of a distant population who have nothing to do with us. Over and over again they cite the unimaginable nature of what took place, as if some barrier stood between us and Auschwitz. Do we really have to accept this—or are we not obliged to make an attempt to understand, precisely in this case? No matter how far that attempt takes us? And whatever the consequences for history?

"Understanding," wrote Hannah Arendt in 1953, ". . . is an unending activity by which . . . we come to terms with, reconcile ourselves to reality, that is, try to be at home in the world." How is that possible in the face of the Holocaust? Hannah Arendt goes on to say that this striving for reconciliation becomes extremely problematic in an age of totalitarianism, in which we suddenly discover that "we have lost our tools of understanding. Our quest for meaning"— which can apparently produce understanding—"is at the same time prompted and frustrated by our inability to originate meaning."[8]

Yet Hannah Arendt draws a different conclusion from the evidence than Sternberger. For it is precisely in a situation in which "our categories of thought and standards of judgment have been destroyed," she writes, that it is necessary to judge.[9] There is a particularly urgent need for the power of judgment in a totalitarian system (because one is otherwise left with no defense against it), but it is also necessary afterward. Judging presumes at least some basis of understanding, however. Maurice Merleau-Ponty even speaks of an obligation to understand what we disagree with or reject.[10]

Judging something without understanding it does not get to the heart of things.[11] Condemning without understanding leads into a dead-end of cheap insistence on our own superiority. And, conversely, understanding without condemning can lead to a position based on no principles at all, or to indifference. Perhaps the connection between understanding and condemning can offer a way out— a way to clarity and the beginnings of a "reconciliation with reality"—at least as time passes and the distance grows.

All the same, are there ultimately limits to what can be "understood"? Within the discipline of history the word *verstehen* originally referred to gaining an empathetic insight into texts and the actions and thinking of individuals. Since the authors and actors were human beings, it was thought, we ought to be able to view them with at least a minimum of empathy, although at the same time the distinctions between epochs and mental horizons had to be preserved. Sternberger says that only what is sensible (*verständig*) can be understood, even if it were only—as in one example he cites— the pride Commandant Rudolf Höss seemed to take in the fact that the gas chambers in Auschwitz were an improvement over those in Treblinka.[12] Sternberger notes, however, that it is precisely the purpose to which they were put, and the fact that the entire plan was actually carried out, that elude understanding. Perhaps one could phrase this differently: maybe(!) the actions and striving (and suffering) of individuals in the system of mass extermination can be understood—but certainly not the totality of what occurred.

However, a different kind of "understanding" is required as soon as the subject turns from the actions and thinking of creatures of our own species to complex events or chains of events. Or at the very least different tools are required. We can view the actions and suffering of individual participants in the battle of Salamis "empathetically," but not the battle as a whole. Nonetheless, it *is* possible to acquire some idea of how fleets maneuver, how a naval battle proceeds, and how such a battle can be decided. Ultimately, it may be possible to "understand" in a different sense, that is, grasp intellectually, why the Greeks won at Salamis. We arrive at this understanding in part by means of a narrative that "arranges" the material in such a way as to suggest a particular view or conclusion. Analogously one can even come to "understand" how extended processes take their course over time, even if they seem perfectly absurd in terms of ordinary logic. Take the fact, for example, that all the well-meaning efforts of the people in charge of making policy for German universities, who are by no means stupid, effectively make the situation worse. It is actually absurd—but if you have observed the process long enough, you "understand" it well, down to the mechanisms involved. And Parkinson's or Murphy's law are similar, except that what functions rather well in such cases with the aid of a little sarcasm, even if one has a heavy heart, fails utterly with an event such as Auschwitz. And the reason it does is because reckoning with such an event at all, even considering the possibility of it, is unacceptable.

Our use of language is a good guide here, as it so often is. We say that something is "impossible" even if it is quite possible, or in fact actually the case. In other words, "impossible" is used to characterize something that is indeed possible, but shouldn't be—something that should not even be thought of as possible. By this standard, only what follows certain rules or occurs within certain limits is possible. And if someone should insist that other things are possible as well, he is not only called a pessimist (and that is bad enough), but can also quickly come under suspicion of trying to conjure them up. Auschwitz cannot and must not be doubted. But at the same time can't we—*mustn't* we—refuse to consider Auschwitz possible and categorically refuse to "understand" it?

At this point it might be well to use instead a less loaded word: Can Auschwitz be *explained?* Philosophers of science distinguish between "explaining" and "understanding" a phenomenon, and so the term is associated more with the natural or social sciences than with the humanities. My hypothesis is as follows: Auschwitz can be explained to no significantly lesser degree than other events in history. The sources never provide every fact necessary to do this, of course. And since there are always differences of opinion regarding the import of particular historical factors and contexts, explanations naturally differ. This is similarly true in the case of Auschwitz. What matters is that well-founded explanations are possible. Let me make an attempt to demonstrate that.

Formerly, scholars used to trace the systematic extermination of European Jews to an order presumably given by Hitler. Recently, however, a second, opposing, view has arisen that sees it as the result of a relatively long, largely bureaucratic, decision-making process driven by different forces. Regional institutions played a particular role. While extermination certainly did not take place against the wishes of the Führer, he did not set the process in motion, nor did he at any point issue a specific order.

In contrast to the orders for implementing euthanasia, a written order for the elimination of the Jews has never been found, and in all probability such an order never existed in writing. Of course, Hitler could have issued it verbally, or expressed his wishes in indirect form.

If we assume that a command from the Führer existed, then we would have to explain how a human being could have issued such a monstrous order. As possible grounds could be cited: anti-Semitism; its connection with various ideas that Jews constituted a "racial" threat to the German people; and its connection with the more general idea, which flourished at the time, that public health could be promoted through government intervention. (Of course, this was usually limited to the forced sterilization of people with genetic disorders, a measure that was discussed by the Social Democrats during the Weimar Republic and practiced in Sweden up to the 1970s.) An increase in anti-Semitism during the period could be traced back to conspiracy theories such as the "Protocols of the Elders of Zion" or the legend of the "stab in the back" at the end of World War I. One would also have to examine the climate in 1918 and afterward, when widespread deprivation and confusion gave rise in parts of some European societies (particularly in a Germany that had become so impoverished) to a peculiar set of expectations and desperate hopes. They provided a foundation for all kinds of ideologies to flourish, in particular gigantic plans for immediate, revolutionary, and radical social change. Liberalism appeared to have grown flabby, and the bourgeoisie had become despised. Some overestimated the changes that technology and politics could bring about, insisting that their ambitious, messianic notions could be accomplished, and a number of people were receptive to these ideas. And if they booked any early successes, then much more could appear possible. A huge increase in the power of the state and cockamamie, crazy-quilt schemes came to seem feasible. In short, a crop of ominous "philosophies" sprang up in the soil of unrealistic hopes and expectations and ran riot. Seen in this context, a belief in such a thing as the "Jewish question" can appear plausible, and it is even plausible that such a belief spread, along with the wish to solve it. Indeed, some Germans became certain that they could take care of it, once and for all, by depriving the Jews of their jobs, their public roles, and their civil rights and by driving them out of the country.

This was all stupid and malignant, to be sure; indeed, the form it took in Hitler and others was an *idée fixe*, what Martin Broszat has called a "pathological form of anti-Semitism."[13] But such a thing does exist. Hitler's ability to perceive reality in this regard was extremely limited or massively damaged. For what had Jews, especially German Jews, done to other Germans, after all? Weren't many of them especially good Germans, in research and business, and physicians and lawyers, as measured by the criteria of education and the language they spoke? Hadn't they fought for their country in 1914 like everyone else, and suffered losses at just as high a rate as other groups in the population, or at an even higher one? And even if some of the unsavory profiteers who aroused hatred and loathing toward the end of the war and in the postwar period were Jewish—what did that have to do with "race"?

We would next have to explain how a man with such obsessional ideas could have built up a large and powerful movement. How could someone with delusions that were in part pathological (even if some of them reflected the times) have become head of the government of a large country, and been granted vast powers that, although formally within the letter of the constitution, violated its spirit? How did he then succeed in removing the remaining legal obstacles to dictatorship? Since many Germans certainly deplored this, how could there have been such an absence of protest in the political class, the bureaucracy, the army leadership, the legal system, and large sections of the population—to such an extent that even Hitler himself was surprised?

In order to explain this, we must go back to the Treaty of Versailles and the widely unpopular Weimar Republic, to inflation, the economic crisis, unemployment—to all the helplessness, fear, and suffering (some of it severe) in a German population that traditionally expected the state to take the lead in solving economic problems. Ultimately, the response of many Germans in this situation was to turn to a radical movement, either on the left or the right. After the defeat of 1918, this population was also clearly longing to regain the status of a great nation. Furthermore, it was also a population in which many young people were flocking to movements with fantastic and visionary programs. Nowadays much of this may strike us as strange and difficult to imagine—not only the degree of poverty and the longing for national greatness, but also the lack of trust in the democratic system (although this last may not be quite as certain as was once thought). All these factors, however, certainly can be *explained*, and scholars have done a great deal to clarify them.

Finally, the lack of resistance to the Führer and the growing numbers of his adherents appear quite plausible if one factors in the mixture of successes and expectations of more success (which repeatedly surprised many doubters), the mixture of terror and dismissal from office, and the expulsion and elimination of opponents of the regime. People were unprepared for the persistence, energy, and ruthlessness of the men now in power, who were taking over the republic not only outwardly, so to speak, but also in people's minds. And one factor should not be underestimated: they did and achieved what no one had considered possible, with new initiatives and a dynamic that outpaced the world's ability to adapt. This no doubt contributed to the fact that the regime, once it was in power and enjoying its first successes, did not moderate its tactics (as is the rule, it is probably correct to say), but on the contrary became even more radical.[14]

Most Germans of this era behaved at first as people tend to do after political upheavals: they tried to adapt. Moreover, a great deal of what the regime was trying to achieve appeared positive in the eyes of many. Its goals held out possibilities that some of the wishes Germans had cherished for years might be fulfilled, and many people identified themselves with those hopes. As so often occurs, limits on freedom and the rule of law were accepted, at least in the beginning. "You can't make an omelet," people say in such cases, "without breaking eggs." If the sensitivity to the fact that suffering and crimes were being inflicted on others, that whole groups were being degraded, was not particularly great, then that can be explained too in retrospect, as outrageous as it may seem. Anti-Semitism forms part of the explanation, as do the tendency to obedience and the apathy of a general public that was relatively defenseless. Some were, of course, already fanatics. Many people simply possessed the ability to look the other way.[15]

Nevertheless, the "night of shattered glass" made some feel embarrassment in addition to rage and fear. The fact that entire population groups put on blinders, that people grew thicker skins, and kept a great deal of their anger bottled up—these phenomena are not inexplicable either, especially if one adds to the equation a dependency on authority that is perhaps stronger among Germans than other people. And the widespread compliance with the regime should appear plausible if, in addition to the factors already mentioned, one adds a tendency still characteristic of Germans today—despite their far more favorable circumstances—namely, an unwillingness for individuals to step forward and take responsibility or act on the courage of their convictions. For we are hardly less cowardly than our parents and grandparents, if it comes to that. There were some admirable examples of courage at that time, it should be said—just not nearly enough of them, unfortunately.

However, with all of this one arrives only at an explanation for the possibility that those in power along with many mid- and lower-level bureaucrats and segments of the population could treat Jews and others without regard to law, take away their rights, and subject them to degradation and violence—all the way down to the very slow tightening of thumbscrews, as Victor Klemperer has noted so precisely,[16] down to the parents who forbade their children to play with their Jewish friends. All of this corresponded to a desire to persuade Jews to emigrate (with a concomitant loss of most of their possessions).

All this was bad enough, but next to nothing in comparison with what followed! As yet there was no talk of murder—apart from the "night of shattered glass" and some isolated cases, and threatening references to a possible extermination of Jews in the future, if war should break out. On January 30, 1939, Hitler announced to the Reichstag, "Once again I will be a prophet: should the international Jewry of finance succeed, both within and beyond Europe, in plunging mankind into yet another world war, then the result will not be a Bolshevization of the earth and the victory of Jewry, but the annihilation of the Jewish race in Europe."[17] Later Hitler made several references to this declaration.

But even given his readiness to carry out threats, and his known ruthlessness, this still does not mean that he was actually prepared to make a decision to exterminate Jews and carry it out, even if specific events should occur. Matters were not that simple even for Adolf Hitler.

In any event, it is certain that plans continued to be made for a good while after the Polish campaign to resettle the Jews outside Germany, mainly in the area of the now German-led "General Government" of Poland, in the parts of Poland incorporated into the Reich as the new "Warthegau," or possibly even in Madagascar.[18] After the opening of the Russian campaign, distant regions in Siberia and on the White Sea were also considered. That would have been fatal for most of the "settlers" in any case, but it would have eliminated the need to murder them.

However, it proved impossible to defeat and conquer the Soviet Union as quickly and easily as Hitler and his followers had first thought. And even earlier the Germans assigned to govern the Warthegau and the rest of Poland resisted the idea of taking in added numbers of Jews. They were in fact eager to get rid of the Jewish populations they already had—and send them further east.

At this point a process got going that was spurred on by many factors. These included food supply problems in wartime, in a country dependent on imports; housing problems, including providing shelter for hundreds of thousands of ethnic Germans repatriated too quickly to the "Fatherland"; a need for supplementary hospital space for soldiers that led to demands to empty mental hospitals; and a desire on the part of Hitler and his administrators not to make the German population (the "Aryans," after all!) suffer any more than necessary. In such a situation Jews (and the mentally ill) came to be seen as superfluous mouths to feed, mere "human ballast."[19] If they were resettled elsewhere, it would be possible to save money, and others could inherit their property—or simply steal it. The living space that Jews had occupied could be turned over to Germans, or in some cases to Poles who had been evicted to make room for Germans elsewhere.

A competition broke out among the *Gau* administrators in the Reich to see who could be the first to make his district *judenfrei*— "free of Jews." The eastern Jews were herded into ghettos, to have them under control, but there was no way to keep these ghettos functioning economically—despite all efforts—mainly since the Jews confined there had previously been robbed of all their property. And since they were terribly overcrowded, famine and disease followed; the Germans lamented the impossible conditions, but were at the same time not displeased (since they provided a desired "demonstration" of Jews' "inferiority"). A great "relocation" was conceived for the East, and the regional administrators there wanted to know what was expected of them. Thus the question was raised in official correspondence, "what is to be done in the end with these displaced populations that are undesirable for the Greater German settlement areas? Is the goal to permanently secure them some sort of subsistence, or should they be totally eradicated?"[20] And so in the discussions taking place in July 1941 the suggestion surfaced "to finish off the Jews unfit for labor through some fast-acting means. This would definitely be more pleasant than letting them starve to death."[21]

In any case, newly formed special squads of the SS had already carried out mass shootings of Jews behind the front of German troops advancing into the Soviet Union.[22] The victims were men only at first, but after about two months women and children were also included. The total number soon reached more than one million.

Beginning in the fall of 1941 plans were made to establish extermination camps in Belzec, Sobibor, Treblinka, Majdanek, and Auschwitz, with gas chambers and large ovens for burning the corpses. The plans included links to railway lines, with precise timetables for trains. Now the Jews in Germany—and also in all the other parts of Europe where the Germans were in control—were sent to the camps and gas chambers. At this point, at the latest, the goal became extermination, without regard to whether the populations had ever been viewed as in the way or superfluous at home. At best some of these prisoners might be used temporarily as laborers—but soon even that came to be viewed as politically undesirable in Germany, despite many requests from leaders of industry not to expel Jews capable of working. Creating "Jew-free" areas became a higher priority than supplying urgently needed labor. On the whole German policy makers were extravagantly wasteful with what they referred to as "human materiel." In terms of the declared goal of winning the war, the process was completely mad.

That all of this took place with the knowledge and consent of the Führer is probable, as mentioned above. His share in it would have to be explained from his original position and also from the dynamics of developing policy on Jews and the pressure to succeed that he had himself created, as well as from his prophecy of 1939, quoted above, and his obsession that Jews should not be allowed to survive if the Germans lost the flower of their youth in the war.

One aspect of the years leading up to the killing on an industrial scale demands an explanation, however. In these years between 1939 and 1941—when the term "evacuation" was still being used, although it now meant into the hereafter, and when the process of dealing with the Jews was acquiring its own intensifying dynamic— how did it come about that the German leadership believed that they could do with the Jews as they pleased, including killing them if they wanted to? (And including the hideous medical experiments; just imagine had organ transplants been possible at that time!) How did it come about that their sole aim—about which there was clearly almost no hesitation or objections—became how to get rid of the Jews as simply as possible? The only questions raised were technical ones about which solutions were most practical. And that was the end of it.

After the war, Rudolf Höss, the commandant of Auschwitz, wrote of his relief at the decision to gas prisoners: "I always shuddered at the prospect of carrying out exterminations by shooting, when I thought of . . . the women and children . . . I was therefore relieved to think that we were to be spared all these bloodbaths, and that the victims too would be spared suffering until their last moment came."[23] The method might pose problems, that is to say, but not the murders themselves. Höss saw himself as responsible only for the method, and for applying it. If he found the thing itself "wrong, completely wrong" after the war, it was mainly because "it didn't serve anti-Semitism at all." Hitler himself also referred near the end of the war to the "more humane means"[24] by which he had made the Jews pay for their supposed guilt for the war, the war dead, and the civilians killed in the Allied bombing raids.

One hesitates even to broach the subject of how the Holocaust could happen—you don't want to go there. But it is explainable, unfortunately, that in a country without a free press, without an opposition party, cut off to a large extent from foreign countries, a fanatic but simultaneously successful leadership could have high approval ratings. The clever use of propaganda helps to explain further why the erroneous belief could become entrenched that a certain group of people was extremely dangerous (especially given high levels of pre-existing prejudice against them). It is explainable that things went so far that many people, and not just members of a special unit like the SS, could become convinced that they were a master race, and that other races deserved only as much space and as many rights on earth as the master race cared to concede—in some cases, none at all. And, above all, it becomes explainable that during the war more than just a small, specially drilled group could be found to carry out directly the policy of exterminating millions; a far larger number of people were involved in the preliminary stages, many of them willingly enough, and some often quite willing to pull the trigger. All this can unfortunately be explained, if one takes the initial situation and calculates the processes of exacerbation, the possibilities for ordinary people to become enmeshed in such processes.

In addition, one must always reckon with a broad spectrum of possible human reactions, especially toward the negative end. The negative tendencies exist in any case, but the German government made specific appeals to them and mobilized them on a particularly massive scale. It must be admitted that the institutional and psychological safeguards that normally work against such mobilization are vulnerable (especially in the twentieth century, when a colossal unleashed dynamic can overwhelm them).

That a man and his followers attempted to murder millions for the sake of an obsession is something that occurred not only in Germany. Certainly Marxism was not the same kind of dark brew; it was based on a theory, and an impressive one at that. The conclusions, however, that Lenin, Stalin, and their confederates drew from it—and the ways in which they tried to impose it first on the peoples of the Soviet Union and then in Eastern Europe—had a pathological aspect, too. They were also profoundly violent on a grand scale (although they cannot be equated with Auschwitz).

A remaining element was obedience—too often a blind obedience, the striving of many to do their duty efficiently, which was offset by so little readiness to do the absolute minimum, to offer passive resistance, let alone to engage in silent or overt acts of sabotage. Terror, fear, and many forms of human weakness played their part, as did mutual expectations, for all actions would inevitably affect other people. Many felt that they could not leave families or co-workers in the lurch; they had to "hold up their end" within the system. Their minds were no doubt focused on the whole and on carrying out their function in their particular setting, without sparing many thoughts for the victims.

As a rule one way of coping was to keep one's thoughts and actions limited to a very narrow area—a possibility aided by modern relations of size. Tzvetan Todorov once traced children's route to the gas chamber, starting with the French police officer who did nothing but identify Jewish children and turn them in, to the engineer who did nothing but drive the trains (as he always had), to the camp commandant, who did nothing but supervise the unloading and selection of the prisoners, and finally to the special squads who did in fact deliver the prisoners to their death in the gas chambers. To this extent the latter were the only ones directly guilty of killing, as it were, but they were victims themselves, not true executioners. This division into separate functions—Todorov speaks of "compartmentalization"—meant that the people at each step had only a very limited degree of responsibility, that of carrying out their particular orders properly.[25] Beyond that people were told (and believed!) that higher levels, particularly the Führer, alone knew what the issues were and what needed to be done. Even Albert Speer, a minister of the Reich, remarked after the war (using the passive voice!) that "one felt one was being represented, never called upon to take personal responsibility."[26] In such circumstances there was little latitude for thinking, or especially for conscience, a simple bad conscience about what one was doing to others and should not have done, and in the extreme case for the distinction between good and evil. In such circumstances clearly only a few (likely to be simple, upright people like Sergeant Schmid)[27] had "a heart in their body," in contrast to the "schizoid apathy" that the court psychologist Gustave M. Gilbert diagnosed in Commandant Höss.[28]

Many Germans also lacked imagination and any desire to acquire a general orientation about their situation. Hannah Arendt later wrote that Adolf Eichmann was unable to imagine the results of the processes he had set in motion. This, too, can be explained. And for the lower ranks we should note—as a slightly mitigating circumstance—that many of them were overtaxed in terms of their education, background, and social position. Thus many "ordinary men" like the members of the Reserve Battalion 101 of the Hamburg police, who before and after the war were ordinary guardians of the public order and family men, were prepared to carry out orders to murder Jews. And this even though their commander, himself deeply shaken by the first order, had explicitly made participation voluntary on that occasion.[29] Of course, generals and officers were also willing to organize shootings of Jews and prisoners, sometimes on a large scale, and even to give orders for them; some also allowed millions of prisoners of war to starve to death.

Todorov cites Arthur Seyss-Inquart, the Reich Commissioner of the Netherlands during the war, as saying that "there is a limit to the number of people you can kill out of hatred or a lust for slaughter, but there is no limit to the number you can kill in the cold, systematic manner of the military 'categorical imperative.'"[30] But, in any event, forming a mental picture of the scale of the entire murderous operation and developing an independent and responsible judgment about it grew harder the longer it went on. And reaching judgments through discussions with others was possible only in tiny groups at best.

And, finally, the war in Eastern Europe was extraordinarily harsh, relentless, and brutal on both sides, especially the war fought against partisans behind the front. And even "normal" wars and revolutions produce (or uncover) a great deal of brutality.

"We are puppets, our strings are pulled by unknown forces," observed Georg Büchner in his play *Danton's Death* in 1835. "What is it in us that whores, lies, steals, and murders?"[31] Büchner appears to have concluded that it was not people as such but only an undetermined component in their makeup that kept the dreadful machinery going—in this instance, the reign of terror after the French Revolution—and he felt "crushed under the terrible fatalism of history." Todorov speaks of "fragmentation" within individuals, "which manifests itself as an alternation between benevolence and malice."[32]

In 1922 Robert Musil recalled: "First we were bustling good citizens, then we became murderers, killers, thieves, arsonists, and the like." And in 1922, one could continue his thought, we are hardworking citizens again: "Life goes on just as before, only a little more feebly, with a touch of the invalid's caution."[33] The disposition to terrible aberrations (and occasionally to excesses) is obviously a given, although it was never exploited in such a way and to such an extent before Auschwitz. These reflections are not intended to excuse anything. The only issue here has been to show that the phenomena can be explained, and it should not be necessary to provide more details to make the point.

What became decisive in Germany was the fact that after a certain time the country had passed the point when institutions or responsible statesmen, generals, and civil servants could still have brought it under control; it was at the mercy of a criminal group with a wide following, who could trample on the law. Some of those who could most easily have prevented these developments went along, while other were either unwilling or not in a position to join ranks to resist or to attempt an assassination—at least not until it was much too late.

All in all the Germans of that era (and not only the Germans) were unequal to the challenges posed by Hitler's regime, in terms of recognizing the degree of danger, taking a stand, acting, and in the possibilities of communicating with one another. A great deal occurred and a great deal was demanded of them that they would not have believed possible (at least at first). And, terribly, most of them could not really imagine it; or if they could, then they soon stopped, becoming hardened to what was happening. They grew used to doing what they had not previously been accustomed to and should not have done. Again, I mean this only by way of explanation.

As to the extent to which this failure was "typical of the Germans," that is a difficult question. Certainly the readiness to obey orders and the inner dependence on authority were greater than they would have been in many other countries; one could call this a lack of defenses against such dependence, or a certain heartlessness, in the sense of being able to suppress subjective feelings to a high degree. Max Weber once mentioned the "specialized training" and "objective" manner of performing tasks "without regard for the individual" concerned, which struck him as characteristic of the bureaucracy of an earlier era.[34] Perhaps Germans have had an inclination to function like this. But it is hardly possible to determine the extent to which that is true objectively and what difference it made with regard to the totality of the crimes committed. And the same holds for German anti-Semitism in comparison to anti-Semitism in other countries.

It is indeed true that the fact that Auschwitz could happen in twentieth-century Europe gives one food for thought, but not in the sense that is usually intended—for it is not all that astonishing.

First of all, killing on an industrial scale was not possible earlier or in other parts of the world; the technology belongs to the twentieth century and to Europe. Similar claims could be made for the organizational ability and the coldness with which it was used, and perhaps also for the expectation that crimes of this magnitude could be undertaken without a real reason. According to Todorov, the degree to which life in the twentieth century had become divided into fields of specialization, complex, and more difficult to view as a whole than ever before contributed essentially to making this unparalleled crime possible.

And it is likely that no such thing as moral progress exists; Jacob Burckhardt did not believe in it.[35] Cultural assets by themselves produce philistines rather than culture. And whether culture can promote the development of human compassion is an open question. It becomes a more serious question as time passes, since new weapons and new technologies are opening up new possibilities both for good and evil all the time. New sensibilities give rise to new weaknesses (and vice versa), and a lack of overview to new perplexities and vulnerabilities. As Walter Benjamin observed in the 1930s, "The astonishment that the things we are experiencing are 'still' possible in the twentieth century is *not* a philosophical kind of astonishment. It does not stand at the beginning of deeper insight, unless it is the insight that the idea of history from which it is derived cannot be maintained."[36] The same presumably applies to the astonishment over Germany and Europe, although one can never get beyond it.

Another question is the extent to which Auschwitz can be depicted and imagined. This is true in terms of the camp's origins and organization, and the events in which perpetrators, victims, and onlookers were involved. But it applies above all to the individual histories of the prisoners, beginning with their identification and degradation before they arrived, and their suffering afterward. We have a great many eyewitness accounts, and we can certainly write much of this history. For some of the victims that history began in the Herwarthstrasse in Essen, a city in which they had lived, perhaps for decades, as respected citizens. Early one morning they were picked up by plainclothes policemen, permitted to collect only a bare minimum of belongings, and herded onto trucks. The story continued in holding areas, freight yards, and trains; it includes the engineer who, after delivering his cargo to the gates of death behind the arch with the slogan *Arbeit macht frei* ("work makes free"), may have relaxed with a sandwich and a thermos of tea. And the story goes on, usually into the "undressing rooms," and in Auschwitz itself to Commandant Höss, who reported that "one woman approached me as she walked past and, pointing to her four children who were manfully helping the smallest ones over the rough ground, whispered: 'How can you bring yourself to kill such beautiful, darling children? Have you no heart at all?'"[37] We have eyewitness reports from the "undressing rooms," and again for the transportation of the bodies to the crematorium. Only from the gas chambers themselves do we have nothing but reports of the screams and groans heard from outside. Here the historian must fall silent, too.

It is also possible to describe the activities of the commandos, including the hideous Christmas of Commando IIb, who had received the order to murder 3,000 Jews and gypsies by the holiday. They were told that if they carried it out quickly enough, they would be able to take part in the Christmas Eve church services.[38] Their commanding officer, Otto Ohlendorf, is said to have delivered a moving speech to his men. And how did the victims feel? Imre Kertész, Auschwitz survivor and winner of the 2002 Nobel Prize for literature, writes, "And what is the truly terribly part? That they were killed? No, that they did not understand their deaths."[39]

Certainly such a depiction is infinitely difficult. Yet what happened does not transcend words entirely, even though General Eisenhower did say, after visiting part of the concentration camp at Buchenwald, "The things I saw cannot be described in words." The American war correspondent Martha Gellhorn also found that, while she could write about much of postwar Germany, Dachau went beyond the limits of what could be expressed. Today this is probably no longer true in the same sense, after we have been confronted with it again and again, although boundaries remain that one cannot pass, and without passing them perhaps the most important things cannot be said. Yosef H. Yerushalmi has said that the most influential depictions of Auschwitz would probably come from writers of fiction.[40] But a depiction that establishes its own boundaries must also be possible for historians, and it is urgently necessary, for the powers of imagination that Eichmann and countless others on the side of the perpetrators lacked must be trained.

One must also write such a depiction from the heart.[41] Although objectivity is doubly and triply called for in view of the terrible events, the emotions of sympathy, pity, outrage, disgust, and desperation can resonate with it. Much can be made extremely vivid in plain and stark words, such as the methodical nature of what was done, the routine that even in sight of the gas chambers was carried out punctiliously, coldly, and heartlessly.

Characteristic fates, experiences, and scenes make it possible to depict the entirety of events vividly but without rhetorical embellishment and exaggeration—for example, the macabre situation at the Jewish Cemetery in Berlin-Weissensee, where some Jewish fugitives hid out for a time in the mausoleum of the noted baritone Josef Schwarz. We can imagine them anxiously huddled, sleeping fitfully, wondering how long their hiding place would remain undiscovered, under the inscription from Psalm 90: "Lord, thou hast been our dwelling place in all generations."[42]

Of course, one limit remains, namely the gulf between perpetrators and victims, and consequently also between the survivors and descendants on both sides. It cannot be bridged, particularly since history continues to transmit a sense of the most profound injuries. However, nothing argues that both sides cannot attempt their own depictions—and respect each others' efforts in the process.

Presumably the real obstacle to dealing with the Holocaust lies in the great resistance we feel when we approach the subject. Imre Kertész observes on this point: "We can not, dare not confront the brutal fact that the low point of human life in our century represents not just a strange and unsettling—'incomprehensible'—story of one or two generations, but a general human potentiality in which we ourselves are included. We are horrified by the ease with which totalitarian dictatorships liquidate autonomous personalities, and human beings transform themselves into well-functioning cogs in the machinery of the state. It fills us with fear and doubt that in a certain phase of our lives so many people, or even we ourselves, could become creatures whom we can no longer recognize at a later date as rational creatures equipped with normal sensitivities and morality, creatures with whom we can no longer identify ourselves. The combination of these three factors evokes the feeling of incomprehensibility in us, and here 'incomprehensible' in fact becomes a synonym for 'unacceptable.'"[43]

And it is for just this reason, I would claim, that it becomes necessary to contradict Sternberger. We *must* do everything to analyze this potential within human beings, to recognize and comprehend it. And if we can explain and depict it, can even imagine it within certain limits, does it then remain truly incomprehensible? We believe that we can understand battles and other complex chains of events after we have studied them long enough, after all, and we can—and must—try to achieve the same with Auschwitz, if only because the urge to understand releases stronger impulses for emotional as well as intellectual forms of comprehension.

In this case no understanding can exist without repeated shocks, condemnation, and despair. All understanding must be hair-raising and horrific by any human standard and lead to the conclusion again and again that one understands nothing. Furthermore, we cannot come to terms with the catastrophe itself; all we can come to terms with is our own situation *after* it—as survivors, which all of us are (although in radically different ways), at least in Europe and the West.

Certainly it is difficult to understand such an enormous political and moral catastrophe without being able to trace it back to causes of similar dimensions. It is difficult when the explanation results— apart from the ideologically criminal intentions of Hitler and others—only from a coincidence of the most varied factors, of organizations, and men, most of whom were, taken singly, hardly dangerous and not in the least criminal. Difficult unless one accepts that the essential foundations of an entire continent failed, in this instance, in one country only. And it is hard to fathom the grand-scale criminal impulses at the same time as all the small crimes, errors, and ignoble acts, the mistakes with far-reaching consequences, all the thoughtlessness and the mere willingness to accept what was happening, without active intention of harm to anyone.

But the alternative would be repression, regret, and ritual. As much as Auschwitz will always elude understanding, it is not acceptable to leave it at that. There will be intervals between occasions that provide shattering reminders, but it is not necessary to wait for them. And last but not least, we must become clearer about the difficulties of comprehension, meaning that the first task is to try to understand how much is incomprehensible. This task might conceivably provide a link between the descendants on both sides.

"The Holocaust is of value," Imre Kertész has said, "because it has led through immeasurable suffering to immeasurable knowledge and thus holds an immeasurable moral reserve."[44] That is a very bold statement, but without courage all of us would have to surrender in the face of Auschwitz—all the historians, all those who lived through the period, and those born afterward. It is all too easy to arrive at the kind of "deep despondency . . . that has its roots in a defense against the historical experience of the break-down and thus also against the cathartic insight that can emerge from it." "If I reflect on the traumatic effect of Auschwitz," Kertész writes elsewhere, "paradoxically I tend to think more about the future than about the past."[45]

The history of what is identified by the rather clumsy term *Vergangenheitsbewältigung* ("coming to terms with the past") has now continued for more than fifty years; in fact, it can only mean working on that part of the past that extends into the present and continues to influence it. The process has a most unsatisfactory history, in that so many shortcomings are evident, yet it remains impressive at the same time because, given what was possible, an extraordinary amount has been achieved.[46] What way of remembering Auschwitz *could* be appropriate, or be considered satisfactory?

The problem was threefold: (1) for people to become aware of the Holocaust, and (2) to realize the dimensions of the extermination of the Jews. (In this context the horrible dispute over whether perhaps only one, two, or three million were killed should be recalled; the claims that maybe there were only several hundred thousand victims or even fewer; the allegations that the victims consisted solely of people who had unfortunately been caught in the crossfire between the front lines.) It was absolutely essential that we grasp the monstrosity of what had been done. And, finally, (3) it was necessary to register how many people actually participated in the extermination process, either directly or indirectly. They included those who actually killed victims, or assisted or acquiesced in their killing; they included large groups such as the Hitler Youth, who marched through the streets of Germany singing *"Wenn das Judenblut vom Messer spritzt, dann geht's nochmal so gut"* ("When Jewish blood spurts from the knife, then things will go twice as well)"—although, it should be added, this was not the song's original text.

The difficulty of accepting that all this had happened involved simple defense mechanisms, not-wanting-to-know, continuing to think in the familiar terms of friend and foe, and resistance to re-education efforts. However, the main complication after the war—one that continues to the present day for members of the older generation—lies in the fact that most members of German society experienced the war from a very different perspective than the one that has come to dominate in the postwar period. The two views were and are extremely difficult to connect with one another.

As time has passed, an essential aspect of this history has been a gradually increasing sense of distance, as the generation that participated in it dies out. In addition, many interdependent relationships have developed between Germany and other countries, and factions formed within the country. A particularly important component is the history of West German identity,[47] which developed in part in contrast to East Germany.

To the extent that people customarily felt themselves to be German, it cost them a great effort to recognize the crimes Germans had committed, which meant at first the crimes of which they were accused. It was easy to consider Hitler and the SS guilty of crimes if one counted oneself as part of "the other Germany," the citizens who had opposed the National Socialist regime. While such people accepted responsibility for Auschwitz, they otherwise wanted to know nothing about it. Germans who belonged to the political left could incriminate conservatives in the civil service, and the protesters of 1968 (mainly students) accused West Germany as a whole of having "fascistic" tendencies (although this view was rightly rejected by the majority). The real sticking point for Germans, including many in leftist circles, lay in considering the *Wehrmacht* (the name of the German army in the Second World War) guilty of crimes. Nearly everyone had close relatives and friends who had fought bravely and given their utmost—for a criminal leader, it is true, and on behalf of a criminal cause, but Germans resisted regarding the army itself as criminal. Too many soldiers had sacrificed too much to accept that. Of course, the greater the distance Germans gained from the past and the more they began to acquire a "post-national" identity as Europeans, the easier it became to shift blame to "the Germans back then" or "the Germans" as a group with whom they no longer felt much sense of identity. Nevertheless, some attempts were still made to avoid facing the situation by referring to "Nazi armies" instead of "German armies" (totally false in terms of both praise or blame). German reunification has altered little in this respect.

The process of self-distancing from "the Germans" reached its peak in the Goldhagen debate of the mid-nineties.[48] Until then Germans had tended to see themselves standing with the earlier Germans in the arena into which stones were being thrown; now they joined the stone throwers. The result was that what "the Germans" of that time had done could not be painted in black enough colors. And the worse it was, the less we—the different people who we now were—had to do with it. The same effect was produced, often below the surface, by revising entire family histories,[49] so that the parents and grandparents who had been Nazi sympathizers or failed to offer any resistance (at the very least) were promoted to "good Germans" who had provided hiding places for Jews. All of this fits in well with the regret and distress that it is appropriate to feel.

It created a situation, however, that must lead to a very different kind of reflection. It is now necessary to seek justice for very many Germans of that era—that is to say, to divide up the conglomerate that is alleged to have participated willingly in all kinds of crimes into more differentiated groups. For they were not all monsters and devils, and it is wrong to assume that they were. We avoid a good part of the whole difficulty of understanding if we overlook the fact that even in the German army—as in the whole population—many people thought and acted with integrity and behaved decently under the most difficult conditions.

In any case, we should stop approaching the problem from the single angle of how many Germans knew how much about Auschwitz.[50] It is true that very many people must at least have known that Jews were being shot, but the more terrible the rumors became, the more difficult they were to credit, certainly for those not predisposed to believe the regime capable of the worst crimes imaginable. What if a wife suspected that her own husband had become entangled in a crime, or children their fathers? To whom could they turn with their suspicions? What could soldiers do with their knowledge, if they were unwilling to desert, organize resistance, or plot to overthrow the regime; how many more people were not in a position to do any of those things?

Nor should it be forgotten that as the war progressed the civilian German population was thinking about the safety of family members, mourning the fallen, and attempting to survive air raids. What priority could they give under such circumstances to terrible rumors? And one should not forget the fear that caused people to keep many things they heard to themselves, the climate of intimidation that kept one from investigating further, and, in some cases, from wanting to know more. One German woman recalled that she and her contemporaries knew just enough to be afraid to ask any more questions. I believe the question of who knew what is quite academic if it is not placed alongside the question of what ordinary people alone could have done with the knowledge if they had it. Most of them could only have repressed it altogether, or pushed it to the back of their minds where it would bother them as little as possible.

Our knowledge after the fact, our fervent wishes that things could have been different, and all our bitter disappointment that they were not, cause us to be too partisan. As we picture the Germans of that time and their situation, we fail to calculate the dangers they faced; we judge them far too much from the safety of hindsight. One cannot get at the phenomenon of Auschwitz if one paints the perpetrators (in the broadest sense of the word) as evil through and through. For the problem consists precisely of the fact that the majority of a nation, neither devils nor monsters, let themselves be co-opted into the service of a monstrous crime step by step, in many small increments, until finally they were willing to participate in it.

At first they waged war in the traditional way (as it was accepted in other countries as well), convinced that if necessary they should give their lives for their country. Later the Russian campaign turned into a war of extermination, with the consent of the senior command, and many rules of traditional warfare no longer prevailed. This meant that many soldiers ended up implicated in crimes, either willingly, by following orders, or by drifting into them one small step at a time;[51] even high-ranking officers let this happen or gave orders to commit crimes. Yet much as I would like to plead in defense of the Germans who acted decently, by and large, I must come to a close.

The difficulty we have in dealing with Auschwitz consists, in sum, mainly in the fact that it is impossible or nearly so to take in all the relevant information and different perspectives, and to fathom it as a whole. I mean by this the near-impossibility of keeping in mind both the perspective from which most ordinary Germans experienced the times (including what they knew and what they could have done something about) and the perspective from which those times must appear to us. A gulf separates the enormity of the diabolical evil as it had to appear during the Third Reich in the person of men such as Adolf Eichmann and the banality of evil, the kind of sordid shabbiness that came to light after the war. There is a chasm between the perpetrators and the victims, between the Germans of then and now. It is extremely difficult, as educated Europeans, to reconcile our view of history and culture with the reality of Auschwitz in the twentieth century. Thoughts of Auschwitz are irreconcilable with present-day reality, so our "statesmen" try to bridge the gulf by passing ineffectual, and highly problematic, resolutions against other countries while making references to the Holocaust. How do we overcome the near-impossibility of finding an appropriate way to commemorate the Holocaust and the fact that we *must* commemorate it? How do we reconcile the insufficiency of language[52] and the necessity of using it? The event remains too enormous, too far beyond ordinary categories for us to keep it before the public and in our own daily awareness in the way it deserves, just as it must have been at the time for those who had some knowledge or an inkling of what was happening. If we remained fully aware of it, we could not go on.

Imre Kertész notes that a prisoner had "to comprehend in order to survive, that is, he had to comprehend what he was surviving." In the meantime, however, the century has continued the history "with a fundamentally different logic, . . . so we can no longer comprehend that we also grasped the preceding [totalitarian] logic. This does not mean that history is incomprehensible, but rather that we cannot comprehend ourselves."[53] In other words, to the extent that we lived through and survived those times and that regime, we cannot fathom all the parts of ourselves or, put more simply, all the parts of our own biographies.

Let me return now to questions I touched on at the beginning of this discussion: Does Auschwitz have a "retroactive power" as

Nietzsche conceived of it? Does it alter our view of earlier history? And is it possible for a historian to interpret Auschwitz as "part of a whole"?

In the traditional view not only does Auschwitz have no meaning itself, unless as a part of the history of human delusions, but it also invalidates retroactively many older assumptions about the meaning of history. In the history—of a country, of a continent, of a world—that leads to Auschwitz, no meaning can easily be found.

If one seeks to reconceive the old assumptions about the meaning of history—which saw it as a path toward an ever- improving world and the continual betterment of humanity—then one can only locate Auschwitz somewhere on that path as a setback of colossal proportions. But I don't believe it is possible to see meaning in Auschwitz even then. One could try to give it a meaning after the fact, as Imre Kertész has proposed, by noting that Auschwitz "has led through immeasurable suffering to immeasurable knowledge and thus contains an immeasurable moral reserve."

Of course, since it is human beings who make history, they would have to make use of this fund. And they would have to accept the responsibility, after Auschwitz, of meeting the high expectations expressed in the old view and of making the world a continually better place. Some attempts are being made to do just that. Nonetheless, the assumption that the goal of all history has been future progress (via the present) remains problematic. As Hannah Arendt put it, this constitutes a "large stumbling-block that no philosophy of history has ever been able to remove: It remains 'always surprising,' to quote Kant himself, 'that the older generations appear to conduct their laborious business solely for the sake of those who will follow after them, . . . that only those born later will have the good fortune to live in the house' that was built by all."[54]

There is, however, another sense in which Auschwitz could exert "retroactive force." This is the view (represented in European history since ancient times, and possibly anticipated in earlier cultures) that historical change is defined by an ever- increasing potential for both good and evil. As the chorus in Sophocles' *Antigone* declares: "There is much that is monstrous, and nothing more monstrous than man." The direction of history, seen in this light, would be determined by human beings' magnificent yet dangerous ability to control the world more and more, without necessarily being able to control themselves. A continuation of this path suggests that the most advanced technological skills could become linked with primitive terrorism in Europe, for example.

Understanding history in this sense would not mean that it had to lead "directly to Auschwitz," to borrow Thomas Nipperdey's phrase.[55] Far from it! But it would make more vividly conscious the risky undertaking that this history represents—namely, immense progress in many areas, but no overall progress that would include both justice and morality. History would bring countless advantages, but potentially just as great risks. Such a conception of history creates an increasingly problematic relationship between the pleasant aspects of everyday life and the possible catastrophes. It is a very open-ended history, not least in its anthropological dimension.[56]

It is difficult to identify oneself with this kind of history, but it is the history of Europe. We could flee from it, taking the view that it is over and done with or by refusing to accept a historical view of the world at all. We can get caught up in simply feeling stricken and appalled, and participate in the rituals designed to assuage such feelings; in Germany, at least, the worse one's conscience is, the bigger the monument one must build to silence it. But traditionally the best part of Europe's legacy is not silence, not repressing unpleasant truths and burdens, but facing up to them squarely. This would mean claiming history as our own in both its heights and depths, its achievements and its unspeakable crimes, accepting it as a challenge and doing our utmost to meet it. In my belief this is possible only if we become aware of our own era at the same time.

Humboldt's challenge to historians was to present every occurrence as part of a whole. It remains relevant, is indeed becoming more urgent than ever, in its call "to depict in each one the form of history in general." To me this means first of all that one must pay particular attention to the crimes, the catastrophes, the victims, and the perpetrators. But the task does not end there, for societies function not only in negative terms; they attempt to produce livable conditions, laws, constitutions, and many other benefits (although for much of history not every member of society was included), and create many different institutions for these purposes. They have their shady and dubious aspects, certainly, but are respected, and rightly so, because they are so able to work beneficially, even though they may at times fail utterly, as in Auschwitz. In other epochs, too, it is necessary to relate in our minds many things that all too easily resist connection, all the varied (and limited) surviving "evidence of those who acted."[57]

In sum, the Holocaust must give rise to a constant ambition: in the words of the poet Hilde Domin,[58] we must keep open the maw of the beast in which we are compelled to live.

6

A Legacy without Heirs?

What Is Our Legacy and What Is It Good For?

Athens and Auschwitz: I have used these two points to mark the beginning and end of the special European path, which so clearly distinguished Europe from all other cultures and, one might say, led it to break through certain barriers, opening up entirely new possibilities of freedom and what it meant to be human, new possibilities for governing society, for knowledge and science, for mastering nature, for technology and capitalism. It is the path on which Europe altered the course of the rest of the world, colonializing some parts of it and opening up others to its influence (along with the United States). Ultimately, the features that had made Europe distinctive became exportable; the modern state, constitutions, efficient civil services, democracy, industry, science, socialism, and many other institutions were transplanted to different soils. Far-flung parts of the world adopted them, sometimes altering or even reversing their intent, sometimes producing violence and upheaval. In some areas borrowed elements remained superficial formalities, existing in name only, but almost always the institutions imported or absorbed from Europe interacted with local traditions to form distinctive combinations. Overall, the differences between Europe (and North America) and the other parts of the world are shrinking—although the polarization might be intensifying.

Hence one of the questions I would like to address here is: How much individuality will Europe and its member nations be able to preserve? For naturally these countries will continue to exhibit distinctive features (and there still remain considerable differences between Western and Eastern Europe, too). A second, related, question is the following: What sort of legacy could Europe still derive today from its history? Of course, Europe's history is not over yet, but what clearly distinguished it on its special path has to a great extent been diffused. Generally speaking, we can say that Europe now stands alongside others rather than particularly standing out— or standing at the center of the world, as Europeans once felt.

We must accustom ourselves to that; we have still not fully comprehended the message that Peter Esterházy wants to send when he writes: "We avert our eyes in shame and look down at the ground— that is what it means to be a European today. 'How many thousands of people can be killed today in the middle of Europe?' That is a typically arrogant European question. As if it were less important and less scandalous when people are killed somewhere that is not in the middle of Europe!"[1] Europe is simply no longer privileged (although naturally Europeans need to be concerned about what happens in their midst).

Of course, one can question whether Auschwitz is the proper symbol for the end of the special European path. Would the battle of Stalingrad or perhaps World War II in its entirety have been a better choice? World War I had suggested that Europe was losing its position of dominance, and World War II brought a definitive end to the continent's central role. Rapid decolonization followed the postwar era. The United States became not only the dominant power in the world, along with the Soviet Union, but also the leader in modern industry and science. In both Asia and Africa the United States took over the Europeans' role, Vietnam being a particularly clear instance. The task of defending Europe against the Soviet Union on its eastern periphery fell to the United States as well, for it was the Americans who had the new atomic weapons and missiles.

American popular culture was becoming an important influence around the globe. So if one needs a particular date, why not take the end of World War II? What particular meaning does the choice of Auschwitz have, or could it have, in the context of a special European path? Does it imply that the Europeans possessed some superior claim to morality before, which Auschwitz caused them to lose?[2] That is a difficult claim to make if one thinks of the many millions who were murdered or perished over the course of European history; during colonialist expansion, Native Americans died in huge numbers, and Africa suffered not only the slave trade, but also outright extermination campaigns, such as that waged against the Herero people in German Southwest Africa. And this is not to mention all the victims within Europe itself.

If we consider the ancient world, matters do not look all that different, although the destruction took place on a smaller scale. The courage of the inhabitants of the little Greek island of Melos, for instance, received a splendid tribute from Thucydides in the "Melian Dialogue."[3] The historian contrasted their stubborn wish to remain free, their faith in the gods and in justice, with the Athenians' hubris when the latter sought to take over the island for no real reason other than to enhance their prestige. When Melos was finally forced to surrender, the Athenians executed the men and sold the women and children into slavery: several hundred men were slaughtered with the sword, probably one at a time, although they had posed a threat to no one. This was not an isolated occurrence. Xenophon reports how the Athenians reacted on learning that they had lost the decisive battle of the Peloponnesian War: "That night no one slept. They mourned for the lost, but more still for their own fate. They thought that they themselves would now be dealt with as they had dealt with others," such as the Melians.[4] The defeat marked the end of the great century of classical Greece.

But to return to World War II, we might also ask whether it is appropriate to view all of that war and its significance for the world through the lens of Auschwitz, as so many Jews and Germans do? This cannot simply be assumed, for many people would disagree, even though Auschwitz is correctly regarded as a crime against humanity, and hence concerns humanity as a whole (if such a thing exists). No, the catastrophe of Auschwitz, the breach of civilization that it represents, constitutes only one aspect of the end of the special European path, within World War II (with which it shares the instigator). But despite all the horrors of that conflict, despite the atomic bombs dropped on Hiroshima and Nagasaki (although an armistice was clearly imminent), Auschwitz appears to me a more powerful symbol even than the war to make the *skandalon*[5] of this end of the path fully clear. It best highlights the challenge that has arisen for our self-definition in terms of history. That is the reason why I have given these discussions the title "From Athens to Auschwitz," and not "From Athens to the Second World War."

My goal, then, is to relate Athens—and Europe and its special path—not only to a world war but to Auschwitz in particular, and to draw conclusions from bringing them together. The history of the special path, unlike the other histories that exist, is defined by the repeated sudden shifts in people's horizons, by extraordinary, and often arbitrary, dramatic changes not only on the surface, but also in the structure of society, of knowledge, and of relationships in the world, down to their foundations.

European history departed further than any other from the conditions provided by nature (although no one would deny the wonders of technology achieved in Asia, which were not limited to regulating the flow of rivers and building canals). Whatever great achievements Europe produced through competition between individuals, cities, and countries, it was also necessary to maintain a balance, so that society could bear the dangers and threats competition brought with it, and the fears that increased with the dangers. All the same, the competitive process resulted in progress that was ultimately not hindered by deference to limits that had to be respected. The directions in which the various forces were striving were too disparate and too much at cross-purposes, and in the long term too lacking in coordination. The process continued because as Europe made advances, the problems and riddles for which new answers needed to be found grew as well. Human beings' potential ability to destroy all life on earth is a consequence of European history and European history alone, if we include Europe's most important offshoot, the United States. Yet the antidotes to the threat of nuclear war stem from the same history, in this case that between West and East. (I am thinking in particular of the Soviet Union, where, despite everything, those at the helm were not desperadoes.) On the other hand, progress always has a positive and negative side to it.

Max Weber conceived of Western history primarily as a process of rationalization.[6] He did not mean rationalization in general (for that is encountered elsewhere), but rather a process affecting our basic understanding of life and the world. And although he did not say so explicitly, one can trace this process all the way back to antiquity, for it was then that the fundamental discovery occurred: men can be citizens, that is, they can participate fully in the practical tasks of governing the community, a discovery that had far-reaching practical consequences. Because the primary institutions were relatively weak, because citizens were free and shared responsibility for their own political order, and because conflicts arose that required interventions at the very core of this order—because of all this, not only was the order of the polity called into question for the Greeks, but also that of the world and the gods. New and radical questions arose about what a human being was, and about what men could and should do. All traditional knowledge, everything that had been taken for granted, all myths and all beliefs ceased to be sufficient, or to put it more precisely, they were sufficient for most people in the long run, but not for everyone, and that made a decisive difference. The Greeks came to view the principles that governed the world in terms of rational knowledge and concepts. The process established in antiquity, which entered Christianity refracted in various ways, was still the driving force in the establishment of civil rights and freedoms in the West, in modern capitalism, in technology and science, and in the modern state and its bureaucracy, to name the most important areas, although the list is far from complete.

In his own era Weber saw potential dangers arising if the process continued still further. Rationalization, he feared, was leading to "specialists without spirit, sensualists without heart," in his famous phrase.[7] Increasing bureaucratization furthered expectations, among both bureaucrats themselves and the general public, that citizens would obediently submit to the dictates of the bureaucratic system. And this led in turn to "people who need order and nothing but order around them, who become nervous and timid if the system shows even a momentary unsteadiness." The result was a "subdivision of the soul," in Weber's words, in which human beings were reduced to functions, and a mentality spread that was based on conformity. Individuals' willingness to make decisions and take risks was curtailed, along with personal initiative and responsibility. And in the end all these factors meshed to form an "iron cage," from which no one could escape. "This order," Weber wrote, "is now bound to the technical and economic conditions . . . which today determine the lives of all the individuals who are born into this mechanism, not only those directly concerned with economic acquisition, with irresistible force. Perhaps it will so determine them until the last ton of fossilized coal is burnt."[8] He saw the possibility on the horizon of a political order similar to the Roman Empire or the New Kingdom in Egypt.

Some of his phrases—"subdivision of the soul," obedient submission to the dictates of the bureaucratic system, curtailment of responsibility—foreshadow the explanation offered by Tzvetan Todorov for why perfectly normal men were prepared to commit the crimes of the Holocaust. To a certain extent the processes of bureaucratization and application of rational principles to all areas of life created essential preconditions for the German mass murder of Jews and other minorities.

Another strand of the same process consisted of belief in progress and its ability to unleash extraordinary forces, which could then be concentrated in the state. Conditions arose that enabled men like Lenin, Stalin, and Hitler to believe that they could develop and carry out gigantic plans to transform their nations and societies rapidly, and to feel as if they had become executors of the will of history itself. In Germany even "racial" genetic characteristics (or, rather, what the National Socialists took as such) became a matter of public policy, with murderous consequences. The Nazi leaders were aided in this undertaking by enormous popular expectations; the population's reactions derived in part from previous disappointments and suffering so bitter that the paranoid labeling of entire ethnic groups as scapegoats found some resonance and met with hardly any resistance among the majority. The result was an interaction between paranoia and hope in countries for which no certain or satisfactory place within the circle of European nations was visible for the foreseeable future. This phase of history was just as much about strivings for power and preeminence among nations as it was about civil and human rights within nations, and to some degree the hopes of the population were abused without scruple.

But I need not describe in further detail how these expectations arose, and how they were used and abused: the process of the special European path, which had been operating since antiquity and gained renewed momentum repeatedly in the modern era, always produced an immense increase in the scope of possible actions. This, however, by no means implied that rational control over these possibilities—or, let us say, the ability to prevent serious abuse—would necessarily grow at the same rate. The expansion of potential did not imply that human beings' judgment and sense of responsibility could keep pace with the growth of the harm they were able to do, and sometimes tempted or encouraged to do.

What Jacob Burckhardt says about the wars of religion can be generally applied to all wars: "Among civilized peoples they are most terrible of all. The means of offense and defense are unlimited, ordinary morality is suspended in the name of the 'higher purpose,' negotiation and mediation are abhorrent—people want all or nothing."[9]

Thus it is not all that difficult to connect Athens and Auschwitz in terms of the long process of development that the West experienced between these two eras. One must just point out the erroneousness of the belief that first arose in the Enlightenment, according to which moral behavior in all classes of society could improve continually (and had done so in the past), keeping pace more or less with other kinds of changes. Burckhardt declared, with respect to the nineteenth century, "our assumption that we live in the age of moral progress is supremely ridiculous."[10]

Certainly we can observe some notable successes in terms of societies becoming more civilized, especially in the last few centuries: it is a development that also occurred, in a different manner, during certain phases in the history of the Greek city-states. Extensive limitations have been established on the use of force within and between nations, and we have become accustomed to pursuing our aims peacefully within the framework of the law. National governments have salutary effects on their populations' behavior through such measures as providing education and police forces, and human ambitions have in the main shifted from glory and fame toward economic goals. Revolutionary attitudes have been reduced in favor of working on reform, and the possibilities for acquiring wealth by peaceful means have increased considerably.

Of course, there are exceptions to the rule. Sometimes events reveal how thin the veneer of civilization is, as Freud pointed out. Civilization can easily display its dark side. As Burckhardt observed: "what we are wont to regard as moral progress is the domestication of individuality brought about (a) by the versatility and wealth of culture and (b) by the vast increase in the power of the state over the individual, which may even lead to the complete abdication of the individual, more especially where moneymaking predominates to the exclusion of everything else, ultimately absorbing all initiative."[11] When people become accustomed to respecting laws and obeying authorities, the effect can be to weaken the very qualities—such as initiative, independence of mind, judgment, and the capacity to offer resistance or sabotage—that are called for in exceptional circumstances. The tendency to law-abiding behavior in all circumstances is probably stronger among Germans than among the French and Italians, for example. What we usually call "culture" is of no use in those exceptional cases where a willingness to break the law is precisely what is called for—or at least not a form of culture that is unsophisticated about political matters. Even when it is not taken over by philistines, "culture" is not necessarily the medium in which the courage to stand up for one's beliefs can flourish—or, if need be, a readiness to engage in conspiracy. (No doubt matters stand differently when a revolutionary movement is growing within a country, or when it is a question of organizing resistance against a foreign power.)

In short, a culture can develop in such a way that exceptional circumstances can overtax its members; their culture has not given them the necessary skills—which in some cases may be an ability to assess the situation properly and predict future developments. To take an example from our own recent past: Can we really grasp the conditions of the totalitarian regime in which our parents, grandparents, and great-grandparents acted or failed to act? Can we picture what these actions consisted of and what they meant—in situations where what was at stake must often have seemed so insignificant? They stepped aside, perhaps without really paying attention or noticing, as happens in daily life—and all at once they were caught in the trap, and compromised. Were they ready to take the next step then, since they felt helpless in any case?

Sebastian Haffner,[12] a law student in 1933, was studying in the library of the Prussian Court of Appeals in Berlin when storm troopers rushed in to eject any Jews in the building. Asked if he was "Aryan," Haffner replied truthfully that he was—and realized in the same instant that he had compromised himself.[13] How many other people would have registered the fact right then and there? How many would have—or could have—drawn the conclusion so soon afterward that they had to emigrate? And how many would have realized so clearly that the new regime had not just let a few things get out of hand, but that the situation was about to become deadly earnest—that things were in fact far worse than they seemed? As Haffner's example shows, it was possible to realize all this. But it probably took a special kind of person to do so. Haffner left Germany. Most people did not realize what was happening and continued to act "normally"; they believed they could maintain their own routines, little knowing that they would ultimately be swept far beyond every civilized routine and all "normality," or perhaps one should say to a very different kind of normality.

"Where do things go from here?" we must now ask. Weber's prediction of the "iron cage" in which we would be trapped does not seem to be coming true. Despite all constraints, many new and previously unimagined kinds of latitude are opening up, along with many different possibilities to slip through the bars of our society into free spaces of all kinds—for it is well known in Western countries that societies are better governed on a long leash. Nevertheless, it seems that the notion of freedom is becoming limited to free space in a personal sense (along with the spaces that can be freed up by bulldozers). Instead of our world becoming frozen, it is on the verge of making colossal new discoveries of which earlier generations could only dream. What is happening now in laboratories could produce immense and rapid changes in the structure of society and also in the political sphere, for both good and for evil.

Less reason than ever exists for assuming that the end of history has arrived or that we have arrived at history's final goal. If many problems that have plagued humankind for millennia no longer occur, at least in our parts of the world—thanks to machines and automation, fertilizers, global trade and communication, modern medicine, the welfare state, and so on—it could certainly be the case that in exchange, and partly as a result, other problems will arise that cause us enormous difficulties. We just don't know which ones yet. They could include continuing hunger, the shameful poverty in large parts of the world, immigration and reactions to it, climatic catastrophes, new devastating diseases, aging of the population (perhaps with the question of where to put old people), new ways of attempting to seize power (such as by Mafia-like groups), specific new forms of political organization (possibly reflecting new divisions between elites and the rest of the population), further specialization of knowledge, and hence new forms of anxiety, unrest, and protest. In any case, it would be very surprising if humanity were soon able to inhabit a place with no clouds on the horizon.

My aim here is not to make prognoses, however. Nor is my question whether we can visualize what may be in store for us very soon, trends that may even have been developing for some time now, although we do not yet perceive them. It is enough to observe in this context that the future is more uncertain than ever and that no clear tendencies have become visible to enable us to predict the direction of change with any probability.

It is relatively clear only that the power of change (if I may call it that), that is, the potential for profound and sweeping transformation of the conditions under which we live, is distributed all around the globe, as are the means to finance the corresponding innovations. Yet our ability to see the whole picture, to keep change under control and direct it, lags far behind. What we face is no longer the alteration of society through direct action (as protesters called for somewhat presumptuously in the slogans of the '60s); rather, societies will be transformed indirectly, by the side effects of countless small actions by people who had no thought of social change in their minds. Or perhaps the goal of transforming society will be replaced by the goal of transforming human beings themselves. There is no reason, however, to assume that some problems will not be dealt with successfully, as has happened again and again in the past. Without doubt, great potential still exists to meet challenges, even unanticipated ones. On the other hand, as history shows repeatedly, not everyone is able to meet them to the same degree and at the same time—or at the right time. Some will succeed better than others, and some forms of dealing with the challenges that arise—some constitutions, legal systems, kinds of knowledge and political organization, cultures—will prove more effective. Some of these responses may have to be developed ad hoc.

The issue will largely be a question, as it is in nature, of how we can best adapt to new conditions. Of course, things need not necessarily be as straightforward as the term "survival of the fittest" suggests. Some unfit people will certainly survive, and may not do badly at all; there will be bread and circuses enough in many regions of the world. Nietzsche presented a certain view of this in his vision of "the last man" in *Thus Spake Zarathustra*.[14] Adaptation is occurring, today as always, and perhaps at a greater rate than before.

At this point the historian must raise a few questions. Clearly we should view the ability to adapt to new conditions as positive for the evolution of species. But what applies to other species does not necessarily apply to the history of human beings, who can make conscious choices about whether to adjust to some new circumstances or not. Rapid adjustment is not wholly compatible, perhaps, with what used to be called character and also responsibility (and perhaps still is), even if what circumstances call for is not adjustment to a new regime, but to a process of change across the board. As Robert Musil observed in 1922: "Since 1914 humanity has revealed itself as a mass that is astonishingly more malleable than we had been accustomed to assume . . . and the war demonstrated to all of us in one monstrous mass experiment how easily human beings can move to the most radical extremes and back again without experiencing any basic change. They change—but what changes is not the *self*." Formerly, people did not really want to accept such an insight, partly because of the "importance ascribed to 'character' in our moral systems," which demanded that people's behavior be a constant, always dependable and predictable.[15] Musil's point is that this is not possible! And what holds for changes in basic life conditions also holds for opposites such as war and peace,[16] except that any adaptation to the former tends to be more lasting than to the latter.

Friedrich Schiller speaks of the capacity inherent in human beings to remain oneself in changing conditions over time and to keep an internal identity as outward circumstances alter.[17] And Theodor Adorno views the potential of the personality ideal preserved in "the power of the individual not to entrust himself to what blindly happens to him," but rather to sharpen his critical awareness and rationality.[18]

It is not necessary to speak of character or personality, however; we can simply observe that people acquire convictions and values through their traditions and life experience and would like to remain true to them. This by no means excludes the possibility that people go on learning, that they change and grow. And overall there can be highly fruitful combinations of adjustments and preservation of the self in a certain elasticity and openness to new experiences, including learning from those younger than oneself. As the saying goes, only those who change remain true to themselves.

A person can absorb many innovations and yet remain of the opinion that, for example, no matter how people dress, they should take some care with their appearance; that language can add new words—by borrowing from other languages, let us say—but that one still ought to strive for a certain level of linguistic cultivation; that the media offer a great deal that people want, but that at the same time should not treat everything that happened the day before as worth forgetting; rather, our news media should be capable of taking a second look at an event from a certain distance, and recalling it to mind. And certainly one can wish for many kinds of innovations in politics without being influenced by every mindless new rumor or trend.

The same principle applies to societies—like democracies, for example—that could have certain fundamental convictions despite all pluralism, and could adopt new ideas not just randomly, but in order to transform themselves.

Yet that becomes difficult if too much changes too fast. Then uncertainty spreads, precisely among those people whose judgment as such tends to be good, as tested axioms and shared ideas no longer hold in the new situation. The problem becomes one of keeping up at all, and the alternatives can easily come to seem either clinging to convictions already held or adapting to everything new. The first can look like rigidity, and the second like a lack of principles. As a result it becomes impossible to discuss many subjects and, if the uncertainty becomes widespread enough, to reach any kind of decision. The ability of a society to practice self-determination becomes problematic (or the areas in which self-determination still functions shrink). At worst what is called "self-determination" amounts simply to accepting developments that have long since taken place or decisions made elsewhere.[19] The momentary situation, the currents of the times, then begin to replace traditional roots, personal biographies, experience, and reflection; *homo sapiens* is taken over by *homo telephonans*. One could add here in Musil's words: "This has always been life's way with man, of course, restructuring humankind from the surface inward; the only difference is that people used to feel that they in turn should contribute something from their inside to their outside."[20]

And so now finally to the questions that form the title of this chapter: A legacy without heirs? and how should we deal with our historical legacy? The legacy of European history would have to be what our ancestors have passed on to us. That is in many respects a desolate field of ruins,[21] with a whole chain of further ruins stretching behind it; but in other respects it represents a huge amount of capital that has enabled humanity, with the investment of intelligence and a great deal of labor, to build on top of the ruins again and again.

We now have at our disposal buildings, the infrastructure of cities and countries, as well as knowledge, practical skills, science, literature, the fine arts, music, theater, institutions, law, social customs, human dignity, and freedom, to list just some of the most important bequests. Many great achievements were made by earlier generations, often at a price of enormous sacrifices in bitter, often violent struggles, and of great suffering (for the advances of one group created conditions under which others suffered as victims, as conquered peoples, slaves, and laborers, or because they were women). Much advancement is only a side effect of actions that had quite different goals, as when conflicts had to be resolved. Even though most of our legacy has been lost, squandered, destroyed, neglected, or simply worn away by time, important advances have been handed down, preserved, sometimes at great effort, and revived again and again. People have searched the past and borrowed elements of it, or rediscovered it, sometimes after centuries, and placed what they retrieved in the service of new goals. Essential components of tradition have lasted, either as a potential or an actuality, surviving even the decline of ancient Greece and Rome.

Starting with what we took over directly from our ancestors, consciously and unconsciously, and with the potential contained in their legacy, we have gone out in recent generations—in Europe, the United States, and many other parts of the world—and added an enormous amount that is new. Admittedly, we have destroyed or trampled on parts of our inheritance, such as pristine landscapes, old city centers, and perhaps archeological sites, along with many intangible certainties.[22] But we have also continually added to it, making discoveries and implementing them.

Thus today we live, to a greater extent than earlier generations, under conditions that have arisen during our own lifetime, and that continue to be transformed at an enormous speed. This does not change the fact, however, that in almost every sphere of life we have built on earlier foundations. Without them, who knows where we would have had to start out—certainly it would not have been in the industrial age, with tools such as modern law and the modern sciences at our disposal. And however far we may have gone from where we started out, all of us are far more the product of history than we tend to believe.

To this extent the legacy of history is something we take for granted. We have internalized much of it—and yet at the same time testimony of the past and earlier cultures can be observed on the outside, too, lying all around us. These facts are self-evident, as is the fact that, in and of itself, the culture handed down to us from earlier millennia is dead. People who do not enliven and make culture fruitful by questioning it or using culture to question themselves are philistines, as Nietzsche insisted. Roots do not grow upwards; they must stretch down into the ground if organisms are to draw nourishment. And here we have arrived at the specific problem of our legacy.

This history can pose a problem only if we understand it not as mere objects we have inherited, but also as a challenge, an obligation, which we can acknowledge and accept—or reject. The normal view is that if a person receives something, he or she owes a debt of gratitude to the giver. But what if the legacy includes not only love, but also infamy and shame, or a highly uncomfortable role in the world? In that case the recipients may not feel all that grateful, and certainly gratitude, to the extent that it is called for, does not constitute their only obligation. Rather, we must regard our legacy as consisting of taking on a set of tasks—some urgently requiring us to preserve and carry on, and others to make reparations.

How descendants deal with this legacy is ultimately up to them (and to how active their consciences are in reminding them of their obligations). And one cannot demand that people devote their whole lives to serving the dead. "Let the dead bury their dead," says the New Testament, after all.[23] In my view the members of the present generation have the right, at least, to consider their own situation as well as the past and to decide on that basis what obligations exist for them. It is not out of the question that they will prove reasonably insightful.

What form could that insight take in our case, in the Europe of today? As a minimum, certainly, the legacy includes preserving our inheritance and maintaining it competently. This also means preserving the memory of what has happened in the past. In its maximum form our legacy emerges from our historic role in the world, and involves obligations toward the peoples whose cultures were destroyed, who were robbed of many life-sustaining traditions, or whose ancestors were enslaved by European conquerors, for example. But one might also express this more cautiously, saying that we in Europe have an obligation toward the peoples whom we have drawn into processes of development in which it has been all too easy for them to fall behind, again and again. Of course, when the maximum obligation is expressed in such general terms, it is difficult to say what practical consequences will result.

In the middle ground also lies a possible responsibility, I believe, to recall the great achievements of European history and to keep them alive—carry them on, at least in Europe. Here I could cite certain ideals or rights that have been revitalized again and again,[24] such as freedom, and the right to freedom. By this I mean the right of individuals to their freedom, not in the sense of a freedom limited to or broken down into little nooks and crannies of private life, but rather a freedom corresponding to the freedom of the community, the freedom of all, in an order that is based on law yet still free, based on cooperation among citizens and on their actual participation in government in the broad sense of the word, and presuming a certain amount of reason and morality. For freedom brings responsibilities with it.

Freedom should also encompass human dignity. As Kant observed, respect for human dignity means that people regard each other as ends, not as means. Such a definition includes the notion of tolerance. Freedom and human dignity entail a further responsibility, however, which is to accept as a necessity our remaining personally alert and open to specific social and political questions that arise—even if they do not force themselves upon our attention or appear to have simple answers—and attempting to come up with answers. It is no accident that freedom arose among the Greeks almost in the same rhythm as their radical questions about the gods, the cosmos, justice, nature, and the proper sphere of human action. The Greeks dared to probe so deeply because they were confident that answers would be forthcoming, no matter how difficult the questions were; ultimately they believed that the world, human beings, and the *polis* could be understood, even if much remained unsolved. Their attitude stimulated research and led to the development of science and philosophy, and when Christianity and its inscrutable God were added to the tradition, people continued to ask questions about them as well.

In all this we could recognize as the legacy of Europe (or at least make a good case for it): freedom, human dignity, responsibility, and knowledge—resulting in a life that is lived consciously, and in some sense autonomously and freely, although never perfectly so. We might add equality, solidarity, possibly also that part of Christian doctrine that calls for loving one's neighbor and compassion for the suffering of others, or at least its secularized offshoots— with the consequence that people acquire a sense of responsibility for others beside themselves, even for strangers. The legacy of European history comes down to this, or so I would claim, and precisely by studying history we can see how precious it is—and how rare.

Whether the world would have been a happier place if this special European path had never existed is another question. Perhaps so. Sigmund Freud made a very skeptical observation on the subject in late 1914: "I do not doubt that mankind will survive even this war, but I know for certain that for me and my contemporaries the world will never again be a happy place. It is too hideous . . . [S]ince we can only regard the highest present civilization as burdened with an enormous hypocrisy, it follows that we are organically unfitted for it. We have to abdicate, and the Great Unknown, He or It, lurking behind Fate will someday repeat this experiment with another race."[25] "We are organically unfitted" is another way of referring to human inadequacy given the challenges we face; the Second World War and Auschwitz revealed this inadequacy more dramatically than ever before, and we may even have to concede that it applies to us as well.

We cannot do away with the special European path, however; history cannot be annulled.[26] Yet even though it led to World War II, Auschwitz, and the Gulag, among other things, that does not mean European history should be reduced to these three phenomena and to the sole message "Never again." Its legacy is not only far richer, but also acutely topical.

Naturally, the question remains of the extent to which we are prepared and able to take up that legacy. If all we do is enjoy life in relative peace and freedom, with a superfluity of consumer goods and institutions that we allow to run more or less on autopilot; if we live in mutual indifference, focused on our small patches of private freedom; if all we do is live and let live, without mutual respect—then that is not taking up our legacy.

More is involved, especially in terms of responsibility. "You can't take responsibility for another human being!" says Dr. Skovronnek to the old District Commissioner von Trotta in Joseph Roth's novel *The Radetzky March,* adding "No one should do that." "My father was responsible for me," counters von Trotta, "and my grandfather was for my father." "Things were different then," replies Skovronnek. "Today not even the Emperor can be responsible for the Monarchy. Yes, it even looks as though God doesn't want to be responsible for the world any more. It was easier then! Every stone was in its place. The roads of life were properly paved. There were stout roofs on the walls of the houses. Whereas today, District Commissioner, today the stones are lying all over the roads, and in dangerous heaps some of them, and the roofs are full of holes, and the rain falls into the houses, and it's up to the individual what road he walks, and what house he lives in." Then the doctor draws the conclusion from all this: "And that's why you should let things go, let everything please itself." Sometimes even his own children seem like strangers to him, he says, "from a time that's yet to come."[27]

Jelacich, another character in the same novel, has a similar feeling that he stands "powerlessly between his ancestors and his descendants, themselves destined to be ancestors, one day, of an entirely different breed . . . At forty, the Master of Horse felt like an old man, and his sons were like bewildering great-grandchildren to him."[28] A few years earlier Musil had written, "We are an early phase"—or, one might say, pre-history.[29]

Roth conceived his novel at the end of the 1920s and published it in installments in the *Frankfurter Zeitung,* beginning in April 1932. Part of the novel's fascination derives from the way the author showed the decline of pre–World War I Europe in a melancholy, multinational empire approaching its end, and whose ruler, in the period in which the bulk of the novel is set, has already celebrated his sixty-year jubilee on the throne and tends to confuse his grandsons with his sons, since otherwise he would feel too old. Yet at the same time the novel depicts a world where virtually nothing seems to be changing, despite the advent of the Social Democrats to power in Austria, despite the demands of the middle classes everywhere in the empire to be granted a share in political responsibility. The novel's point of departure is reminiscent of descriptions by both Max Weber and Tzvetan Todorov: every citizen has his place and is responsible in his own small circle—while the emperor is responsible for the empire (including the Jews among his subjects, who hold him in high regard for that reason),[30] and God is responsible for the world. Then that ceases; no one can cope any more, because the order is disintegrating—and one can only let things run their course. The younger people must figure things out for themselves! There is no bridge, but there is supposed to be a new beginning: a new age, and a new lineage, whose founders will be the characters' own children.

Today there are, as always, many entities and institutions that bear responsibility for matters both large and small, but we no longer feel that our society is like the Austro-Hungarian Empire, which—at least in retrospect—seemed to be protected and secured by the emperor and God. If we take a closer look at our own society, we find no inherent solidity or firmness; instead it has become the responsibility of us all, although to different degrees. It is well ordered, here in Europe, or at least in Western Europe. But there is no visible guarantee anywhere that it will remain so, given all the rapid change that is occurring. No responsible authority exists, since politics can deal with only a small percentage of change. To the extent that "all of us" are the authority, responsibility can be perceived only as a kind of "as if": as if it mattered what we do and leave undone, what things we bother or don't bother to think about.

One fact can be established, however: the European legacy includes at least the attempt to achieve some clarity about our own situation, to acquire an overview of what is going on, and also to make sure that we know what the consequences are, for ourselves and our own community and for the world. People have striven for this same goal for thousands of years, both among the Greeks and in the modern era, and not just in narrow circles but in broad segments of society. They also did so in a multitude of ways and in a wide variety of disciplines, in science and literature and myth, in music and the arts, in the theater as well as in city planning and architecture.

The changes both large and small that were always occurring provided stimuli (as did the causes of those changes and the necessities for them). And they were made possible and easier through the fact that not only recent traditions existed to draw on, but also older ones, especially the Greek and Roman past. There were not only models and types but antitypes, works and movements offering virtually infinite possibilities for interpretation—not to mention the wealth of stimuli from other parts of the world.

I see this as the most important legacy of European history (without wishing to deny that there are other avenues of access to it). And it strikes me as still highly relevant today. And everyone is a potential heir to it, at any point on the globe, who is willing to accept it. Here I am concerned primarily with Europe itself. And the question is whether there is perhaps not a shortage of heirs, or to put it more precisely, a lack of ability and willingness in our society to lay claim to this inheritance, or to a particular view of it.

Continuing a culture is not a question of preserving monuments, as essential as that is, but of continuing to absorb the past, of creating new links to it and drawing new inspiration from it. What counts is not occasionally going back to one aspect, visiting one or the other monument, but of a certain continuing presence, handing it on and fostering it in new generations. For the openness to culture that one must wish for, particularly in times of rapid change, can only be prepared openness, so to speak, that can perceive significance in several forms.

It is difficult to say how much of that is still possible today. The conditions leading to an absence of history, which I mentioned in the first chapter, might also be cited for culture, with others added to them. Presumably a certain connection exists between history and culture, for to a significant extent it is historical consciousness—living tradition—that in the end imbues a given era with culture. Such tradition is subject to many kinds of change, to be sure, and people use and build on different bits and pieces of it at one time or another. Nevertheless, it also constitutes a whole that must be supported on a sustaining foundation, one that even in our day includes the Greeks and Romans. This remains valid even if sudden bursts of rapid change bring with them new quandaries and uncertainties; in the long term the foundations must remain.

In history, as in other spheres of public opinion, perseverance and optimism are indispensable; we historians must act as if our work might actually be needed one day. And thus we move on to our second question: What is history good for?

I see five main ways in which history (beyond the limited circles of professionals and enthusiasts) can become important again in the future. I have already mentioned the first two: history can provide a sense of orientation in one's own time, and assist in the process of self-determination. It can help us decide how the European Union should develop, for instance (should the EU ever decide to concern itself with more than agricultural policy, military interventions, and the standardization of tax rates on interest income). The same applies to what history can convey about how history itself comes to pass, how change occurs and what role individuals play in it. A third function would be to gather information from earlier epochs that might illustrate possible scenarios for the future.[31]

The field that historians cultivate and tend is one in which human beings have created a multitude of societies and political and economic structures, torn them down, and replaced them with others. One way to conceive of history is as the sum total of an immense number of experiments in living.

Of course, it is not possible to devise experiments as such, as if human societies were chemistry laboratories. Human experiments are not permissible (except on a very limited scale in medicine). In history, however, many experiments have already been performed, so to speak, without our participation, independently of us—we need only to evaluate them, whether it be ways of obtaining food or the arrangement of living spaces, forms of communal living or organizations on different scales; we can examine the organization of belief, forms of subjugation and revolt, relationships between men and women, types of warfare, and much, much more.

All kinds of new questions have become relevant in recent times or are beginning to appear so. Questions about suffering in history, about how many "men who make history" can be endured, and about the history of hubris. What are human limits? The history of balancing between tradition and the future is becoming interesting, the history of fear, but also particular aspects of the history of language (such as under what circumstances words really register and become part of the living language, or simply disappear without having any effect at all, as so often happens today). We could also study the history of what is determined either by the past or the present; we could investigate how societies have been reshaped in the past, or responded to dramatically new situations; we could look at periods in which change accelerated. And, finally, those of us alive today must deal with the question of whether a new era is beginning for a new type of human being, as it seemed to Joseph Roth (i.e., whether the rate of acceleration will decrease at some point, as Koselleck presumes, or whether it will just continue to increase—and we must simply accept the fact and adapt, a response for which the nineteenth century offers certain parallels). And also we must deal with examples in history for how human beings have succeeded in controlling change (or failed); this is a new perspective that is providing us today with a different window on the past and hence a different view of the present.

All of these also provide examples of how history looks different in retrospect. "In fear and trembling finally to grasp all that human-ity is capable of—that is indeed a precondition of modern political thought," as Hannah Arendt understood after Auschwitz.[32]

In short, our societies will also need history in the future, if only because it is the study of change and of possibilities. For it should not be assumed that our societies will dispense with self-determina-tion and circumspection in the future. And this lends importance to a fourth function, namely, historiographic synthesis. For at the very least, one thing history does do is investigate how factors in differ-ent epochs are connected, how they affect another, and how they contribute to regeneration and change. History tells us how such a process of either regeneration or change looked to people liv-ing through it, how they viewed and experienced it, how it affected them.

In this framework it becomes important to make history vivid and imaginable, particularly its cruel and unexpected sides. Han-nah Arendt's observation that Eichmann could not imagine the ef-fects of his action stands in a long tradition. In 1914 Karl Kraus de-scribed his own era as one "in which things are happening that you couldn't have imagined, and in which things will inevitably happen that you still cannot imagine; if you could imagine them, then they wouldn't happen."[33] Oddly enough, Arthur Schnitzler also com-plained at that time about the impossibility of imagining events, about the inability of even creative and inventive people to imagine things.[34] But the powers of imagination must be of many different kinds, for as the old and still valuable saying goes, the devil doesn't enter through the same door twice.

Finally, one last point: there is a special need for history in times of change, because it help us study and grasp unsimultaneities of the simultaneous, and especially because it offers always new and different examples of great interest for the interaction of change, adaptation, and the striving to remain true to oneself and one's con-victions. We must define ourselves as individuals in the present particularly in view of our origins and traditions. In order to understand ourselves, we must know what we have received from the past.

This was a particularly fruitful experience in the generation to which Weber, Musil, Benn, and Roth belonged. In their cases, particularly under the influence of Nietzsche and the First World War, their parents' firm values, religious faith, and the humanistic schools in which they were educated, on the one hand, and the way they later perceived themselves led to great tensions.

The torment and productivity once produced by the tension between the God of revelation and human nature was caused here by the tension between tradition and the present.

Musil's "man without qualities" is revolted by the "lethargic acceptance of changes and conditions, this helpless contemporaneity, this mindlessly submissive, truly demeaning stringing along with the centuries, just as if he were suddenly rebelling against the hat, curious enough in shape, that was sitting on his head." When this happens he is riding in a "luminous, swaying box," probably a streetcar that appears to him like "a machine in which several hundred kilos of people were being rattled around, by way of being propelled into 'the future.' A hundred years earlier they had sat in a mail coach with the same look on their faces, and a hundred years hence, whatever was going on, they would be sitting as new people in exactly the same way in their updated transport machines . . . Instinctively he got to his feet and made the rest of his way on foot. In the more generous confines of the city, in which he now found himself, his uneasiness gave way to good humor again."[35]

Musil's character thus felt the age in which he had been born to be a pure accident.[36] Time shaped human beings first in one way, then in another, in a completely arbitrary manner; they could easily have been very different; they weren't in control. Defenseless, helpless, without a plan, they were jolted back and forth in history, and then had to shift into the next mode. The man without qualities was clearly incapable of "creating something from within and bringing it forth," to live with his century without being its creature, in Schiller's words. He could not simply accept what he was and, working on that material in one way or another, bring forth his own self.

How "demeaning" it was just to "string along with the centuries," however, to be passively jolted along as if in some kind of conveyance—to become aware of that in the clear and shocking way Musil did was possible only if he came from a world of stability, where even change had once appeared meaningful.

Gottfried Benn is considered to have been anti-history. There are a whole series of statements that make that only too clear.[37] They refer to a history of events, however, and perhaps to many kinds of historical processes, but not to the transformation that he felt had affected him. What is the issue in "The Modern Ego" and "The Last Ego"—to cite only two titles—if not a historical definition of his own location? "The biography of the ego is unwritten," observed Benn in 1920. Ten years later he spoke of the "history of the psyche from antiquity to Expressionism." Finally, in the "Conversation of the Three Old Men," he wrote, "People say 'human beings,' but they forget their mutations." He found that "the psychological interior of an ego striving for an experience and then processing this experience in the sense of development" had stepped into the shadows, with the ego living on loss, "isolation of the centers, without psychological continuity, without a biography, without a history having taken place centrally."

A clear awareness of the epoch finds expression here, which reveals rather too *much* sensitivity to the historical changes Benn was enduring than too little. For what was disintegrating was not one race, one continent, or one social order, but an entire design for creation, which no longer had a future: "The Quaternary Period tipped over backwards." One could expound on this point by bringing in Benn's statements about antiquity and the role it played in the pre-history of the modern world: "The ego emerged, trampled things down, fought; in order to do so it needed means, material, and power." Or his various commentaries on his own era, as when he speaks of "movements without people to carry them," or when he says on January 18, 1945, "If we are honest, as creatures, as beings, we no longer see ourselves in relation to *anything at all,* neither in the past nor in the future." Again and again the tension between the conditions in which he is living and the conditions into which he was born—his family, his father, the vicarage, his school, and everything they stood for—becomes almost palpable. We sense how vulnerable Benn was to this tension, and how he struggled with it, like so many of his contemporaries.

What his generation experienced and had to come to grips with in many different ways seems to me to reveal with particular clarity how difficult it is to attain a sense of self-assurance and self-assertiveness in times of upheaval or rapid change. It is a problem with history. For many people, tackling the problem helps them at least to endure history. And that is important, for as Hannah Arendt observes, "humanly speaking, it is endurance which enables man to create durability and continuity."[38]

I would like to close with three quotations. One of them I quoted earlier in these lectures. Jacob Burckhardt calls the study of history "not only a right and a duty; it is also a supreme need: It is our freedom in the very awareness of universal bondage and the stream of necessities."[39] The second quotation also comes from the great historian from Basel: "if in misfortune there is to be some fortune as well, it can only be a spiritual one, facing backward to the rescue of the culture of earlier times, facing forward to the serene and unwearied representation of the spirit in a time which could otherwise be given up entirely to things mundane."[40] But as my very last word I would like to use Hegel's conclusion to his lectures on the *Philosophy of History:* "Farewell."

Notes

1. The Absence of History

1. In the late twentieth century there was a great deal of dispute over a supposed German "special path." It was said to have been not only a "particular path," in the sense that it was one of many particular paths taken by different nations, but also a unique one that distinguished Germany from *all* others (whose paths were thus asserted to have been general and "Western"). One hears very little of this nowadays. When I speak of a European special path in this book, in all probability what does not apply to Germany *does* apply to the Continent: Europe followed a path that differed from that of *all* other cultures (as different as they may have been from one another) in essential ways. Compare my remarks at the beginning of Chapter 2.

2. See Christian Meier, *Die Welt der Geschichte und die Provinz des Historikers* (Berlin: Wagenbach, 1989), 147ff. For practical suggestions, see Christian Meier, "Geschichtswissenschaft in der heutigen Welt," *Saeculum* 40 (1989), 188ff.; Meier, "Aktuelle Aufgaben der Geschichtswissenschaft und der Geschichtsvermittlung," *Aus Politik und Zeitgeschichte* 40–41 (1988); Landeshochschulstrukturkommission, *Stellungnahmen und Empfehlungen zu Struktur und Entwicklung der Berliner Hochschulen* (Berlin: 1992), 179ff. See also Jürgen Osterhammel's article in *Geschichte in Wissenschaft und Unterricht* 46 (1995), 253ff.

3. Reproduced in an expanded version in Christian Meier, *Entstehung des Begriffs "Demokratie"* (Frankfurt: Suhrkamp, 1970). Further remarks on the subject in other versions and situations under the same title can

199

be found in *Verantwortung und Ethik in der Wissenschaft: Berichte und Mitteilungen der Max-Planck-Gesellschaft München,* no. 3 (1984), and *Diogenes* 168 (1994), 25ff.

4. Professional historians can get along quite well without society taking an interest in their work (as long as they are paid), but teaching and research go better, and are often more fruitful when interest is present, other things being equal.

5. Johann Wolfgang von Goethe, *Elective Affinities,* translated by Judith Ryan, in *The Sorrows of Young Werther; Elective Affinities; Novella,* Goethe's Collected Works, vol. 11 (New York: Suhrkamp, 1988), 121. The familiar "serenity prayer" written by Reinhold Niebuhr makes a similar point: "God grant me the serenity to accept the things I cannot change; courage to change the things I can; and wisdom to know the difference." See Elisabeth Sifton, *Das Gelassenheitsgebet: Erinnerungen an Reinhold Niebuhr* (Munich: Hanser, 2001).

6. Compare the letter written by the poet Gottfried Benn to F. W. Oelze on January 18, 1945: "If we are honest, as creatures and existences we no longer see ourselves in relation to *anything at all,* either in the past or in the future; we stand alone, silently but also trembling in ourselves. That must now be transferred to every verse, every line, every sentence, and it must also stand by itself and hold up *everything;* for there is no other support—no relationship, no faith, no hope, no illusion. Something seeks and finds its expression, and then its life is over: think about how many things Nietzsche saw himself in relation to, for instance, from the past and from the future! Everything, really! But we don't. That is what is new, what is decisively new about us." Benn, *Briefe an F. W. Oelze, 1932–1945* (Wiesbaden: Limes Verlag, 1977).

Bruno Snell offers a good example of the older view: "Man, at least Western man, attempts to steer his future course with a will and a purpose. But since he cannot very well plan in a vacuum, since he must accept the guidance of given facts, he orientates his search along the bearings of his own past. The question: 'what do I want to do?' is in his mind always linked with the further question: 'What am I and what have I been?'" Snell, *The Discovery of the Mind in Greek Philosophy and Literature,* translated by T. G. Rosenmeyer (1953; rpt. New York: Dover, 1982), 261.

7. This is my designation for the prevailing tendencies of generalizing social perception. Despite the fact that within a society differing or op-

posing perceptions can prevail in certain groups or camps and be the subject of conflict between them, it happens again and again that certain perceptions in society are so powerful as a whole that they are generally considered to be correct, and that a gravitational force works in their favor. This is not to say that they are shared by the majority; it is sufficient that they are expressed with particular force—for a certain time. For example, the gravitational force of perception may pull in the direction of "everything is corrupt"; then all possible other cases appear to be exceptions to the rule. Or vice versa. Thus a society can tend to believe that security conditions are good, and observations to the contrary will not carry much weight, or will be categorized as exceptions. Or vice versa. And again: for a certain time. Those who have the gravitational force of perception on their side will not be under as much pressure to explain or justify their point of view. The process of titration offers an illustration of this shift: a chemist gradually adds many drops of an essence to water, and for a long while there is no reaction. Then suddenly, in an instant, the liquid takes on a different color. A transition, that is to say, from quantity to quality—which can of course happen with prevailing opinions, perceptions, and so on in a quite similar manner.

8. Johann Gustav Droysen, *Historik*, vol. 1, ed. Peter Leyh (Stuttgart–Bad Canstatt: Frommann-Holzboog, 1977).

9. Jacob Burckhardt, *Reflections on History*, translated by M. D. Hottinger (1943; rpt. Indianapolis: Liberty Classics, 1979).

10. Johann Wolfgang von Goethe, *Poems of the West and East: West-Eastern Divan / West-Östlicher Divan*, Bi-Lingual Edition of the Complete Poems, translated by John Whaley, Germanic Studies in America, no. 68 (Bern: Peter Lang, 1998), 189.

11. Compare, for instance, Jacob Burckhardt's observation in *Reflections on History*: "let us remember all we owe to the past as a spiritual *continuum* which forms part of our supreme spiritual heritage . . . The only peoples to renounce this privilege are, first, barbarians, who accepting their cake of custom as pre-ordained, never break through it. They are barbarians because they have no history, and vice versa" (p. 38).

12. Ibid., 40.

13. Jacob Burckhardt, *Judgments on History and Historians*, translated by Harry Zohn (Boston: Beacon Press, 1958), 224.

14. Robert Musil, "Helpless Europe," translated by Philip H. Beard, in

Musil, *Precision and Soul: Essays and Addresses,* ed. Burton Pike and David S. Luft (Chicago: University of Chicago Press, 1990), 116–117. See also Musil, *The Man without Qualities,* translated by Sophie Wilkins (New York: Knopf, 1995), vol. 2, 996.

15. Musil, "Helpless Europe," 121.

16. Similar observations can also be made in the field of art, of course, such as the "progressive shortening of the periods in which styles of production remain dominant." Hermann Lübbe, *Die Aufdringlichkeit der Geschichte: Herausforderungen der Moderne vom Historismus bis zum Nationalsozialismus* (Graz: Styria, 1989), 48. Lübbe also speaks of the "increasing temporal density of innovation": "As the rate of innovation increases, so does the speed at which things become out of date. As a result the amount of time shrinks that a certain constancy of aesthetic structures allows us to recognize as the present." Incidentally, Francis Bacon predicted that the pace of new inventions would speed up; see Reinhart Koselleck, "Fortschritt," in O. Brunner, W. Conze, and R. Koselleck, eds., *Geschichtliche Grundbegriffe: Historisches Lexikon zur politisch-sozialen Sprache in Deutschland* (Stuttgart: Klett, 1975), vol. 2, 402. For earlier observations on acceleration during the entire modern period, see Reinhart Koselleck, *The Practice of Conceptual History: Timing History, Spacing Concepts,* translated by Todd Samuel Presner et al. (Stanford, Calif.: Stanford University Press, 2002).

Whether acceleration can always be clearly distinguished from speed is another question. Particularly important in this context is Burckhardt's interpretation of crises as "accelerated processes." Beyond a certain point—namely, the point where people can no longer really get by using their old opinions, values, and so on—acceleration means giving up habits. A certain adaptation is probably always possible. When demands grow too great, then a fairly large gap can open up, at least for sensitive people. Their ability to tolerate acceleration becomes overtaxed.

17. Older people can easily begin to suspect that they are no longer real members of the contemporary age. No one said it better than Tacitus, in very different circumstances: "Ut ita dixerim, non modo aliorum sed etiam nostri superstites sumus" (*Agricola* 3, 2).

18. More on this topic follows in Chapter 3.

19. Hannah Arendt, *On Revolution* (New York: Viking Press, 1963), 45.

20. Burckhardt, *Reflections on History,* 39. Compare also *Judgments on History and Historians,* 224; letter of July 2, 1871, in *Briefe an seinen Freund Friedrich von Preen 1864–1893* (Stuttgart: Deutsche Verlags-Anstalt, 1922), 36.

21. Commenting on these ways of orientation, Hans Freyer noted that "the older systems of philosophy wanted to provide an orientation for man in the world in which he lived. In the period that began with the *querelle des antiques et des modernes,* reached its apex in the Enlightenment, and appears to have ended with Nietzsche, historical philosophy had a central place in thinking. Man now oriented himself in historical time, i.e. he located his own place between past and future: at a particular stage in the progress of reason, in a certain phase of the class struggle, at a particular point in the history of European Nihilism." Freyer, *Theorie des gegenwärtigen Zeitalters* (Stuttgart: Deutsche Verlags-Anstalt, 1955), 74. And today?

22. Droysen, *Historik,* vol. 1, 369, 272. On the concept of "workers" or "agents" in history, see Droysen, *Outline of the Principles of History,* translated by E. Benjamin Andrews (Boston: Ginn, 1893), 43–44, 84–85.

23. The determination is not always so palpable, however, because we can feel quite free to do all kinds of things without consequences or at least apparently without consequences (as far as our trash is concerned) in the niches (along with possibilities for travel) opened up to us increasingly by that very process of change in the conditions of production.

24. Botho Strauss sees things differently: "The mind does not like to accept that everything is unfortunately pointing toward precisely those circumstances that are already showing signs of being inevitable." Strauss, *Die Fehler des Kopisten* (Munich: Hanser, 1997), 8.

25. On the problem of prognoses, see the section "Historiker und Prognose," in Christian Meier, *Das Verschwinden der Gegenwart* (Munich: Hanser, 2001). On the increased difficulty in times of comprehensive change, see Hermann Lübbe, *Geschichtsbegriff und Geschichtsinteresse: Analytik und Pragmatik der Historie* (Basel: Schwabe, 1977), 325–326 and 130. Here, too, one could say that there is nothing new under the sun: "Frankly, in view of the instability and uncertainty of human affairs, it is almost impossible to give you an unalterable rule either for your private conduct or for governing the states and territories that I will bequeath to you" (from instructions of the Holy Roman Em-

peror Charles V to his son, dated January 1548, as quoted by Heinz Schilling in the *Frankfurter Allgemeine Zeitung*, February 26, 2000).

26. By contrast Gottfried Benn, speaking of his own era, refers to "movement without people to carry it." Benn, "Akademierede," *Gesammelte Werke*, ed. Dieter Wellershoff (Wiesbaden: Limes Verlag, 1959), vol. 1, 433–434.

27. See Lutz Niethammer, *Posthistoire: Has History Come to an End?*, translated by Patrick Camiller (London: Verso, 1992). From this perspective Peter Sloterdijk could write: "The grand HISTORY of old turns out to have been an evolutionary stratagem, which could not reveal itself if it was to remain effective: an active, auto-hypnotic myth. Today this secret has been let out and used so as to take effect. Perhaps HISTORY was just a fairy-tale of the violent might of reality, which paid off so long as its target group could be used to become subject of the fairy-tale action and to weave their personal histories into HISTORY." Cited in Niethammer, ibid., 49. Niethammer also discusses Alred Heuss's *Verlust der Geschichte* (Göttingen: Vandenhoeck and Ruprecht, 1959) in this context, at 49–50.

28. One could also, in the narrower sense, cite Arnold Gehlen's observation: "Man's need to free himself from the yoke of circumstances is fundamental and lies at the core of his constitution. Philosophers, politicians, and physicians are probably the most important kinds of people to act on this need nowadays, and the sequence of these men— Fichte, Marx, and Freud—is thus meaningful in itself." Gehlen, "Über die Geburt der Freiheit aus der Entfremdung," *Philosophische Anthropologie und Handlungslehre*, vol. 4 of *Gesamtausgabe* (Frankfurt: Klostermann, 1983), 379. Of course, this principle was somewhat violated by the youthful revolutionaries of 1968. Compare Jean Améry's interesting article, "Expeditionen jenseits des Rheins," *Merkur 25* (1971), 38ff. And, from another angle, see Niethammer, *Posthistoire*, note 15, p. 20. For the "nations that do not belong to the Club of Rome," see Niethammer, ibid., note 8, p. 152.

29. *Politics* 1318b4, quoted from Aristotle, *Politics: Books V and VI*, translated with commentary by David Keyt (Oxford: Clarendon Press, 1999), 43.

30. For more on this topic, after Niethammer, see Francis Fukuyama, "The End of History?," *The National Interest* 16 (1989), 3ff. See also Christian Meier, "Vom 'fin de siècle' zum 'end of history'? Zur Lage der

Geschichte," *Merkur* 44 (1990), 809ff. How far Niethammer's recommendation of "history from below" (*Posthistoire*, 149–151) can advance history is highly questionable in view of the difficulties in imagining this history (see below) and the complicated mediation between macro- and micro-history. Compare Christian Meier, "Notizen zum Verhältnis von Makro- und Mikrogeschichte," in Karl Acham and Winfried Schulze, eds., *Teil und Ganzes,* vol. 6 of *Theorie der Geschichte* (Munich: Deutscher Taschenbuch Verlag, 1990), 111–140.

31. Droysen, *Historik,* 272.

32. That is, the twelve years of the Third Reich, 1933–1945.—translator's note.

33. My interpretation appeared as "Debatte: Goldhagen und die Deutschen," *Internationale Zeitschrift für Philosophie* 1 (1997), 119ff. For a different view, see Jörn Rüsen, *Zerbrechende Zeit: Über den Sinn der Geschichte* (Cologne: Böhlau, 2001), 296.

34. I would like to point out here that a connection to history for young people is "normally" achieved in families through stories told by older members; see, for example, Alfred Heuß, "'Geschichtliche Gegenwart,' ihr Erwerb und ihr Verlust," *Gesammelte Schriften* (Stuttgart: F. Steiner, 1995), vol. 3, 2237ff. Another entirely different approach that makes for an interesting comparison can be found in Sudhir Kakar, *The Colors of Violence: Cultural Identities, Religion, and Conflict* (Chicago: University of Chicago Press, 1996), 25–37.

35. Freyer, *Theorie des gegenwärtigen Zeitalters,* 226. One could also cite here certain formulations of Gottfried Benn's, such as "the psychological interior of an ego striving for an experience and then processing this experience in the sense of development stepped into the shadows." Or "behind this stands another, much more general anti-historical tendency." Or "this ego, that lives on loss, frigidity, isolation of the centers, without psychological continuity, without a biography, without a history having taken place centrally." Benn, *Werke,* vol. 1, 432, 436. It would be an interesting task to investigate the topic of Benn and history in depth. I have published a few observations as "Gottfried Benn und die Griechen," *Jahrbuch der Bayerischen Akademie der schönen Künste* 1 (1987), 259ff. On the subject of experience, compare Hans Blumenberg, *Lebenszeit und Weltzeit* (Frankfurt: Suhrkamp, 1986): "The proportion of the world that can be experienced in one's own lifetime is shrinking, despite the mechanisms for saving time, so that all we

can do is make up for the experiential deficits that concern each of us as individuals. Even mid-life crises are linked to an awareness that a lifetime, such as each person gets only one of, is not enough to experience everything that is called 'the world.'"

36. G. W. F. Hegel, *Elements of the Philosophy of Right*, edited by Allen W. Wood and translated by H. B. Nisbet (Cambridge: Cambridge University Press, 1991), §184, p. 222. There is an interesting formulation for the state in Burckhardt: "It was not engendered by the abdication of the self-seeking of its individual members. It *is* that abdication, it *is* their reduction to a common denominator, in order that as many interests and egoisms as possible may find permanent satisfaction in it and, in the end, completely fuse their existence with its own." *Reflections on History*, 70.

37. Here I should perhaps point out Freyer's observation on the lack of prerequisites in secondary systems in *Theorie des gegenwärtigen Zeitalters*, 180.

38. "This self-accelerating temporality robs the present of the possibility of being experienced as the present, and escapes into a future within which the currently unapprehendable present has to be captured by historical philosophy." Reinhart Koselleck, "Modernity and the Planes of Historicity," in *Futures Past: On the Semantics of Historical Time*, translated by Keith Tribe (Cambridge, Mass.: MIT Press, 1985), 18. In this essay Koselleck is referring to the eighteenth century.

39. This need not occur in the same way as Schiller once proposed. In the interpretation of Odo Marquard: "Someone who defines history as the long march into the universal and as the path of the individual's dissolution into the species must logically assume, to repeat the passage from Schiller that I quoted earlier, that 'all prior ages have striven . . . to bring about our humane century' . . . ; he thus becomes a kind of 'committed' reporter who—as a sort of William Tell, but equipped with microphone and camera rather than crossbow and arrow, and rejoicing and inciting rather than lying in wait—reports, regarding mankind in its present, late European phase: 'It has to pass through this narrow passage. There is no other path to freedom. Here mankind will complete its task, and necessity is on its side.'" Marquard, "Universal History and Multiversal History," in *In Defense of the Accidental: Philosophical Studies* (Oxford: Oxford University Press, 1991), 65.

40. Thomas Mann, "The Sorrows and Grandeur of Richard Wagner," in

Pro und Contra Wagner, translated by Allan Blunden (Chicago: University of Chicago Press, 1985), 92.

41. Alfred Heuss, *Verlust der Geschichte,* 60. In his day Heuss saw (and expressed) much that has only become clearer in the present day. I could quote several passages on how much we are occupied by a highly transitory present and are much too strongly conditioned by its diverse phases for it to give us much food for thought. Here is just one: "The burden/strain lies in this case not at all in the sheer abundance of material . . . , but rather in the necessity to become emotionally engaged, to be affected by events connected with an unpleasant feeling that man does not really have them under control, events that must therefore arouse a double aporia, both practical and theoretical."

42. See Hannah Arendt, "Geschichte und Politik," *Fragwürdige Traditionsbestände im politischen Denken der Gegenwart* (Frankfurt: Europäische Verlags-Anstalt, 1957), 81.

43. See Koselleck, "On the Disposability of History," *Futures Past: On the Semantics of Historical Time,* 198–212.

44. *Die Fehler des Kopisten,* 96. The passage continues: "And this faint still expels sighs like 'worldwide web,' 'apocalypse of nature,' or 'disintegration of values.' This is indicated not by pale cheeks and lips, but by swooning talk, which testifies much more credibly to the lost consciousness of the *entirety* of the world than the strain on the senses, which it doubtless represents, would lead one to suppose."

45. For another aspect of theater, compare Botho Strauss's observation: "It is striking how modern theater wants to be relevant to its own time—and only its own time, and how awkward its attempts are. It fails to be relevant to itself, as a place that offers the strongest opposition to the complete illusionality [*Verscheinung*] of the world." *Die Fehler des Kopisten,* 84.

46. Horst Siebert, president of the Kiel Institute for World Economics and a former member of the German Council of Economic Experts. The quotation comes from Siebert's article "Odysseus am Mast der Ökonomie," *Frankfurter Allgemeine Zeitung,* April 19, 1997.

47. Compare what Kant writes in the third thesis of his *Idea for a Universal History from a Cosmopolitan Point of View:* "It remains strange that the earlier generations appear to carry through their toilsome labor only for the sake of the later, to prepare for them a foundation on which the later generations could erect the higher edifice which was

Nature's goal, and yet that only the latest of the generations should have the good fortune to inhabit the building on which a long line of their ancestors had (unintentionally) labored without being permitted to partake of the [good] fortune they had prepared." Immanuel Kant, *Selections*, ed. Lewis White Beck (New York: Macmillan, 1998), 417. See also Hannah Arendt, *Fragwürdige Traditionsbestände*, 109. Jacob Burckhardt observed: "There is, however, one error which we must not impute to the philosophers alone, namely, that our time is the consummation of all time, or very nearly so." *Reflections on History*, 34. And Max Weber described his own time in terms of "specialists without spirit, sensualists without heart; this nullity imagines that it has attained a level of civilization never before achieved." *The Protestant Ethic and the Spirit of Capitalism*, translated by Talcott Parsons, 2d ed. (London: Allen & Unwin: 1976), 182. Compare also Botho Strauss: "I would like someone to explain to me how someone from *our* time could look down on an earlier one!" *Die Fehler des Kopisten*, 97.

48. This must be what Reinhart Koselleck means when he writes, "It is becoming apparent that certain processes of acceleration in our highly diversified society have reached their satiation point . . . It could turn out that the acceleration up to now has indicated only a transitional phase, after which the relative proportions of 'permanence' and 'survival' [*Dauer, Überdauern*] and 'change' and 'transformation' [*Veränderung, Wandel*] will have to be reordered with respect to one another." *Zeitschichten* (Frankfurt: Suhrkamp, 2000), 199, 200–201.

49. Alexis de Tocqueville, *Democracy in America and Two Essays on America*, translated by Gerald Bevan (London: Penguin, 2003), 15–16.

50. Burckhardt, *Judgments on History and Historians*, 217.

51. The expression was coined by Max Weber in his essay "'Objectivity' in Social Science and Social Policy," in *The Methodology of the Social Sciences*, edited and translated by Edward A. Shils and Henry A. Finch (New York: Free Press, 1949), 79. He means by it the knowledge that cause and effect are regular, a prerequisite for linking specific causes with specific effects, for instance in history. I would understand "nomological knowledge" in the wider sense as the set of fundamental beliefs to which we tend to resort when we must recognize, understand, classify, or judge something as right or wrong, possible or impossible, true or false, and also as either important or unimportant. What this set of beliefs consists of is not easy to describe or even necessarily con-

scious—we feel or sense some things rather than knowing them—and they are not universally shared within a particular society; see Christian Meier, *Die parlamentarische Demokratie* (Munich: Hanser, 1999), 53ff. All the same, as a rule societies allow their children to grow into certain beliefs or even inculcate them. And then one "knows" that corruption is wrong, for example, or that impairment of democracy is unacceptable. Depending on the expectations that "one" acquires in this way, certain things are considered possible and others not.

News reports and personal accounts are judged predominantly on the basis of these expectations to be true or false, or are received skeptically. The Argentinian author Elsa Osorio reports that she was accused of exaggerating in her report on the treatment of the children of Argentinian dissidents, when she wrote that mothers were shot and the children adopted by military officers. The military hospital on the Campo de Mayo had a special gynecological ward for this reason. The planes also took off from there to drop prisoners into the Rio de La Plata, who thereby "disappeared." Without doubt the questions put to Osorio express one of the greatest obstacles in the path to recognizing truths in our time: the "knowledge" of what is possible and impossible all too often prevents people from making appropriate distinctions between true and false. This is just one more confirmation of the "old experience," noted by Lorenz von Stein, "that people prefer to be wrong in their accustomed chain of reasoning than right in an unaccustomed one." "Zur preußischen Verfassungsfrage," *Deutsche Vierteljahrs Schrift*, 1852, vol. 1, 4. Compare also James Madison's remark in the *Federalist Papers*, no. 49: "The reason of man, like man himself, is timid and cautious when left alone, and acquires firmness and confidence in proportion to the number with which it is associated."

Nomological knowledge can vary considerably. It can change both in content and in intensity, and in the degree to which it is shared, as can be observed, for instance, in the fifth century B.C. The teachings people had absorbed—at home, from myths, and prevailing opinion—ceased to be sufficient. A gap opened between older traditions and what was considered appropriate at the present time. On the one hand, armies were still accompanied by a seer when they took the field, and prayers were offered before battle. On the other, military commanders devised bold and comprehensive strategies in which they left no role for the gods. The problems that grew out of this and many other kinds of discrepancy were presented in Greek tragedy in a highly skillful manner; see Christian Meier, *The Political Art of Greek Tragedy*, translated by Andrew Webber (Cambridge: Polity, 1993), and Meier, *Athens: A Portrait of a City in Its Golden Age*, translated by Robert and Rita Kimber (New York: Metropolitan/Holt, 1998), 270–276, 312, 452–453.

Eric Hobsbawm sees things quite differently with regard to England: "The old traditional England . . . relied on the enormous strength of custom and convention. One did, not what 'ought to be done,' but what *was* done: as the phrase went, 'the done thing.' But we no longer know what 'the done thing' is, there is only 'one's own thing.'" Hobsbawm, *On History* (New York: New Press, 1997), 264. A graphic example is offered by the shift of nomological knowledge in beliefs about what is allowed and forbidden in the area of sexuality (in the process that began with the breaking of taboos in a libertarian spirit and has led to universally available pornography). See Botho Strauss, *Die Fehler des Kopisten*, 82.

Of course, the meanings and in some cases the normative connotations of words are also based on nomological knowledge. As early as 1793 the *Schleswig Journal* noted that "words whose reverberation previously had an indescribable force . . . have now lost all significance" (quoted in Koselleck, *Futures Past*, 252–253). Theodor Adorno spoke of the severing of the relationship between matter and expression, in *Minima Moralia: Reflections from a Damaged Life*, translated by E. F. N. Jephcott (London: Verso, 1978), 137. Stefan Zweig wrote (at the time of the First World War, not the Second): "the word still had power . . . The moral conscience of the world had not yet become as tired or washed-out as it is today. It reacted vehemently to every obvious lie, to every violation of international law and of humanity, with the whole force of centuries of conviction." Zweig, *The World of Yesterday: An Autobiography*, translated by Cedar and Eden Paul (London: Cassell, 1987), 185–186.

Or for a statement that might be from the present day, there is Karl Jaspers' comment to Golo Mann in a letter dated January 25, 1947: "You point to the most paralyzing factor for the *clerc* of our epoch, namely the question: for whom do we write? . . . You know how exhilarating it is to receive even the tiniest echo, or a sign that people are expecting something from us. We seem to have been given the task of writing for a purely conceptual audience—in the hope that a real one will appear at some point. There is no audience as yet in Germany. Everything published disappears as if it had fallen into a muddy swamp; it sinks and vanishes without a ripple, as if nothing had happened. Maybe the stones will collect at the bottom and some day a tip of the mountain will show above the muck." Jaspers, *Briefwechsel 1945–1968,* ed. Renato de Rosa (Berlin: Springer, 1983). Botho Strauss speaks of an "extraction of meanings in all our values, words, and designs." *Die Fehler des Kopisten,* 103. See further Christian Meier, "Herausforderung einer Akademie in sich verändernder Zeit," *Jahrbuch der Deutschen Akademie für Sprache und Dichtung* (1997), 65ff.

"We were lacking the concepts with which to absorb what we experienced; or perhaps lacking the feelings whose magnetism sets the concepts in motion," wrote Robert Musil in 1922 ("Helpless Europe," 117). A contemporary voice asks: "What happens to the world and to people in a time when language is no longer fit for clear questions, and people cannot construct any clear questions from their language? In which many people use the language and in which the language of the people is used, but neither people nor language are capable of clear questions? What if that is not only true of me, but is also true of our time or at least people in our time?" Dževad Karahasan, *Schahrijârs Ring* (Berlin: Rowohlt, 1997; German translation of *Šahrijarov prsten* [Sarajevo: Bosanska knj., 1994]), 168. Probably a comment by Hannah Arendt also belongs in this context: "The words we use in everyday language acquire the specific weight that guides our usage and keeps us from uttering thoughtless cliches from their many associations. Such associations rise automatically and unmistakably from the store of great literature with which that particular language is blessed." Cited by Elisabeth Young-Bruehl, *Hannah Arendt: Leben, Werk und Zeit* (Frankfurt: Fischer, 1986), 18. Nomological knowledge can be upset by profound change, becoming splintered and weak—until, perhaps, a new form develops as people become used to the new situation and speed (or acceleration).

52. Quoted in Hildegard Hamm-Brücher, *Der Politiker und sein Gewissen* (Munich: Piper, 1991), 63.

53. *Gay Science,* translated by Josefine Nauckhoff and edited by Bernard Williams (Cambridge: Cambridge University Press, 2001), §196, p. 140.

54. As Goethe's character Odoardo says: "the times must come to our aid. The times must take the place of reason, and within our expanded hearts nobler motives must supplant baser ones." *Wilhelm Meister's Journeyman Years*, translated by Krishna Winston, Goethe's Collected Works, vol. 10 (New York: Suhrkamp, 1989), 382 (Book 3, Chapter 12).

55. "One could in fact already see some distance. Everything already lay very close together; sometimes all the sails were already next to one another, from Salamis and the sails of the *Mayflower* and from the regattas at Cannes," says the Ptolemaist in Benn, *Werke*, vol. 2, 234. "Continents depicted by a projection system, centuries as the shifting of clouds, fates summed up in a phrase . . . an architecture with its own balance," writes Benn in *Der Roman des Phänotyp*, ibid., 186. See also Niethammer, *Posthistoire*, 26.

56. *Histories* I, 1, 2.

57. Arendt, "Understanding and Politics," *Partisan Review* 20 (1953), 377.

2. Around 1500

1. Jacob Burckhardt, *Reflections on History*, translated by M. D. Hottinger (1943; rpt. Indianapolis: Liberty Classics, 1979), 31.

2. Ibid., 31–34.

3. Ibid., 40.

4. For more on the subject of a "special path," see Jürgen Lütt, "Eurozentrismus? Der europäische Sonderweg und der Orient," in Helga Breuninger and Rolf Peter Sieferle, eds., *Markt und Macht in der Geschichte* (Stuttgart: Deutsche Verlags-Anstalt, 1995), 97ff.

5. One could cite, for example, the surprise in many quarters at Edward Said's polemics against the distinction made between Europe and the Orient. See *Orientalism* (New York: Vintage, 1979). The book, however, contains a number of false interpretations; for more on them, see Lütt, "Eurozentrismus." Furthermore, various distinctions necessarily recur again and again: compare Ian Buruma and Avishai Margalit, "Occidentalism," *New York Review of Books*, January 17, 2002.

6. *The European Miracle: Environments, Economies, and Geopolitics in the History of Europe and Asia* (Cambridge: Cambridge University Press, 1981).

7. Max Weber, *Wirtschaft und Gesellschaft: Die Wirtschaft und die gesellschaftlichen Ordnungen und Mächte,* in *Gesamtausgabe Max Weber,* Part I, Bd. 22, Teilband 5, *Die Stadt,* ed. Wilfried Nippel (Tübingen: Mohr, 1999), 111–112, 23.

8. Musil, "Helpless Europe," translated by Philip H. Beard, in *Precision and Soul: Essays and Addresses,* ed. Burton Pike and David S. Luft (Chicago: University of Chicago Press, 1990), 121.

9. The best sources on this topic besides E. L. Jones's *The European Miracle* are probably Max Weber's *The Protestant Ethic and the Spirit of Capitalism* and Weber's other works on the sociology of religion; David Landes, *The Wealth and Poverty of Nations: Why Some Are So Rich and Some So Poor* (New York: Norton, 1998); and William H. McNeill, *The Pursuit of Power: Technology, Armed Force, and Society since A.D. 1000* (Chicago: University of Chicago Press, 1982).

10. See Günter Abramowski, *Das Geschichtsbild Max Webers* (Stuttgart: Klett, 1966), 68.

11. Landes, *Wealth and Poverty of Nations,* 45–59.

12. McNeill, *Pursuit of Power,* 45.

13. On the fleet and expedition, see Landes, *Wealth and Poverty of Nations,* 93–98; McNeill, *Pursuit of Power,* 44–46.

14. Burckhardt, *Reflections on History,* 123–124. Could it be that both the leaders and members of such a society think more about—or at least differently about—the entirety of culture and the world that are to be preserved (and in their norms for behavior) than people in modern Europe, where some at least viewed this whole more as a framework, so that more free maneuvering room was left for individuals, and more and stronger contrasts arose (along with the willingness to deal with and settle competing claims)? It would then be an interesting challenge to determine how Greek and Roman antiquity differed in this respect from both later Europe and other high cultures. Compare Burckhardt, ibid., 127.

15. McNeill, *Pursuit of Power,* 48–50.

16. Max Weber, *The Religion of China: Confucianism and Taoism,* translated and edited by Hans H. Gerth (Glencoe, Ill.: Free Press, 1951), 13–14. See also Wilfried Nippel's introduction to Max Weber, *Wirtschaft und Gesellschaft: Die Wirtschaft und die gesellschaftlichen Ordnungen und Mächte,* 20ff.

17. *Histories* I, 1ff.

18. See, for example, Eugen Wirth, "Fernhandel und Exportgewerbe im islamischen Orient," in Breuninger and Sieferle, eds., *Markt und Macht,* 122ff.

19. Burckhardt, *Reflections on History,* 333. This translation does not include the final sentence about Asia having ceased to pose a threat to Europeans: "Es ist denkbar daß Asien für Europa gestorben sei." See Burckhardt, *Über das Studium der Geschichte: Der Text der "Weltgeschichtlichen Betrachtungen" auf Grund der Vorarbeiten von Ernst Ziegler nach den Handschriften,* ed. Peter Ganz (Munich: Beck, 1982), 241. In this passage one senses the historian's horror and despair: "There are (or at any rate there seem to be) absolutely destructive forces under whose hoofs no grass grows . . . Timur in particular was horribly devasting with his pyramids of skulls and walls of lime, stone and living men. Confronted with this picture of the destroyer, as he parades his own and his people's self-seeking through the world, it is good to realize the irresistible might with which evil may at time spread over the world. In such countries, men will never again believe in right and human kindness." At the same time Burckhardt ultimately holds out "the consolation we have divined": "Yet he may have saved Europe from the Osmanlis. Imagine history without him, and Bajazet and the Hussites hurling themselves simultaneously on Germany and Italy." *Reflections on History,* 333. What a time, which had to be "consoled" about horrors of world history that had occurred more than four centuries earlier! What an awareness of history! Even if such awareness had not shrunk a great deal since then, would it have been able to "recover" from Hitler, Stalin, Pol Pot, and many others?

20. See the summary in Abramowski, *Das Geschichtsbild Max Webers,* 69.

21. Weber, *The Religion of China,* 228.

22. This is the conclusion pointed to by Marx's observation, "mankind always takes up only such problems as it can solve." Karl Marx, *A Contribution to the Critique of Political Economy,* translated by N. I. Stone (Chicago: Charles H. Kerr, 1904), 12.

23. Gottfried Schramm has endeavored to show what such a combination *can* mean, using the example of Copernicus, in "Europas vorindustrielle Modernisierung," in *Deutschland und Europa in der Neuzeit: Festschrift Karl Otmar Freiherr von Aretin* (Stuttgart: F. Steiner Verlag Wiesbaden, 1988), 214–215.

24. For more on the topic of labor, compare Christian Meier, "Arbeits-

auffassungen in archaischer und klassischer Zeit," *Berichte und Abhandlungen der Berlin-Brandenburgischen Akademie der Wissenschaften,* special issue 9 (2001), 19ff.

3. Athens and Rome

1. "Quidquid recipitur, ad modum recipientis recipitur." See Otto Bardenhewer, ed., *Die pseudo-aristotelische Schrift Ueber das reine Gute, bekannt unter den Namen "Liber de causis"* (Freiburg: Herder, 1882), prop. 10, p. 174. Many similar citations exist from the Middle Ages; see the article "Rezeption und Rezeptivität," in the *Historisches Wörterbuch der Philosophie,* ed. Joachim Ritter (Darmstadt: Wissenschaftliche Buchgesellschaft, 1971–).

2. For information on the process of cultural formation there, see Christian Meier, *Athens: A Portrait of the City in Its Golden Age,* translated by Robert and Rita Kimber (New York: Metropolitan Books, 1998), Chapter 3.

3. A good overview on Phoenician cities can be found in Wolfgang Röllig, "Phönizier und Griechen im Mittelmeerraum," in Helga Breuninger and Rolf Peter Sieferle, eds., *Markt und Macht in der Geschichte* (Stuttgart: Deutsche Verlags-Anstalt, 1995), 45ff. Jacob Burckhardt refers to them as the "first example of a free, unchecked mobility and industry." *Reflections on History,* translated by M. D. Hottinger (1943; rpt. Indianapolis: Liberty Classics, 1979), 167.

4. A great deal that would distinguish Israel in the future was not developed until the exile and afterward. It would be interesting to know whether Samuel's astounding description of the rights of a king stems from the early time (1 Samuel 8).

5. *Reflections on History,* 126.

6. In addition to the vertical solidarity that exists, say, between noblemen and their vassals or politicians and their clientele (usually in the sense of a *do ut des*), there exists the fundamental possibility of horizontal ties among, and combined efforts by, people of more or less the same social standing. Then those below oppose those above, and it becomes more important, say, for the citizens of a town to remain united than for individuals to seek advantage for themselves by cooperating with people of higher rank. This phenomenon was quite marked in Greek cities (see Meier, *Athens,* 258, 402–403). To some extent, however, co-

operation in the form of horizontal solidarity must be at work in every democracy, for there are definitely shared interests in law, having a voice, respect for the representative assembly, and so on, to which differences in particular interests ought to take a back seat.

7. Karl Reinhardt, *Von Werken und Formen* (Bad Godesberg: H. Küpper, 1948), 36.

8. See Christian Meier, "Arbeitsauffassungen in archaischer und klassischer Zeit," *Berichte und Abhandlungen der Berlin-Brandenburgischen Akademie der Wissenschaften,* special issue 9 (2001).

9. On public places and the public sphere, see Tonio Hölscher, *Öffentliche Räume in frühen griechischen Städten* (Heidelberg: Universitäts-Verlag Winter, 1998). There is no more comprehensive study available. Some observations can be found in Jacob Burckhardt, *Griechische Kulturgeschichte* (Darmstadt: Wissenschaftliche Buchgesellschaft, 1977), vol. 4, 143ff., 243.

10. See Christian Meier, *The Greek Discovery of Politics,* translated by David McLintock (Cambridge, Mass.: Harvard University Press, 1990), 82–87; Meier, "Die Griechen—die politische Revolution der Weltgeschichte," *Saeculum* 33 (1982), 133ff.; the section "Die Entstehung einer autonomen Intelligenz bei den Griechen," in Meier, *Die Welt der Geschichte und die Provinz des Historikers* (Berlin: Wagenbach, 1989), 70ff.

11. For more on Solon, see Christian Meier, *Athens,* 57–71. For Anaximander, see Jean-Pierre Vernant, *The Origins of Greek Thought* (Ithaca, N.Y.: Cornell University Press, 1982), 119–127.

12. Fragment 16, in Ernst Diehl, ed., *Anthologia lyrica Graeca* (Leipzig: Teubner, 1954–).

13. See Christian Meier, *Politik und Anmut,* revised ed. (Stuttgart: Hohenheim Verlag, 2000).

14. Burckhardt returned again and again to Athens and Florence, the two "great centers of intellectual exchange" and breeding grounds of culture. See *Reflections on History,* 100–101, 169–171. "These places produced from among their own citizens a disproportionate number of great individuals, through whom they continue to act on the world. That is not the result of 'great educational facilities,' as in the big or even middle-sized cities of our day; all 'great educational facilities' can produce their inflated nonentities . . . and beyond that, mere universal faultfinding. What happened was the stimulation of supreme powers by the exceptional" (p. 101).

15. The phrase quoted is found in a copy of "Reflections on World History" made by A. von Salis. See Peter Ganz, ed., *Über das Studium der Geschichte: Der Text der 'Weltgeschichtlichen Betrachtungen' auf Grund der Vorarbeiten von Ernst Ziegler nach den Handschriften* (Munich: Beck, 1982), 514–515. It is thus possible that Burckhardt's remarks are not reproduced with complete accuracy. However, clear parallels to the hypothesis stated there can be found elsewhere in Burckhardt's work, for example, "Never again have people felt such a pressing need for poetry" (referring to bards), *Griechische Kulturgeschichte*, 2, 36. There we also find the observation: "Nothing is more alien to us than a people that asks not about the news of the day, but eagerly insists on hearing a detailed account of the gods and heroes, which have remained sketchy and frightening, even though they are the people's own creation. How beautiful and full of life they are in these presentations!"

16. See *Die unheimliche Klassik der Griechen* (Bamberg: C. C. Buchners, 1989), 26. Hölscher's book is probably the most important statement on the topic in recent years.

17. *Reflections on History*, 250.

18. For the aspects that are important to me in this context, see Christian Meier, *The Political Art of Greek Tragedy*, translated by Andrew Webber (Cambridge: Polity, 1993), and Meier, *Athens*.

19. This is probably correct, even if in another genre, the discipline of history (despite all "suppositions of meaning" that still play a role in it, and have since ancient times), the scholarly principle of following strictly what can be discovered by empirical methods predominates, and in particular the insight that much in history depends on contingencies. See Christian Meier, *Die Entstehung des Politischen bei den Griechen* (Frankfurt: Suhrkamp, 1980), 395–401.

20. *Reflections on History*, 128.

21. Plato, Letter 7, 325e, in *The Collected Dialogues of Plato*, ed. Edith Hamilton and Huntington Cairns (Princeton, N.J.: Princeton University Press, 1963), 1575.

22. See Paul Zanker, *The Power of Images in the Age of Augustus* (Ann Arbor: University of Michigan Press, 1988).

23. Paul Veyne, ed., *Vom Römischen Imperium zum Byzantinischen Reich*, vol. 1 of *Geschichte des privaten Lebens* (Frankfurt: S. Fischer, 1989), 15.

24. Luke 14, 26.

25. Max Weber, *Ancient Judaism,* translated and edited by Hans H. Gerth and Don Martindale (Glencoe, Ill.: The Free Press, 1952), 4. For more detailed discussions of Weber's views, see Wayne A. Meeks, "Die Rolle des paulinischen Christentums bei der Entstehung einer rationalen ethischen Religion," in Wolfgang Schluchter, ed., *Max Webers Sicht des antiken Christentums* (Frankfurt: Suhrkamp, 1985), 363–385; and John G. Gager, "Paulus und das antike Judentum: Eine Kritik an Max Webers Interpretation," in ibid., 386–403.

26. Ernst Schulin reports that Herbert Spencer was of this opinion. See Schulin, "Das alte und neue Problem der Weltgeschichte als Kulturgeschichte," *Saeculum* 33 (1982), 164. Looking at the quotation Schulin cites in context, however, one finds that Spencer was only objecting to claims regarding the high value of a classical (as opposed to a scientific) education: "Had Greece and Rome never existed, human life, and the right conduct of it, would have been in their essentials exactly what they now are: survival or death, health or disease, prosperity or adversity, happiness or misery, would have been just in the same ways determined by the adjustment or non-adjustment of actions to requirements." Spencer, *Autobiography* (London: Williams and Norgate, 1904), vol. 2, 37. In general, continuing influences of antiquity should not be seen only in the adoption of direct models, the view taken by M. I. Finley, for example, in *The Legacy of Greece: A New Appraisal* (Oxford: Oxford University Press, 1981).

27. Veyne, ed., *Vom Römischen Imperium zum Byzantinischen Reich,* 16.

28. President Mbeki of South Africa recently posed this question during a state visit, noting that the only thing the Chinese admiral Cheng Ho had taken from Africa was animals for the emperor's zoo.

29. *Reflections on History,* 46.

30. Nietzsche, *We Philologists,* no. 116, *The Complete Works of Friedrich Nietzsche,* ed. Oscar Levy (New York: Russell and Russell, 1964), vol. 8, 159. See also no. 29, where Nietzsche notes a "preference for antiquity," which has "arisen from prejudices," including "a false idealisation of humanitarianism, whilst Hindoos and Chinese are at all events more humane"; ibid., 127.

4. Deeds and Contingencies, Politics and Processes

1. "Chains of interdependence become more differentiated and grow longer; consequently they become more opaque and, for any single

group or individual, more uncontrollable." Norbert Elias, *What Is Sociology?*, translated by Stephen Mennell and Grace Morrissey (London: Hutchinson, 1978), 68. See also 96–97, 132–133, and 140–142.

2. Christian Meier, *Res publica amissa: Eine Studie zu Verfassung und Geschichte der späten römischen Republik*, 3rd ed. (Frankfurt: Suhrkamp, 1997), 159–160, xlvi. For more on the context of the crisis without an alternative, see ibid., xliii–liii and 201–205.

3. Reinhart Koselleck, "On the Disposability of History," in Koselleck, *Futures Past*, translated by Keith Tribe (Cambridge, Mass.: MIT Press, 1985), 211.

4. The German joke depends on the fact that the verb *denken* ("think") is irregular, while *lenken* ("guide," "steer") is regular. The correct past tenses are *dachte* and *lenkte*, but if, like little Johnny, you use the parallel form *lachte*, you have the past tense of the verb "to laugh."—translator's note.

5. Meier, *Die Entstehung des Politischen bei den Griechen* (Frankfurt: Suhrkamp, 1980), 327ff., 334, 384–385, 388ff., 419ff. Another view is presented in Jan Assmann, *Das kulturelle Gedächtnis: Schrift, Erinnerung und politische Identität in frühen Hochkulturen* (Munich: Beck, 1992). But Assmann confuses a king's account of his reign with the understanding of history. Compare Christian Meier, "Aktueller Bedarf an historischen Vergleichen: Überlegungen aus dem Fach der Alten Geschichte," in Heinz-Gerhard Haupt and Jürgen Kocka, eds., *Geschichte und Vergleich* (Frankfurt: Campus, 1996), 248ff.

6. Georg Büchner, letter to Wilhelmine Jaeglé, 1834, in Büchner, *Complete Works and Letters*, translated by Henry J. Schmidt, vol. 28 of The German Library (New York: Continuum, 1986), 260. How modest Herodotus seems by contrast: "chance controls men rather than men controlling chance" (Book 7, 49, 3); "there's no more terrible pain a man can endure than to see clearly and be able to do nothing" (Book 9, 16, 5). See Herodotus, *The Histories*, translated by Robin Waterfield (Oxford: Oxford University Press, 1998), 425 and 547.

7. Letter to Joseph Bloch from September 12–22, 1890, in *Marx Engels Werke*, vol. 37 (Berlin: Dietz, 1967), 464.

8. "Zur preußischen Verfassungsfrage," *Deutsche Vierteljahrs Schrift*, 1852, no. 1, 1. Compare also Rainer Specht: "The popular trend to democratization assumes that individual participation can be significantly extended with regard to both information and decision-making, but as the size and complexity of information mechanisms in-

crease, the relative average information of individuals decreases, and as the socialization of political decisions increases, the average weight of political decisions by individuals inevitably decreases as well." Specht, *Innovation und Folgelast* (Stuttgart–Bad Cannstatt: Frommann-Holzboog, 1972), 226–227.

9. Friedrich Engels, *Herrn Eugen Dürings Umwälzung der Wissenschaft* (1878; rpt. Berlin: Dietz, 1948), 351. Compare the prognosis from the year 1895, that the Germans who voted for the Social Democrats "will grow into the decisive power in the country, as spontaneously, as unstoppably, and at the same time so quietly . . . as a process in nature, and all other forces will have to bow down before it, whether they want to or not." Introduction to Karl Marx, *Klassenkämpfe in Frankreich,* in *Marx Engels Werke,* vol. 22 (Berlin: Dietz, 1963), 524.

10. Armand Jean du Plessis, duc de Richelieu, *Political Testament of Cardinal Richelieu: The Significant Chapters and Supporting Selections,* translated by Henry Bertram Hill (Madison: University of Wisconsin Press, 1961), 82–83 (Part 2, Chapter 4).

11. The first quotation is from Otto von Bismarck, *Die gesammelten Werke* (Berlin: Stolberg, 1924–), vol. 13, 304. The second comes from a letter to his wife, Johanna, dated March 23, 1887. See Otto Vossler, "Bismarcks Ethos," *Geist und Geschichte: Von der Reformation bis zur Gegenwart* (Munch: Piper, 1964), 253. "My influence on the events that have carried me is indeed overestimated, but certainly no one will assume that I can make history happen." Speech of April 16, 1869, in *Die Gesammelten Werke,* vol. 11, 37ff. "One cannot make history, but one can learn from it how one should conduct the political life of a great nation according to its development and its historical mission." Address of July 20, 1892, in ibid., vol 13, 668ff., also in H. Rothfels, ed., *Bismarck und der Staat* (Darmstadt: 1958), 86.

12. Adolf Hitler, *Speeches and Proclamations, 1932–1945: The Chronicle of a Dictatorship,* vol. 1, edited by Max Domarus and translated by Mary Fran Gilbert (London: I. B. Tauris, 1990), 214. In September 1935 Hitler said in a speech: "We . . . have been chosen by Fate to make history in the loftiest sense of the word. What millions of people are deprived of has been given to us by Providence. Even the most distant posterity will be reminded of us by our work." *Speeches and Proclamations,* vol. 2 (1992), 711.

13. Hitler, ibid., vol. 2, 1057.

14. Hans-Ulrich Thamer, *Verführung und Gewalt: Deutschland 1933–1945* (Berlin: Siedler, 1986), 577.
15. Quoted in ibid., 572.
16. Heinrich von Treitschke, *Deutsche Geschichte*, vol 1., 2d ed. (Leipzig: 1879), 28; *Politik: Vorlesungen gehalten an der Universität zu Berlin*, vol. 1, 2d ed. (Leipzig: 1899), 6; vol. 2, 2d ed. (1900), 59–60. See also Alfred Heuss, *Gesammelte Schriften* (Stuttgart: F. Steiner, 1995), vol. 1, 222.
17. One need only recall the many occasions when political leaders declare that some event is "historic." Is this a kind of flight from the lack of profundity in the present to the textbooks of the future?
18. For more on the notions of Providence and Fate, see Rainer Lepsius, *Demokratie in Deutschland* (Göttingen: Vandenhoeck & Ruprecht, 1963), 242, and Alfred Heuss, *Versagen und Verhängnis: vom Ruin deutscher Geschichte und ihres Verständnisses* (Berlin: Siedler, 1984).
19. Karl Marx, "The Eighteenth Brumaire of Louis Bonaparte," in *Later Political Writings*, edited and translated by Terrell Carver (Cambridge: Cambridge University Press, 1996), 32.
20. See Pericles' plan for a war that might last a long time (Thucydides 1, 141, 2ff.; 2, 13, 2ff.), a war that in Thucydides' view had every prospect of success, being well calculated and based on superior numbers (2, 65; compare also 7, 28, 3). All the same Thucydides was well aware of the role that chance can play in battle (for instance, 1, 78, 1; 1, 122, 1; for the war itself, 2, 61, 3). He also stresses in the debates he reproduces the ever-present difference between planning and outcome. Clearly, in his view the superiority of troops and calculation on the Athenian side was so great that even a whole series of unfortunate accidents would not have led to their defeat. For the Achilles heel of these plans, see Christian Meier, *Athens: A Portrait of the City in Its Golden Age*, translated by Robert and Rita Kimber (New York: Metropolitan Books/H. Holt and Co., 1998), 457–460.
21. For more on this topic, see Assmann, *Das kulturelle Gedächtnis*.
22. The unlikelihood of such a history is underscored by the few exceptions, such as Aristotle's account of the relationship between constitutional history and demography, and that between the composition and orientation of the citizenry and the organization of the army. *Politics* 1286b 8ff., 1297b 16ff.
23. *Politics* 1261a 39.

24. *Athenaion Politeia* 8, 5. For more on Solon's efforts, see Christian Meier, "Die Gewalt und das Politische," *Berlin-Brandenburgische Akademie der Wissenschaften*, Jahrbuch 1994, 179; *Athens*, 57–71.

25. Immanuel Kant, "Idea for a Universal History from a Cosmopolitan Point of View," in *Selections*, ed. Lewis White Beck (New York: Macmillan, 1998), 415–416.

26. As Alexis de Tocqueville observed, "Everywhere we look, the various events of people's lives have turned to the advantage of democracy: all men have helped its progress . . . both those who fought on its behalf and those who were its declared opponents . . . and everyone has joined the common cause, some despite themselves, others unwittingly, like blind instruments in the hands of God." Tocqueville, *Democracy in America and Two Essays on America*, translated by Gerald Bevan (London: Penguin, 2003), 14.

27. Christian Meier, "Fragen und Thesen zu einer Theorie historischer Prozesse," in Karl-Georg Faber and Christian Meier, eds., *Historische Prozesse: Theorie der Geschichte, Beiträge zur Historik* (Munich: Deutscher Taschenbuch-Verlag, 1978), vol. 2, 41–42.

28. Adam Ferguson, *An Essay on the History of Civil Society*, ed. Fania Oz-Salzberger (Cambridge: Cambridge University Press, 1995), 119.

29. Statistics played a role in observing this great difference, as Kant noted in his "Idea for a Universal History from a Cosmopolitan Point of View," 415. Other factors included the devaluation of action, experiences of the enormous potential of productive labor, and breakthroughs in knowledge and practical technology, among many others—creating a cumulative effect that deserves further study. Much that is characteristic of antiquity would emerge far more clearly from a contrast with these developments. Hannah Arendt discusses the subject in *Fragwürdige Traditionsbestände im politischen Denken der Gegenwart* (Frankfurt: 1957), especially pages 110ff., and in *Vita activa* (Stuttgart: Kohlhammer, 1960).

30. Albert O. Hirschman, *The Passions and the Interests: Political Arguments for Capitalism before Its Triumph* (Princeton, N.J.: Princeton University Press, 1977). He discusses Vico, Mandeville, Smith, Kant, and Hegel, among others.

31. A particularly good example of the conviction that the *demos* did possess virtue is provided by Pericles' eulogy for the fallen in Thucydides, 2, 36ff.

32. See especially "The History of Subordination," section 2 of Part 3 of *An Essay on the History of Civil Society,* 118–131.
33. See Hannah Arendt, "Das Entstehen der Gesellschaft" (the emergence of society), in *Vita activa,* 38–40.
34. For more on the distinction between *Historie* and *Geschichte,* see the article "Geschichte, Historie" in O. Brunner, W. Conze, and Reinhart Koselleck, eds., *Geschichtliche Grundbegriffe: Historisches Lexikon zur politisch-sozialen Sprache in Deutschland* (Stuttgart: Klett, 1975), vol. 2, 593.
35. "Idea for a Universal History from a Cosmopolitan Point of View," 423.
36. "That here an uninterrupted continuity of work may exist and remain; that every insight, once gained, is retained in human consciousness; that the community of the learned and those striving for knowledge, in which every one may have only a grain of sand to add to the great structure, feels itself united and preserves the knowledge it has acquired, in order to build on it further." Johann Gustav Droysen, *Historik,* ed. Peter Leyh (Stuttgart–Bad Canstatt: Frommann-Holzboog, 1977), vol. 1, 326.
37. This holds even if things then turn out as General von Stumm observes in Robert Musil's novel: "I'm a member of a ministerial council. At a meeting everyone proposes what he likes and thinks right, and in the end something comes out that no one really wanted, the so-called outcome. I don't know if you follow me—I can't express it any better." Musil, *The Man without Qualities,* translated by Sophie Wilkins (New York: Knopf, 1995), vol. 2, 844.
38. As one of Goethe's characters says in *Elective Affinities,* "It is terrible that one can't learn anything for life anymore . . . Our ancestors held firm to what they had learned in their youth; but we have to learn everything over again every five years if we are not to be totally behind the times." Johann Wolfgang von Goethe, "Elective Affinities," translated by Judith Ryan, in *The Sorrows of Young Werther; Elective Affinities; Novella,* Goethe's Collected Works, vol. 11 (New York: Suhrkamp, 1988), 113. However, the proportions of what changed and what remained the same were different in that era. In general, the following holds: "No details could be adduced that would not also have been possible before, but all the relationships had shifted a little." Musil, *The Man without Qualities,* vol. 1, 56.

39. Jacob Burckhardt wrote: "Only the study of the past can provide us with a standard by which to measure the rapidity and strength of the particular movement in which we live." *Reflections on History,* translated by M. D. Hottinger (1943; rpt. Indianapolis: Liberty Classics, 1979), 46.

40. Machiavelli, "Discourses," book 3, 43, in *The Chief Works and Others,* translated by Allan Gilbert (Durham, N.C.: Duke University Press, 1965), vol. 1, 521.

41. See *Res publica amissa,* and Christian Meier, *Caesar,* translated by David McLintock (London: HarperCollins, 1995), 190–203, 349–363,

42. "It [i.e., morality] next subsided in ever greater collapse and then began to topple headlong in ruin—until the advent of our modern age, in which we can endure neither our vices nor the remedies needed to cure them." Livy, Preface, *The Rise of Rome: Books One to Five,* translated and edited by T. J. Luce (Oxford: Oxford University Press, 1998), 4.

43. That is probably not a matter of the possible conceptions, but rather of the possible positions. If there is no power (alternative) that can make the structural change its cause—or, to put it differently, as long as no massing of discontent occurs—the order itself can hardly be put on the agenda. Of necessity, everything will remain as it is. What Jacob Burckhardt observes for castes and the old French aristocracy probably also holds true, for example, for "two-thirds societies" (i.e., modern advanced societies where two-thirds of the population is affluent, while one-third remains un- or under-employed): they are "absolutely incorrigible even when a large number of their members clearly see the abyss. For the moment it is more unpleasant to join forces with men of like mind and be doomed to *certain* destruction than to have the feeling that a cataclysm *may* come." *Reflections on History,* 225. Individual statements and actions, however, are less important in this context than particular constellations. What it means when a republic exhausts itself in everyday matters—when the order that is wearing down cannot be placed on the agenda (so that the majority can express its wish to preserve it)—can be studied especially well in Cicero's thinking and despair in the late Roman Republic. See "Cicero: Das erfolgreiche Scheitern des Neulings in der alten Republik," in Christian Meier, *Die Ohnmacht des allmächtigen Dictators Caesar: Drei biographische Skizzen* (Frankfurt: Suhrkamp, 1980), 103ff.

44. That a world government is not a particularly promising possibility, if

it is possible at all (especially against the will of the only remaining world power, which can consequently do whatever it likes), was recently demonstrated concisely and incisively by Wolfgang Sofsky, "Globale Illusionen," *Universitas* 57 (Stuttgart, 2002), no. 1, 83ff.

5. Auschwitz

1. Wilhelm von Humboldt, "Über die Aufgabe des Geschichtsschreibers," *Werke* (Stuttgart: Cotta, 1960), vol. 1, 590.
2. Friedrich Nietzsche, *Gay Science*, translated by Josefine Nauckhoff and edited by Bernard Williams (Cambridge: Cambridge University Press, 2001), §34, p. 53.
3. Compare Christian Meier, *Vierzig Jahre nach Auschwitz*, 2d expanded ed. (Munich: Beck, 1990), 38ff.
4. Dolf Sternberger, "Unverstehbar—Noch einmal: Noltes These," *Frankfurter Allgemeine Zeitung*, April 6, 1988. Compare the line in Lessing's play *Emilia Galotti*: "whoever does not lose his mind over certain things, does not have a mind to lose" (Act 4, Scene 7). See Gotthold Ephraim Lessing, *Nathan the Wise, Minna von Bernhelm, and Other Plays and Writings*, ed. Peter Demetz (New York: Continuum, 1991), 122.
5. Sternberger is here using the German word *verstehen*, "to understand," in the special limited sense of "to feel empathy," "to be able to put oneself in someone else's place," as in the saying *alles verstehen heißt alles verzeihen*, "to understand everything is to forgive everything."—translator's note.
6. "Unzusammenhängende Notizen über Geschichte," *Merkur* 41 (1987), 737.
7. Martin Broszat, *Nach Hitler: Der schwierige Umgang mit unserer Geschichte* (Munich: 1986), 100 and 161. Iring Fetscher expresses a similar thought in Jürgen Habermas, ed., *Stichworte zur "Geistigen Situation der Zeit"* (Frankfurt: Suhrkamp, 1979), vol. 1, 121: "No matter whether we are historians or sociologists, we have analyzed fascism as if it were a phenomenon of some remote civilization with hardly any relevance to ourselves."
8. Arendt, "Understanding and Politics," *Partisan Review* 20 (1953), 377 and 383.
9. Ibid., 382.

10. Maurice Merleau-Ponty, *Humanism and Terror: An Essay on the Communist Problem*, translated by John O'Neill (Westport, Conn.: Greenwood Press, 1980), xxv.

11. I have borrowed this phrase from Rudolf Pfisterer, "Geburtsurkunde als Todesurteil," *Treffpunkte* 115 (1990). See also Christian Meier, "Verurteilen und Verstehen," in R. Augstein et al., eds., *Historikerstreit* (Munich: Piper, 1987), 48ff.

12. *Commandant of Auschwitz: The Autobiography of Rudolf Höss*, translated by Constantine FitzGibbon (London: Weidenfeld and Nicolson, 1959), 197–198.

13. Broszat, *Nach Hitler*, 195ff.

14. Martin Broszat, *The Hitler State: The Foundation and Development of the Internal Structure of the Third Reich*, translated by John W. Hiden (London: Longman, 1981), 353–354.

15. Quite notable remarks on this ability, which we still possess today (and which is often necessary for survival), can be found in Robert Musil's essay from 1921, "Nation as Ideal and Reality," in Musil, *Precision and Soul: Essays and Addresses*, ed. Burton Pike and David S. Luft (Chicago: University of Chicago Press, 1990), 101–115. But what Hannah Arendt wrote remains valid: "What first appeared to the victims and survivors as a shameful failure has now become clear to the entire world: the frightening indifference, the rigid adherence to political rules of behavior, which had long since lost their validity in view of the total collapse of moral and intellectual order in Europe." In such a situation even good people could do the worst, but certainly not the best thing. They decided in favor of the lesser evil, without realizing that this cannot lead to anything good. Quoted in Elisabeth Young-Bruehl, *Hannah Arendt: Leben, Werk und Zeit* (Frankfurt: 1986), 539.

16. Victor Klemperer, *I Will Bear Witness: A Diary of the Nazi Years*, 2 vols., translated by Martin Chalmers (New York: Random House, 1998–1999).

17. Quoted in Max Domarus, *Hitler: Speeches and Proclamations 1932–1945*, translated by Chris Wilcox (Würzburg: Domarus Verlag, and Wauconda, Ill.: Bolchazy-Carducci, 1997), vol. 3, 1449.

18. After conquering Poland, the Germans annexed the western part of the country, naming it the *Warthegau*. (A *Gau* was an administrative district within the Reich.) They established a "General Government" for the rest of Poland. One of the most important books on "resettlement"

policy is Götz Aly, *"Final Solution": Nazi Population Policy and the Murder of the European Jews,* translated by Belinda Cooper and Allison Brown (London: Arnold, 1999).

19. Ibid., 215.
20. Ibid., 221.
21. Ibid., 214.
22. "SS" refers to *Schutzstaffel,* that is, "protective echelon," the elite armed corps of the National Socialist Party.—translator's note.
23. Höss, *Commandant of Auschwitz,* 165.
24. Quoted in Eberhard Jäckel, *A Blueprint for Power,* translated by Herbert Arnold (Middletown, Conn.: Wesleyan University Press, 1972), 66.
25. Tzvetan Todorov, *Facing the Extreme: Moral Life in the Concentration Camps,* translated by Arthur Denner and Abigail Pollack (New York: Metropolitan, 1996), 153–154 and 128–129.
26. Quoted in ibid., 151.
27. Anton Schmid was an Austrian who ran a small radio shop in Vienna before being drafted into the German army. He was posted in Wilnius (Lithuania) where between late summer 1941 and January 1942 he hired more than a hundred Jewish men for an army workshop, thereby saving them from execution. He also requisitioned army trucks and personally drove some 300 people to other cities where Jews were not yet being rounded up. His efforts were discovered, and he was executed by firing squad in April 1942. Sergeant Schmid is remembered as one of the righteous Gentiles at the Yad Vashem memorial in Israel, and in 2000 a German army base in Rendsburg, Schleswig-Holstein, was named after him.—translator's note.
28. G. M. Gilbert, *Nuremberg Diary* (1947; rpt. New York: Da Capo, 1995).
29. Christopher Browning, *Ordinary Men: Reserve Police Battalion 101 and the Final Solution in Poland* (1992; reissued New York: Harper-Perennial, 1998).
30. Quoted in Todorov, *Facing the Extreme,* 125.
31. Georg Büchner, *Danton's Death,* in *Complete Works and Letters,* translated by Henry J. Schmidt, vol. 28 of *The German Library* (New York: Continuum, 1986), 90.
32. Todorov, *Facing the Extreme.* The book has a section called "Fragmentation," at 141–157; the quotation is from page 143.

33. Robert Musil, "Helpless Europe," translated by Philip H. Beard, in *Precision and Soul*, 117.
34. Max Weber, *Wirtschaft und Gesellschaft*, 5th ed. (Tübingen: Mohr, 1972), 562.
35. Jacob Burckhardt, *Reflections on History*, translated by M. D. Hottinger (1943; rpt. Indianapolis: Liberty Classics, 1979), 102–103.
36. Walter Benjamin, "Über den Begriff der Geschichte," *Gesammelte Schriften*, vol. 1, part 2 (Frankfurt: Suhrkamp, 1974), 697.
37. Höss, *Commandant of Auschwitz*, 149.
38. Todorov, *Facing the Extreme*, 148–149.
39. Imre Kertész, *Galeerentagebuch* (Berlin: Rowohlt, 1993), 163.
40. Yosef H. Yerushalmi, *Zakhor: Jewish History and Jewish Memory* (Seattle: University of Washington Press), 1996.
41. See, for example, W. G. Sebald's work on a similar topic, *On the Natural History of Destruction*, translated by Anthea Bell (New York: Random House, 2003). An extreme example of how the air raids can be depicted is Gert Ledig's novel *Payback*, translated by Shaun Whiteside (London: Granta, 2003).
42. Peter Reichel, *Politik mit der Erinnerung: Gedächtnisorte im Streit um die Nationalsozialistische Vergangenheit* (Munich: Hanser, 1995), 215.
43. Kertész, *Eine Gedankenlänge Stille, während das Erschiessungskommando neu lädt* (Reinbek bei Hamburg: Rowohlt, 1999), 21.
44. Ibid., 68.
45. Imre Kertész, "Die exilierte Sprache, *Frankfurter Allgemeine Zeitung,* November 6, 2000.
46. For more on the problem of remembering, forgetting, and repression, see Christian Meier, "Zum öffentlichen Umgang mit schlimmer Vergangenheit in Geschichte und Gegenwart," in *Berichte und Abhandlungen der Berlin-Brandenburgischen Akademie der Wissenschaften* 3 (Berlin: 1997), 59ff. For more on what has and has not been achieved, see Peter Steinbach, *Nationalsozialistische Gewaltverbrechen und die Diskussion in der deutschen Öffentlichekeit nach 1945* (Berlin: Colloquium, 1981); Christian Meier, *Vierzig Jahre nach Auschwitz.*
47. "Because it is unbearable to think the tiny word 'I' in connection with the word 'Auschwitz.' 'I' in the past conditional: I would have. I might have. I could have. Done it. Obeyed orders." Christa Wolf, *A Model Childhood*, translated by Ursule Molinaro and Hedwig Rappolt (New York: Farrar, Straus and Giroux, 1980), 230. For a longer discussion of

the subject, see Christian Meier, "Die andere Mauer in den deutschen Köpfen," *Das Verschwinden der Gegenwart* (Munich: Hanser, 2001), 36ff.

48. The German translation of Daniel Jonah Goldhagen's book *Hitler's Willing Executioners* was published in August 1996, and in September Goldhagen toured Germany to promote it. His speaking engagements, interviews, and appearances on television generated an enormous amount of debate in the country.—translator's note.

49. For more on this, see Harald Welzer, "Stille Post: Tückische Erinnerung—Die Nazizeit im Familiengespräch," *Frankfurter Allgemeine Zeitung*, November 25, 2000.

50. A comment by Imre Kertész on this topic: "'Did the German population know about the concentration camps?' What a question! It's something for scholars to debate. What does it mean, to 'know about' something? As time passes, of course, it comes to mean something completely different. But as long as it is the norm for people to be stripped of their possessions, terrorized, drafted, and made to serve as soldiers; as long as they are put in prison, given limited access to consumer goods and nothing to eat; as long as their houses are being bombed—in short, as long as all of life is abnormal, abnormal phenomena fit easily into the natural order of the abnormal. Later, it turns out that knowing about certain things represents a form of guilt, so one's memory begins to change, and in the light of the altered memories knowledge changes as well. Thus it becomes possible for a person not to have known about anything. And perhaps he is not even telling a lie; he is simply considering what he did not do during the time in question, what he could not do, because his consciousness was different then and hence also his knowledge.—But can you explain that to a scholar, to a scholar of *history*?" *Galeerentagebuch*, 164.

51. Musil wrote of the *Weg der kleinsten Schritte*, "the path of the smallest steps," in a posthumously published fragment, "Theoretisches zu dem Leben eines Dichters," in *Tagebücher, Aphorismen, Essays und Reden*, ed. Adolf Frisé (Hamburg: Rowohlt, 1955), 811.

52. Kertész, "Die exilierte Sprache."

53. Kertész, *Eine Gedankenlänge Stille*, 22.

54. Hannah Arendt, *Fragwürdige Traditionsbestände im politischen Denken der Gegenwart* (Frankfurt: Europäische Verlags-Anstalt, 1957), 109.

55. Thomas Nipperdey, *Nachdenken über die deutsche Geschichte* (Munich: Beck, 1986), 186.
56. One could apply to it—as to all history—Jacob Burckhardt's observation that "anyone who cannot look at good and bad together (in sum: living things and fate) should leave history alone and read novels that always end happily." *Über das Studium der Geschichte: Der Text der "Weltgeschichtlichen Betrachtungen" auf Grund der Vorarbeiten von Ernst Ziegler nach den Handschriften,* ed. Peter Ganz (Munich: Beck, 1982), 127.
57. Raymond Aron, *Dimensions de la Conscience Historique* (Paris: Plon, 1961), 180.
58. Hilde Domin, a poet who has received many awards, was born into a Jewish family in Cologne in 1909. She left Germany in 1932 and completed a doctorate in political science in Italy. She spent the 1940s in the Dominican Republic, where she taught and began writing poetry. She took her *nom de plume* from the city of Santo Domingo, where she lived. Domin and her husband returned to Germany in 1954.—translator's note.

6. A Legacy without Heirs?

1. Peter Esterházy, *Thomas Mann mampft Kebab am Fusse des Holstentors: Geschichten und Aufsätze,* translated by Zsuszanna Gahse (Salzburg: Residenz, 1999), 137.
2. "The belief in civilization is a Eurocentric myth, one in which the modern era worships itself. It lacks a real foundation. Before they were exterminated, 'savage' peoples were by no means savage, as this myth claims, and 'civilized' peoples are nothing like as tame as they would like to see themselves. Butchering people in large numbers is no privilege of earlier eras. Violence is the fate of the species. What changes is just the forms it takes, the times and places, the technical efficiency, the institutional framework, and its legitimatory meaning." Wolfgang Sofsky, *Traktat über die Gewalt* (Frankfurt: S. Fischer, 1996), 224.
3. Thucydides, *History of the Pelopennesian War,* Book 5, Chapter 17.
4. Xenophon, *A History of My Times (Hellenica),* translated by Rex Warner (1966; New York: Penguin, 1979), 104.
5. This word means "offense" in ancient Greek.—translator's note.
6. For more on the subject of rationalization, see Friedrich H. Tenbruck,

"Das Werk Max Webers," *Kölner Zeitschrift für Soziologie und Sozial-psychologie* 27 (1975), 669ff.; Stefan Kalberg, "Max Webers Typen der Rationalität: Grundsteine für eine Analyse von Rationalisierungs-Prozessen in der Geschichte," in W. Sprondel and C. Seyfarth, eds., *Max Weber und die Rationalisierung sozialen Handelns* (Stuttgart: Ferdinand Enke, 1981), 9ff.

7. Max Weber, *The Protestant Ethic and the Spirit of Capitalism*, translated by Talcott Parsons, 2d ed. (London: Allen & Unwin, 1976), 182.

8. Ibid., 181.

9. Jacob Burckhardt, *Reflections on History*, translated by M. D. Hottinger (1943; rpt. Indianapolis: Liberty Classics, 1979), 88.

10. Ibid., 103.

11. Ibid.

12. "Sebastian Haffner" is the pseudonym of Raimund Pretzel (1907–1999), a lawyer who left Germany in 1938. He settled in London, where he became a successful journalist and author. In order not to endanger his family he began writing as "Sebastian Haffner," a name he then retained. He is the author of *The Meaning of Hitler* (1979) and *Defying Hitler: A Memoir* (2003).—translator's note.

13. Sebatian Haffner, *Defying Hitler: A Memoir*, translated by Oliver Pretzel (London: Weidenfeld & Nicolson, 2002), 119–123.

14. Friedrich Nietzsche, *Thus Spake Zarathustra: A Book for All and None*, translated by Thomas Common, revised by Oscar Levy and John L. Beevers (London: G. Allen & Unwin, 1967), 10.

15. Robert Musil, "Helpless Europe," translated by Philip H. Beard, in Musil, *Precision and Soul: Essays and Addresses,* ed. Burton Pike and David S. Luft (Chicago: University of Chicago Press, 1990), 120–121.

16. "The New Man who is produced in this process is . . . at any given moment the non-prestructured product of the process-progress set in motion and kept functioning by himself." Carl Schmitt, *Politische Theologie II: Die Legende von der Erledigung jeder politischen Theologie* (Berlin: Duncker & Humblot, 1970), 125.

17. Friedrich Schiller, *On the Aesthetic Education of Man: In a Series of Letters,* translated by Elizabeth M. Wilkinson and L. A. Willoughby (Oxford: Clarendon Press, 1967), eleventh and twelfth letters, 73–83.

18. Theodor Adorno, "Glosse über Persönlichkeit," *Kulturkritik und Gesellschaft*, Gesammelte Schriften, vol. 10, part 2 (Frankfurt: Suhrkamp, 1977), 643–644.

232 · Notes to Pages 183–185

19. Let me recall here two contrasting images that once had something going for them. First, as the "good old man" says to Wilhelm Meister: "My domestic equipment excites your attention. You see here how long a thing may last; and one should make such observations now and then, by way of counterbalance to so much in the world that rapidly changes and passes away. This same tea-kettle served my parents, and was a witness of our evening family assemblages; this copper fire-screen still guards me from the fire, which these stout old tongs still help me to mend; and so it is with all throughout. I had it in my power to bestow my care and industry on many other things, as I did not occupy myself with changing these external necessaries, a task which consumes so many people's time and resources . . . Tenacity of our possessions . . . in many cases gives us the greatest energy." Wilhelm replies: "Yet you will confess . . . that no man withstands the change which time produces." "That, in truth! (the old man then says) . . . but he who holds out longest has still done something. Yes! even beyond the limits of our being we are able to maintain and secure; we transmit discoveries, we hand down sentiments as well as property." Johann Wolfgang von Goethe, *Wilhelm Meister's Travels,* translated by Thomas Carlyle (Boston: Ticknor and Fields, 1865), vol. 2, 239–240 (Chapter 9). And, second, an observation by Friedrich Nietzsche: "history belongs to the preserving and revering soul—to him who with loyalty and love looks back on his origins; through this reverence he, as it were, gives thanks for his existence. By tending with loving hands what has long survived he intends to preserve the conditions in which he grew up for those who will come after him—and so he serves life." *On the Advantage and Disadvantage of History for Life,* translated by Peter Preuss (Indianapolis: Hackett, 1980), 19 (opening of §3).

20. Musil, *The Man without Qualities,* translated by Sophie Wilkins (New York: Knopf, 1995), vol. 1, 443.

21. Compare Benjamin's "angel of history": Walter Benjamin, "On the Concept of History," paragraph ix, in *Selected Writings* (Cambridge, Mass.: Belknap Press, 1996–), vol. 4, 392; also Gerhard Kaiser, *Benjamin, Adorno: Zwei Studien* (Frankfurt: Athenäum-Fischer-Taschenbuch-Verlag, 1974).

22. According to the Aga Khan, tourism is the modern "-ism" that causes the most damage; of course, taken literally, this is impossible, but if we subtracted a few "-isms" would it be so wrong?

23. Matthew 8, 22.
24. The following passage by Jacob Burckhardt makes for an interesting comparison: "let us remember all we owe to the past as a spiritual *continuum* which forms part of our supreme spiritual heritage. Anything which can in the remotest way serve our knowledge of it must be collected, whatever toil it may cost and with all the resources at our disposal." *Reflections on History,* 38. However, it requires an observation by George Orwell to bring this up to date: "It was not by making yourself heard but staying sane that you carried on the human heritage." Cited in Imre Kertész, *Galeerentagebuch* (Berlin: Rowohl, 1993), 15.
25. Sigmund Freud and Lou Andreas-Salomé, *Letters,* translated by William and Elaine Robson Scott (New York: Norton, 1972), 21.
26. And who would want it to be? No one would want to live without hot showers, microwave ovens, anesthesia, birth-control pills, television, and cell phones. Uniminaginable!
27. Joseph Roth, *The Radetzky March,* translated by Michael Hofmann (London: Granta, 2002), 268.
28. Ibid., 326–327.
29. Musil, "The German as Symptom," translated by Burton Pike and David S. Luft, in *Precision and Soul,* 178.
30. For Roth's own attitude, see David Bronsen, *Joseph Roth: Eine Biographie* (Cologne: Kiepenheuer & Witsch, 1974), 102ff.
31. "In a world of rapid innovations, old ways of life are the least subject to pressure, because they are already old. In the end the modern acceleration of change turns out to serve slowness of pace: it is typical of the rapid tempo of obsolescence that the faster the latest trend goes out of style, the faster old styles can become new again. Everyone who has been around for a while knows that." Odo Marquard, *Philosophie des Stattdessen: Studien* (Stuttgart: Reclam, 2000), 73.
32. Hannah Arendt, "Organisierte Schuld" (written in November 1944), *Die Wandlung* 1 (1945), 344. See the introduction to the German edition of Arendt, *Eichmann in Jerusalem: Ein Bericht von der Banalität des Bösen* (Munich: Piper, 1986), 16.
33. Karl Kraus in a lecture given on November 19, 1914; quoted in Hans Weigel, *Karl Kraus oder die Macht der Ohnmacht* (Vienna: Christian Brandstätter, 1986), 177.
34. In a passage about the relationship between imagination and insanity written in February 1915, Arthur Schnitzler observed: "The inability of

people, even imaginative people, to conceive or picture something new is extraordinary, taking one by surprise again and again. It can only be explained as an inner defense, which has arisen gradually over the course of time, against the ghastliness of the world. If one could imagine what dying is like, then in a certain sense it would be impossible to live." *Aphorismen und Betrachtungen,* ed. Robert O. Weiss (Frankfurt: S. Fischer, 1967), 201.

35. Musil, *The Man without Qualities,* vol. 1, 391. A passage from *Elective Affinities* may make for an interesting comparison, as an example of the "historicization" of human life from the early years of this process: "'As life draws us on,' she [Charlotte] replied, 'we think we are acting of our own free will, choosing our activities and amusements, but really, if we look more closely, we are simply obliged to follow the pitch, the inclination of our time.'" Johann Wolfgang von Goethe, "Elective Affinities," translated by Judith Ryan, in *The Sorrows of Young Werther; Elective Affinities; Novella,* Goethe's Collected Works, vol. 11 (New York: Suhrkamp, 1988), 213.

36. See in particular Musil's essay "The German as Symptom" (1923), in *Precision and Soul,* 150–192.

37. Gottfried Benn, *Gesammelte Werke,* ed. Dieter Wellershoff (Wiesbaden: Limes, 1959), vol. 1, 7 (note 18), 337, 432, and 436; vol. 2, 388. Letter to Oelze of January 18, 1945, *Briefe an F. W. Oelze 1932–1945* (Wiesbaden: Limes Verlag, 1977). For Benn's "anti-historical tendency," see *Gesammelte Werke,* vol. 1, 383 and 432.

38. Hannah Arendt, *On Revolution* (New York: Viking Press, 1963), 91.

39. Burckhardt, *Reflections on History,* 40.

40. Jacob Burckhardt, *Judgments on History and Historians,* translated by Harry Zohn (Boston: Beacon Press, 1958), 224.

Index

235